SOCIAL REGULATION IN MARKETS FOR CONSUMER GOODS AND SERVICES

David T. Scheffman and Elie Appelbaum

Social Regulation in Markets for Consumer Goods and Services

PUBLISHED FOR THE ONTARIO ECONOMIC COUNCIL BY
UNIVERSITY OF TORONTO PRESS
TORONTO BUFFALO LONDON

©Ontario Economic Council 1982
Printed in Canada

ISBN 0-8020-3384-9

Canadian Cataloguing in Publication Data
Scheffman, David T., 1943–
  Social regulation in markets for consumer goods
  and services

  Bibliography : p.
  ISBN 0-8020-3384-9

  1. Consumer protection – Canada – Economic aspects.
  2. Consumer protection – Law and legislation – Canada
  – Economic aspects. 3. Consumer protection – Ontario
  – Economic aspects.   I. Appelbaum, Elie.   II. Ontario
  Economic Council.   III. Title.
  HC120.C63S33   381'.34'0971   C82-094248-0

This report reflects the views of the author and not necessarily those of the Ontario
Economic Council or of the Ontario government. The Council establishes policy
questions to be investigated and commissions research projects, but it does not
influence the conclusions or recommendations of authors. The decision to sponsor
publication of this study was based on its competence and relevance to public policy
and was made with the advice of anonymous referees expert in the area.

Contents

Preface

This study presents an economic analysis of social regulation in markets for consumer goods and services with applications to such regulation in Canada, particularly Ontario. Social regulation, that is, regulation concerned with the 'quality' or safety of goods and services or their method of production, encompasses a major portion of what governments do. Such regulation incurs both costs and benefits, often of a major magnitude. In this study we identify the main costs and benefits of such regulation, suggest a methodology for rational government policy formulation and evaluation, and critically evaluate social regulation in markets for consumer goods and services in Ontario and, to some extent, in Canada.

It has been our intention to direct the study to the broad audience of those interested in government regulation. For economists the study summarizes much of the literature on social regulation and develops some new theoretical analyses. For policy-makers the study thoroughly develops the economic methodology for policy formulation and evaluation and critically evaluates the desirability of various existing and proposed policies – all, we hope, in a non-technical manner. For those interested in 'law and economics' issues, we provide a summary, from an economic perspective, of the legal basis of social regulation in Canada and Ontario, with particular attention to the division of powers between the federal and provincial levels and its economic implications. Finally, we provide a brief summary of the social regulatory activities of the provincial government in Ontario, organized according to ministerial responsibility.

Many people have provided us with information, suggestions, and other forms of support in the course of this research. Professor Ben Hovius of the University of Western Ontario Law School provided much of the legal background for Chapter 5. John Todd (the OEC project leader for this study) helped us develop the terms of reference for the study and made many helpful suggestions throughout our research. We also benefitted from the comments of participants at two review seminars at the OEC. We particularly benefitted from the careful review of our manuscript by two anonymous referees.

Several people in the government helped us by providing information. Alan Gordon, associate secretary of cabinet (Ontario), and his assistant, Susan Gaitskell, were extremely valuable in providing us with information on regulatory activity in Ontario. In addition, we interviewed several other people in government, and we are grateful for their assistance. Finally, each of the Ontario ministries provided us with a summary of their regulatory activities.

One of us (Scheffman) was a visiting scholar in the department of economics of the University of Minnesota during part of the time this research was conducted. Finally, Mrs Marg Gower and the typing pool of the department of economics at UWO deserve special thanks.

SOCIAL REGULATION IN MARKETS FOR CONSUMER GOODS AND SERVICES

1

Introduction

The decade of the 1970s began with the completion of the legislative enactment by the federal and provincial governments of much of the basic platforms of the consumerist and environmentalist movements of the 1960s and apparently ended with a serious questioning of some of these and other government actions. If 'environmental protection' and 'consumer protection' were watchwords of the beginning of the decade, 'deregulation' threatened to supplant them at the end of the 1970s. The reasons for this amazing apparent turn-around in public sentiment are complex, but the marked change in the economic climate over the decade was certainly an important factor. Another factor was that the sheer volume of increased regulatory activity in the post-war period would be difficult to ignore. As an indication of the growth of regulation, the Economic Council of Canada's (ECC) interim report on regulation showed:

the number of pages of federal regulatory statutes increased by almost 350 per cent between 1886 and 1970;

between 1949 and 1978, the number of statutory instruments, including regulations, made pursuant to federal regulatory statutes increased by over 200 per cent, or more than twice the increase related to other statutes not primarily aimed at altering economic behaviour;

the number of pages of federal subordinate legislation related to transportation alone increased from 922 pages in 1949 to 4,419 in 1978;

the average number of statutory instruments per federal statute increased by almost 50 per cent between 1949 and 1978;

in 1886, federal regulatory statutes averaged 20.8 pages; between 1906 and 1970, the average length increased from 26.5 pages to 29; those enacted between 1970 and 1978 averaged 31.8 pages;

in Ontario, the number of pages of regulatory statutes increased from 515 in 1877 to 1,494 in 1927, and to 3,140 in 1970, and in Saskatchewan the number increased from 944 in 1909 to 3,611 in 1978.

(ECC, 1979b, 7)

Although some groups perceived that the regulatory activity of all levels of government had increasingly impinged on personal freedom, we are more struck by how quickly the apparent *costs* of such activity were appreciated. The uncertainty of the post-OPEC economy certainly contributed to this appreciation. In our view, however, of greater importance was the fact that the costs of recently enacted government regulations were not properly anticipated by the public, the business community, or the governments themselves. On reflection, this lack of preparation is not surprising, since the process by which much of the regulation was developed, passed into law, and implemented apparently often did not consider estimates of the costs of regulation to be an important input into the policy-making process.

A serious investigation of the costs of regulation in Canada has only just begun. A meeting of the first ministers in early 1978 mandated the ECC to study economic regulation at all levels of government, and its final report, due at the end of 1980, will provide some of the first comprehensive evidence on the costs of regulation in Canada.

There can be no doubt that the costs of regulation are significant. For example, the increase in the price of automobiles due to federal safety and emissions requirements in the United States was estimated by Weidenbaum (1979) to be $665.87 per car. (The figure would presumably be similar for Canada.)

Estimates of the aggregate costs of regulation in the United States include Weidenbaum (1979) and Denison (1978). Weidenbaum estimated that the aggregate costs of the federal regulation of business in the United States was $102.7 billion (U.S.) in 1979, which was approximately 5 per cent of GNP, or almost $500 per capita. Of the $102.7 billion figure, $4.8 billion, comprising the budgets of the various federal regulatory bureaus, was estimated to be the administrative costs of federal regulation, and $97.9 billion was estimated to be the costs of compliance. The compliance costs included the direct costs of meeting various standards, the costs of paperwork arising from the regulations, and the loss of productivity and employment resulting from the regulations. Denison estimated that business productivity in the United States in 1975 was reduced by 1.4 per cent because of the impact of pollution and job safety regulations. Although such estimates of aggregate costs are necessarily imprecise, most scholars of regulation in the United States would agree that the costs of regulation are significant, and this conclusion could also be expected to be valid for Canada, given the broad similarity of the regulatory climates of the two countries.

Thus it is clear that regulation has increased in Canada and that it has probably imposed significant costs. Naturally, regulation is presumed by policy-makers to have benefits. In this study we shall identify major sources of costs and benefits of certain types of regulatory actions, and we shall argue that estimates of the costs and benefits should be a requisite for national policy-making.

DEFINITION OF 'SOCIAL REGULATION' AND TERMS-OF-REFERENCE OF THE STUDY

The purpose of this study is to develop an economic analysis of 'social regulation' in markets for consumer goods and services and use this analysis to evaluate such regulation in Ontario. Social regulation is a new term. It was coined to differentiate certain forms of economic regulation from 'traditional economic regulation,' which is concerned with the regulation of price, output, rate-of-return, and the number of agents (typically producers or sellers) in a market. Examples of traditional economic regulation include agricultural price supports; minimum wage legislation; regulation of airline fares, trucking rates, etc.; and limitations on the number of electric and natural gas companies and taxis in various localities. In contrast, *social regulation* is concerned with the regulation of the 'quality' or safety of goods and services or their method of production.[1]

Social regulation, broadly defined, encompasses a major portion of what governments do. It includes diverse regulations such as: environmental protection legislation (which is usually directed at regulating methods of production), safety standards (for automobiles, children's clothing, drugs, etc.), licensing of doctors (designed to control both the number and 'quality' of practitioners), regulation of the content of radio and television broadcasts (which includes such 'quality' components as 'Canadian content'), movie and magazine censorship, agricultural grading standards, 'blue laws' (e.g., the regulation of business hours on Sunday), regulation of the sale of alcoholic beverages and tobacco, mandating corrosion warranties for new cars, and the prohibition of the sale of substances such as marijuana and saccharin. Even this short list of examples of social regulation testifies to the extent and diversity of such regulation in Canada.

Most forms of social regulation can be placed in one of four categories: (1) environmental protection, (2) consumer protection, (3) safety regulation, and

1 For similar definitions of social regulation see Lilley and Miller (1977), *Proceedings* ... (forthcoming), and Economic Council of Canada (1979b).

(4) SOCIAL regulation ('social regulation with a capital S'), which we shall define as regulation directed primarily at social rather than economic goals.[2] The objectives of SOCIAL regulation are to control public (and private) morality, protect and enhance 'culture,' protect and enhance the 'national identity,' etc. A significant element of SOCIAL regulation is paternalism – policies implemented because society believes that individuals do not know what is best for them. Examples of SOCIAL regulation include 'blue laws,' movie and magazine censorship, Canadian content requirements for radio and television broadcasting, and the various laws regulating public (private) morality.

Naturally, a comprehensive general investigation of social regulation is too ambitious a goal for a single study. Therefore, the scope of our research will be limited in several respects. For example, since there is already an extensive literature on environmental protection regulation (see the bibliography), including research which examines environmental protection regulation in Ontario (see Dewees et al., 1975), our study will not address this topic. SOCIAL regulation is difficult to scrutinize, since quantifying the benefits of such regulation is difficult. (None the less, we shall argue below that the costs of such regulation should be considered in the policy-making process). Therefore such regulation will be considered only superficially here.

In this study we shall confine our interest to social regulation in markets for consumer goods and services. Most of such regulation falls under the 'consumer protection' or 'regulation of safety' headings. However, restriction of our attention to consumer goods and services markets precludes a consideration of some major topics falling under these two headings, including, for example, occupational safety regulation. This restriction is justified in that many of these topics have been adequately addressed elsewhere (studies of occupational safety regulations include Owens and Schultze (1976), Miller and Yandle (1979), and Smith (1976)),[3] and social regulation in markets for consumer goods and services, a major topic in itself, heretofore has not been given adequate scrutiny.

Although our terms of reference are restrictive relative to the general topic of social regulation, except for environmental protection legislation and some instances of SOCIAL regulation, the previously enumerated examples of social regulation arise in markets for consumer goods and services. Therefore, the 'net' we are casting in this study is still quite large.

---

2 Such regulation could also be termed 'cultural,' 'paternalistic,' etc., but these terms have pejorative connotations. Although in our view some types of SOCIAL regulation deserve these negative connotations (e.g., 'blue laws'), we should certainly not advocate a removal of all forms of all such regulation.

3 Many of the issues arising in occupational safety can be addressed with the analysis developed in Chapters 2 and 3.

Our research is intended to provide four main contributions. First, we develop an economic analysis of social regulation in markets for consumer goods and services which sets out a general framework for rational policy-making and extends the economic theory of social regulation in several respects. Our second contribution is an abstract, annotated with our economic analysis, of the legal basis of social regulation in Canada. The focus of this abstract is an examination of the division of regulatory powers between the federal and provincial governments. Our third contribution is a summary of the social regulatory activities of the provincial government in Ontario. Some of the particular regulatory activities of the provincial government will also be scrutinized, using the economic analysis we develop. Finally, we have assembled an extensive bibliography of the literature relating to social regulation.

AN OUTLINE OF THE STUDY

This study has two parts. In the first part, comprising Chapters 2 to 4, the economics of rational policy formulation and the economic theory of social regulation in markets for consumer goods and services are developed. It has been our intention to direct the study to the broad audience of those interested in government regulation. Therefore, although there is a limited use of mathematics in Chapters 2 to 4, we have tried to provide enough explanation so that readers who are not mathematically adept can understand the arguments. Building on the economic analysis developed in Chapters 2 to 4, the second part of the study, comprising Chapters 5 to 7, summarizes the legal basis of social regulation in Canada, summarizes and critically reviews social regulation in Ontario, and provides our policy recommendations. The discussion in these chapters draws heavily on the economic analysis developed in the preceding chapters. The study concludes with an extensive bibliography of the literature relating to social regulation.

We begin the study in Chapter 2 with an explanation of the methodology of economic policy analysis and then apply this methodology in a general way to analyse the economic case for social regulation in markets for consumer goods and services. We explain that an economic case for such intervention may be made if market imperfections have resulted in a market failure, that is, a situation in which a market is unable to allocate resources efficiently. The major potential sources of market failure (market power, externalities, uncertainty, etc.) are defined and explained, and the general case for intervention by social regulation based on these potential sources of market failure is critically evaluated. We then enumerate the major types of regulatory instruments and discuss their applicability to various basic situations. The chapter concludes with a summary of various political and economic theories of the 'demand for social regulation' (i.e., explanations as to why social regulation arises).

Chapter 2 is in essence a highly concentrated summary of the economic literature bearing on social regulation in markets for consumer goods and services. In Chapters 3 and 4 new analysis is presented which is used to examine some of the basic issues described in Chapter 2. The model we develop in Chapter 3 provides a general framework for analysing problems arising in markets in which reliability or safety is an important characteristic of the good (or service) provided. The market's determination of the reliability or safety of the product produced, the price of the product, and the division of liability in the event of product failure are described by the model. In addition, the market's ability to generate and provide information about product reliability and safety to consumers is considered. Then the efficiency of the market-determined level of safety, compensation for product failure, and information is analysed and the desirability of various forms of government intervention (social regulation) is evaluated. The efficiency and desirability of policies such as setting quality or safety standards, mandating warranties or producer liability for product failure, recalls, and regulating advertising, all of which are used in some form in Ontario, is thoroughly discussed.

The analysis developed in Chapter 3 argues that there may be significant impediments to efficiency in markets in which consumers have uncertainty about the quality of the goods or services being offered for sale. A general discussion of possible remedies for such efficiencies is also provided in Chapter 3. A common type of regulation used for situations in which consumers cannot adequately determine product or service quality is the setting of standards for the inputs or technology used in the production of the product or service. A primary example is occupational and professional licensing or certification. Such regulation generally requires that to perform the services in the regulated occupation or profession, a practitioner must meet certain educational and experience standards. We are particularly interested in such regulation, because the province of Ontario has an extensive system of occupational licensing and certification.

In Chapter 4 we develop a model of occupational licensing. This model allows us to consider the desirability and effects of occupational licensing regulations which are directed at controlling both the number of members of an occupation and their 'quality.' Both types of controls are common to occupational licensing in Ontario (discussed in Chapter 6), a regulation which typically controls numbers by the use of an apprenticeship system, and control 'quality' by a combination of formal and "on-the-job" educational requirements. We conclude the chapter with an empirical example which bears out the theoretical predictions of the model.

Chapter 5 marks the beginning of the institutional portion of the study. In this chapter we provide a summary of the legal basis of social regulation in Canada. The economic aspects and effects of the law are emphasized, drawing heavily on the analysis developed in Chapters 2 to 4. We begin Chapter 5 with a discussion of the division of social regulatory powers between the federal and provincial levels prescribed by the British North America Act and the relevant case law. The purpose of this discussion is to reveal and evaluate (using the analysis developed in Chapters 2 to 4) the general social regulatory actions the two levels of government are engaged in, and to indicate the limits on such actions and the desirability of such limits. Specific attention is then given to the regulation of advertising in Canada and Ontario (an issue given prominence in Chapter 3) and to the legal remedies available to the two levels of government and to consumers for cases of product failure. The chapter ends with a summary of the major economic issues arising from the earlier discussion.

In Chapter 6 social regulation by the provincial government in Ontario is explicitly considered. The major social regulatory actions used in the provinces are catalogued according to provincial ministerial responsibility. Some of the major social regulatory programs (e.g., occupational licensing) are critically evaluated, using the analysis developed in Chapters 2 to 4.

Chapter 7 concludes the study with a brief summary of the preceding chapters and a statement of our major policy conclusions.

2
The economics of social regulation: an overview

The purpose of this chapter is to explain and analyse some of the possible economic justifications for social regulation and to evaluate the various possible regulatory instruments. In the main the material in this chapter represents a condensation of the body of economic literature bearing on social regulation. In the following two chapters some original economic models will be presented, and certain aspects of social regulation will be analysed in greater depth. In Chapter 5 the economics of the legal basis of social regulation in Canada will be thoroughly considered.

We realize that economic arguments are not the only determinant of policy decisions. However, economics can and should play an important role in the policy formulation and evaluation processes for three reasons. First, any social regulatory activity has a potentially important impact on the allocation of scarce resources or the distribution of income and wealth, that is, important economic effects. These economic effects will usually consist of both economic benefits and costs, and economics provides a methodology for evaluating these benefits and costs. The second role for economics in policy formulation is that the economic aspects of a problem themselves may suggest the need for a policy action. Such economic justifications for social regulation will be the focus of this chapter. Finally, economics can be useful in policy formulation in that it may suggest the most appropriate action for achieving a desired objective, even if the objective is basically social rather than economic. For example, if for purely social reasons society wishes to decrease aggregate alcohol consumption, economics suggests that it would be more efficient (although perhaps not more 'fair') to levy taxes on alcohol than to ration its use.

We shall begin this chapter by giving an overview of economic methodology. Then, the various possible economic justifications for social regulation will be discussed (some specific issues will be more thoroughly developed in the following two chapters). The third section of the chapter will critically evaluate the basic types of policy instruments. Finally, we shall survey some of the theories as to why and in what form social regulation arises.

THE METHODOLOGY OF ECONOMICS

Introduction
Economics is concerned with the allocation of scarce resources and the distribution of income and wealth. In recent years the public at large has become more aware that virtually all resources available to society (even clean air and water) are scarce; that is, they are not unlimited in supply. With this awareness has come an increasing realization that policy decisions affect society's allocation of its scarce resources; thus, policy decisions necessarily involve *trade-offs*. As it is often phrased in introductory economics texts, a choice by society for more 'guns' has a cost in terms of less 'butter.'

The general populace apparently realizes that increased defence expenditures will generally 'cost' other government programs or that having less inflation may 'cost' more unemployment, at least in the short run. Thus, the basic trade-offs involved in traditional macro-economic policy are now widely appreciated. There is apparently a growing realization that social regulatory activity also involves trade-offs. Certainly there exists a wider appreciation of the fact that having clean water can be costly, having safer cars means more expensive cars, etc. – trade-offs which the naïve early environmental and consumer movements often failed to recognize. Of course the fact that safer cars or water are not costless does not in itself suggest that society should not require such safety. In evaluating the desirability of such a policy, however, the costs and benefits should be considered.

One of the important characteristics of social regulation is that its costs are often difficult to discern, because there are often important *indirect* effects of such regulatory activity. As an illustration, although it should be obvious that requiring manufacturers to build safer cars will be likely to result in more expensive cars, a less obvious indirect effect could be that people drive less safely. This might occur because safer cars reduce the risks of unsafe driving and therefore may reduce the incentives for safe driving. (In Peltzman, 1975, it is argued that auto safety regulations in the United States resulted in an increase in pedestrian fatalities – presumably resulting from drivers operating their vehicles less safely because of the increased protection afforded by the safer cars.) Similarly, a stringent policy designed to ensure the efficiency of new drugs may result in a delay in the use of some effective drugs and a slow-down in the rate of innovation of new drugs. (In Peltzman, 1973 it is argued that the 1962 Drug

Amendments in the United States had these effects.)[1] Although Peltzman's *quantitative* conclusions have been questioned (see, for example, McGuire et al., 1975 or Peltzman, 1973), all economists would agree that social regulation can often have significant indirect effects. Economics is useful in that it often pinpoints what the direct and indirect effects of a regulatory action will be, and it provides a methodology for quantifying costs and benefits.

The methodology of economics explicitly recognizes that decisions involve trade-offs. Given society's available resources and technology, a variety of *consumption bundles* are feasible in the economy during any time period (or over time). Taking the simple textbook example of a society that can produce only guns and butter, society could have a consumption bundle comprised mainly of guns, or butter, or various intermediate bundles. Because resources are limited, having more guns will force society to sacrifice some butter. Thus having more guns 'costs' butter, and this cost is termed the *opportunity cost* of guns.

As an example more relevant to the issue at hand, part of the opportunity cost of having safer cars is that more resources (labour and materials) will probably have to be used to construct a safer car. Notice that although the automobile manufacturers *apparently* bear the direct costs of a policy which requires safer cars, society in fact bears the costs, because the increased use of resources in automobile manufacturing reduces the amount of resources available for other uses. Furthermore, the increased costs borne by automobile manufacturers will generally be passed on to their customers in some form – probably higher prices.

The important problem which must be faced in evaluating and formulating social regulatory policies is that such policies will generally affect the consumption bundle available to society. Economics provides a methodology for evaluating the *economic* effects of policies. The economic effects of policies are evaluated in terms of their effects on (1) the *efficiency* of resource allocation, and (2) the *equity* of the resulting distribution of income and wealth.

A policy is *efficient* if the aggregate benefits accruing to all members of society exceed the aggregate costs, and the excess of benefits over costs is as great as that of any mutually exclusive policy. Benefits from social regulatory activity may include increased output of certain goods and services, increased 'quality' of certain goods or services, increased 'safety,' or reduced input requirements. Costs resulting from social regulatory activity may include decreased output of certain goods and services, reduced 'quality' of certain goods and services, reduced 'safety,' or increased input requirements.

Naturally, one of the problems involved with measuring the costs and benefits of social regulation is the difficulty of measuring the 'value' of quality or safety.

---

1 For other studies of the Drug Amendments see Grabowski and Vernon (1976) and Grabowski (1976).

This issue will be discussed below. When only quantities of goods or services or inputs are involved, the market provides an evaluation of costs and benefits. For example, if a certain policy (e.g., expanded agricultural research) will result in increasing the production of wheat by 1 million bushels a year and wheat is valued at $20 a bushel, it is reasonable to argue that one component of the benefits of the policy can be valued at $20 million per year. We shall see below that implicit market valuations can often be used, at least to a limited extent, to value quality and safety.

The efficiency criterion makes it clear that both benefits and costs must be considered in evaluating policy alternatives, and in many cases the criterion provides a basis for measuring benefits and costs on a common scale, namely willingness to pay in dollars on the part of all people affected. However, society is obviously concerned not only with *aggregate* economic costs and benefits. In most cases an efficient policy (i.e., one for which the aggregate benefits exceed the aggregate costs) will make some groups worse off. As one illustration, imposition of effluent standards may reduce wages or employment in some industries, and safety and emission standards for automobiles may adversely affect automobile manufacturer shareholders.

Traditional economic methodology argued that efficiency and equity were separate issues. This is because in a simplified model of reality, any equity goal of society could, in principle, be achieved by a lump-sum redistribution of resources. However, modern economics has increasingly recognized the interdependence of efficiency and equity. This interdependence arises from four sources. First, despite intuition to the contrary, the existence of positive aggregate net benefits is neither necessary nor sufficient for compensation of losers by gainers to be feasible, even if such redistribution were costless.[2] Second, any sort of redistribution scheme will use resources because of administrative costs. The third source of interdependence is that any *feasible* redistribution scheme will distort the allocation of resources. (For example, income taxes obviously affect people's work decisions.) Finally, in most cases governments do not carry out such redistribution to compensate losers.

Therefore, any sensible evaluation of public policy must go beyond the simple calculation of aggregate net benefits. Instead, if a policy has important differential effects over various groups in the population, the net benefits over the groups must be considered. When we speak of benefits and costs throughout this study, it should be understood that differential effects should be identified.[3]

---

2 See Boadway (1974). Compensation itself may have general equilibrium effects which change relative prices.
3 For discussions of how distributional effects might be integrated into cost-benefit analysis, see Sugden and Williams (1978) and Boadway (1974).

The efficiency of the market allocation
One of the most important contributions of modern economic analysis has been to prove that an idealized market economy will, in the absence of certain 'imperfections' (described below), allocate society's resources efficiently. The concept of efficiency being used in this context is *Pareto efficiency*. An allocation is Pareto efficient if it is not possible to benefit any individual without decreasing the well-being of at least one other individual (where the well-being of individuals is measured in terms of their own perceptions). Alternatively, if an allocation is not Pareto efficient, it is possible to alter it in such a way that some individuals are better off and none are worse off. Full (Pareto) efficiency requires that prices be equal to the marginal *social* costs of production and prices. This condition insures that the full social costs of production are minimized and that prices correctly reflect social costs.[4] Our earlier definition of an efficient policy (positive aggregate net benefits) is based on the Pareto concept of efficiency. To see this, if lump-sum redistribution is possible, an efficient policy by our definition can result in some groups' being better off and no one being worse off, since aggregate net benefits are increased – that is, the policy results in a Pareto improvement.

Notice that the Pareto criterion does not choose a unique efficient allocation. The efficient allocation derived from an idealized market economy is only one of many possible efficient allocations. In our guns and butter example an economy can be Pareto efficient producing mostly guns or mostly butter. In particular, the Pareto criterion is devoid of equity concerns. Thus, an allocation which gives most of society's resources to a small group of individuals can be Pareto efficient. The Pareto methodology is based on the traditional economic view of the separation of efficiency and equity issues. As was previously mentioned, efficiency and equity objectives cannot, in practice, be considered totally independent. None the less, efficiency is a useful concept for policy evaluation. For example, if one is interested in creating a particular distribution of income, it seems obvious that if there is more than one feasible policy, that the one that distorts efficiency least should be chosen.

The economic methodology used to evaluate any proposed government intervention begins with the recognition that an idealized market economy, free of imperfections, allocates resources efficiently. This idealized market economy, termed the model of perfect competition by economists, assumes a frictionless world of atomistic economic agents. In such a world each agent is assumed to be perfectly informed and is too small to have any effect on market

---

4 For a more thorough development of the concept of Pareto efficiency see Hirshleifer (1976) and Orr (1976).

prices. Furthermore, the actions of any agent are assumed to have an imperceptible economic impact on any other agent.

Since such an idealized economy has been shown to allocate resources efficiently, an argument for government intervention on the grounds of economic efficiency must start with the existence of an important deviation from the idealized market economy, that is, the existence of a market imperfection. The argument here is that if some imperfection has resulted in the market's allocation of resources being inefficient, there *may* be a policy action that would restore efficiency. The failure of a market to allocate resources efficiently is termed a *market failure*, and imperfections which result in market failure are termed *potential sources of market failure*.

It should be stressed here that the existence of an inefficiency is not in itself a justification for a government action. Government action incurs costs which must be balanced against the benefits of the action. In many cases it may not be possible to design a government action the benefits of which justify its costs.

Potential sources of market failure do not necessarily lead to actual market failures and therefore do not in themselves justify intervention. This is because, as we shall see below, there are often market or non-market institutions which satisfactorily ameliorate potential sources of market failure. By definition, an inefficient allocation involves potential benefits to at least some through changing the allocation. Therefore there are economic incentives to 'cure' inefficiencies and so the private economy will often find a means of dealing with potential sources of market failure. For example, the idealized perfectly competitive model assumes that the actions of any individual agent do not have perceptible economic effects on any other agent, and this assumption clearly doesn't hold for spouses, in that the well-being of one spouse presumably affects the well-being of the other. Although this is a potential source of market failure, spouses obviously have the ability to allocate their resources efficiently in the face of this externality (i.e., they will recognize their interdependence and allocate their resources appropriately), so that no policy action is called for in this case.

As another illustration, although automobile accidents are obvious examples of externalities[5] (one type of a potential source of market failure), a case for government intervention must go beyond the recognition of this fact. One important institutional arrangement which must be considered in this context is personal liability laws, which at least to some extent deal with this externality.[6] Therefore, to evaluate an argument for government intervention based on

5 An externality exists when the economic actions of one economic agent have a perceptible *non-market* effect on another agent. Externalities will be discussed below.

6 The allocative role of the law will be developed later in this chapter and in Chapters 3 and 5.

efficiency grounds the institutional arrangements specific to the problem at hand must be considered, since the market may have found a way of dealing with the perceived imperfection.

If the market has not found a way of dealing with an imperfection so that a market failure exists, it may none the less be impossible to design a remedy which attains full efficiency, and indeed, in some cases it may not even be possible to increase efficiency, because intervention is not costless. In evaluating the desirability of a proposed remedy, the benefits of the remedy must be balanced against its costs. In many cases the costs of the remedy will exceed its benefits.

As one example, consider the traffic congestion we observe in large cities. There is a significant potential source of market failure involved with traffic congestion – the externality arising because drivers do not take into account the fact that being on the road at busy times imposes costs on other drivers. It is clear that the allocation of traffic is not efficient and that the costs of inefficiency are significant.[7] Not enough commuters use public transportation or car pools or adjust their time of travel. Full efficiency can be attained only if it is possible to affect directly commuters' behaviour. In principle, this could be accomplished by taxing commuting, where the tax rate would depend on the particular journey and the time of day it is taken. Naturally, the administrative costs of such a remedy generally would be prohibitive. Therefore, full efficiency cannot be expected to be attainable and traffic congestion remains an uncorrectable market failure. However, efficiency may be improvable (not to the point of full efficiency) by policies such as subsidization of public transportation, designated lanes for buses and car pools, etc. – policies which are now widely used.

Measurement of costs and benefits [8]
As mentioned earlier, measurement of costs and benefits of social regulation is often complicated by the fact that quality or safety often must be evaluated. This requirement will necessarily inject a degree of subjectivity into the measurement process, but of course any policy choice at least implicitly makes subjective choices in such matters.

There are at least two basic methods by which costs and benefits can be assessed when quality or safety features are prominent. First, as with ordinary goods, a market valuation of quality or safety may often be discerned. In our

---

7 See Frankena (1980).
8 For a lucid text on cost-benefit analysis see Sugden and Williams (1978). For examples of cost-benefit analyses of social regulation, see Lave and Seskin (1970), Miller and Yandle (1979), Montador (1977), Morin (1977), and other literature listed in the bibliography.

earlier example of a policy which resulted in an increase in the production of wheat of one million bushels, with wheat valued at $20 a bushel, we argued that one component of the benefits of the policy could be valued at $20 million. It is obviously more difficult to value a policy which increases the safety of automobiles. None the less, consumers, by their market choices, often reveal an implicit valuation of increased safety. For example, if seat-belts were optional (as was the case prior to recent safety regulations), *some* evidence on consumers' valuation of the increased safety provided by seat-belts could be discerned from the observed willingness to pay for this optional feature and its price. (Of course, there are potential difficulties with this methodology – e.g., consumers may not correctly perceive the relationship between seat-belts and safety, or may not value safety sufficiently because of subsidized medical insurance.) Such a methodology has been used by economists to measure the cost of an accident, an illness, and even the value of a life. Although such measurements are by their nature imprecise and are necessarily controversial, they can provide a useful input into the policy formation and evaluation process.

A second methodology that can be used when quality or safety components are important is to evaluate the quantifiable economic benefits and costs of a policy and view these benefits and costs in conjunction with the technical effects of the policy on quality or safety. As an illustration of this methodology, consider a policy which attempts to reduce the number of accident fatalities by requiring certain safety equipment on cars. Two effects of such a policy can be quantified. First, what are the costs of the policy? Second, by how much will the policy reduce the number of accident fatalities? This latter aspect, although difficult to quantify precisely, can often be measured within tolerable limits of error by highway and traffic engineers and safety experts. A typical output of such a measurement methodology would be that for a cost of N per year (in increased resources used in auto manufacturing) the policy would be expected to reduce the number of accident fatalities by n per year (or alternatively, would reduce the probability of an accident fatality by P per cent). With this methodology a policy-maker can identify the costs of achieving a given level of 'safety' and can easily compare different proposed policies.

Although any measure of quality or safety – being necessarily subjective and often imprecise – is less than ideal, the formal measurement of benefits and costs is an essential component of rational policy formulation. Recognition of costs and benefits forces the policymaker to consider explicitly the trade-offs involved.

A detailed exposition of methods by which costs and benefits of social regulatory activities can be evaluated is beyond the scope of the present study. The interested reader is referred to Lave and Seskin (1970), Colantani et al. (1976), Friedlander (1978), and our bibliography for studies using such methods.

POTENTIAL SOURCES OF MARKET FAILURE

In this section we shall enumerate and assess the potential sources of market failure which, in the absence of suitable institutional arrangements, may justify intervention by social regulation. In addition, the following two chapters will present models which are used to consider some of the issues addressed here in greater depth. Although the institutional focus of this study is social regulation in markets for consumer goods and services in *Ontario*, the question as to which level of government is more appropriate for attempting to remedy a specific problem will largely be deferred to the second part of the study. Our concern here and in the following two chapters will be an evaluation of the case for government intervention in general.

Market power

An economic agent is said to have *market power* if he can exert significant control over the price and/or output in a market. When an agent has market power, it will generally be in his interest to exercise that power, an action which results in a market failure. A *market structure* in which no agent has market power is competitive. Non-competitive market structures (i.e., markets in which some agents have market power) include monopoly, oligopoly, and monopolistic competition.[9] In the simple textbook case of a monopoly (a market with a single seller and no potential competitors), it is in the monopolist's interest to restrict output below the efficient level, which raises price above social marginal cost. In this simple textbook model the 'quality' of the good is taken as given, and only relatively recently has the economics literature begun seriously to address the question of the relationship between market structure and the 'quality' of goods and services produced.

Since the textbook monopolist restricts the *quantity* of his output, it was commonly believed that it would also be in the monopolist's interest to restrict the *quality* of his output (below the efficient level). A series of papers (Wicksell, 1934, Martin, 1962, Kleiman and Ophir, 1966, Levhari and Srinivasan, 1969, and Schmalensee, 1970) suggested that this was the case. However, in two important papers Swan (1970a,b) questioned this conclusion and in fact argued that if by 'quality' one meant *durability*, then quality in this sense might be independent of market structure.

To see why this result might occur, consider the following simple model of the market for razor blades (adapted from Levhari and Peles, 1973). Assume that razor blades differ only with respect to the number of shaves per blade (not, for

---

9 For a description of various market structures see Scherer (1980).

example with respect to the 'comfort' of the shave). Although this is a limited aspect of quality, it is commonly believed that a monopolist will produce a product which wears out faster. This example will show that this is not necessarily true. Since in such a world consumers will only be interested in the number of shaves per blade, the demand for razor blades can be written

$$Qn = f(p/n), \quad f' < 0 \tag{1}$$

(i.e., the demand for shaves is a decreasing function of the price per shave), where Q is the number of blades demanded, n is the number of shaves per blade, and p is the market price of blades (so that p/n is the price per shave). Writing this demand function in inverse form we have

$$p = g(Qn)n, \tag{2}$$

where q is a decreasing function of (Qn). Suppose for simplicity that the industry cost of producing Q blades, each of which provides n shaves per blade, can be written

$$c(Q,n) = b(n)Q, \quad b' > 0, \tag{3}$$

that is, there are increasing marginal costs of durability and constant marginal production costs.

A monopolist would choose Q and n so as to maximize his profits, that is, Q and n are chosen to maximize

$$g(Qn)nQ - b(n)Q, \tag{4}$$

where $g(Qn)nQ$ is total revenue and $b(n)Q$ is total costs. If we let N be the total number of shaves provided ($N = nQ$), this problem is equivalent to choosing N and n to maximize

$$g(N)N - N(b(n)/n). \tag{5}$$

From (5) it is easily seen that the monopolist chooses n, the number of shaves per blade, so as to minimize $b(n)/n$, the average cost per shave. But of course a competitive industry will minimize this same quantity. (If it did not, a firm could offer a blade of different durability at the market price and make profits.) Thus, in this example market structure has no effect on 'quality' (as measured by durability), so that the general relationship between quality and market structure is at best ambiguous. This conclusion is borne out by subsequent literature such as Schmalensee (1979) and Su (1975). This argument will be extended in the following chapter, where it will be shown that the relationship between the warranty coverage offered and market structure is also ambiguous.

Why does this result obtain? In the standard simple monopoly model it is clearly in the monopolist's interest to minimize the costs of producing his chosen level of output. Our example is a somewhat subtle version of this result. The apparent widespread belief that monopoly will lead to lower quality is evidently based on the notion that a monopolist can exploit his customers. This is true, in the sense that he can raise his price, lower his output, or vary the quality of his product, *subject to the demand of his customers*. For example, in the simple monopoly model the monopolist cannot set both the price and output, since the final outcome must be on his demand curve. He cannot raise both his price and his output level. Similarly, the monopolist does not have scope to vary the quality of his product without incurring effects on his price and output level. Although he can lower the quality of his product, as long as this situation is perceived by his customers the price he receives will fall. Thus, it should not be surprising that it is not necessarily in the monopolist's interest to reduce quality. Indeed, it is conceivable that it might be in a monopolist's interest to produce a good with 'excessive' quality, for which he could charge an 'excessive' price. As we will see in the next chapter, this conclusion is valid, even if changes in quality are not perfectly perceived by his customers.

What is the practical import of the ambiguity of the relationship between market structure and quality? The standard market power argument (restriction of output) forms the basis of the economic case for anti-combines legislation and the regulation of 'natural' monopolies (e.g., Ontario Hydro). However, as we have seen, market power does not have an a priori predictable effect on the 'quality' or safety of the goods or services produced.[10] Therefore, any case for government intervention with the market production of quality or safety based on an argument that the market structure is not competitive must be based on the specifics of the particular case.

Externalities

An externality exists when the economic actions of one economic agent (consumer or producer) have a perceptible *non-market* effect on another agent. For example, if a fossil-fuel-burning electricity generating plant is located near me, I may be forced to 'consume' some of the smoke and dust it produces (or to incur expenses to reduce my consumption of smoke and dust). Similarly, when someone runs into me with his car, I must 'consume' the effects of the accident. Our earlier example of traffic congestion is yet another example. Finally, if my neighbour keeps his yard well tended and cultivates a beautiful garden, I 'consume' some of the benefits of his activities from the enhancement of the local

10 The relationship between market structure and safety is examined in Chapter 3.

scenery. Thus, externalities may be positive (beneficial) or negative (harmful).

Externalities are a potential source of market failure to the extent that they represent *unpriced transactions*. In the power plant example the negative externality associated with the coal and dust produced in the generation of electricity is a cost borne by the affected parties, but this cost may not be recognized by the managers of the power plant. The *social costs* of electricity generation in this case include both the private costs (i.e., the costs of labour, materials, depreciation, etc.) of electricity generation *and* the external costs. Efficiency requires that the marginal *social* cost of electricity generation equals the price consumers pay. Even when the power plant is operated as a perfectly competitive (price-taking) firm, unless the managers are forced to recognize the costs of the externality, inefficiency will result, because only *private* marginal costs will be used in profit maximization calculations. This inefficiency may take the form of an inefficient level of production of electricity or of socially inefficient methods of production of electricity.

In the automobile accident example, if the offending driver does not take into account the social costs of his causing an accident, an inefficiency may result in the form of his being insufficiently careful in his driving or in his choice or maintenance of the car.

One way to view the externalities problem is that there are not enough markets for all the sorts of interactions that take place, which results in involuntary transactions. In the power plant example if there was a market in which the power plant could 'sell' its production of smoke and dust, an equilibrium, if it existed,[11] would be efficient. Non-existence of equilibrium or prohibitive market set-up and transactions costs may preclude the market from arriving at a solution.

Another way to view the problem of externality-created market failure is that there is an inadequate assignment of property rights.[12] In this view what goes wrong in the power plant example is that although the power plant dirties the air, since no one 'owns' the air, no one can be assigned the costs of air pollution. If the power plant owned the air and 'sold' it to consumers (competitively), the externality would be reflected in consumers demand for clean air, so that the power plant would recognize the trade-off between production and air pollution. Although this example is far-fetched, the assignment of property rights often leads to the efficient remedying of externalities if the number of parties involved is sufficiently small. It is now known, for example, that in the classic

---

11 One problem with externalities is that they may introduce a non-convexity which precludes the existence of equilibrium. See Starrett (1972) and Scheffman (1975).
12 See Dales (1968).

economics textbook example of a positive externality – an apiary and orchard located in the same area – it is common for the apiary and orchard owners to recognize their interdependence and make contractual agreements (see Cheung, 1973).

Thus, the legal system has an important part to play in the efficient allocation of externalities, because the legal system specifies both property rights and the rules of liability for damages.[13] Except for the automobile accident type of externality, and the role of legal liability in allocating externalities, (which we shall return to later), the major types of externalities relevant to social regulation in Ontario are environmental (e.g., pollution) and locational. Since these issues have been fully discussed elsewhere (even for the particular case of Ontario) we shall not address them here.[14]

Public goods[15]

A *pure* public good is a good (or service) which has the property that one agent's consumption of it does not affect the ability of other agents to consume it, and no agent can be excluded from consuming it. The classic example of a pure public good is national defence. It is generally argued that pure public goods are sources of market failure, because private markets will be unable to supply such goods efficiently as a result of the *'free rider problem.'*

To clarify the nature of the free rider problem consider the following simple example. Suppose an economy with 100 identical consumers has one private good, denoted X, and one pure public good, denoted G. Suppose that each unit of G is produced at a cost of 100 units of X. Because the consumers are identical, presumably each consumer would be required to pay one unit of X for each unit of G supplied. Efficiency then requires that G be supplied at a level at which each of the identical consumers would find his well-being unchanged by a one-unit reduction in G combined with a one-unit increase in X (for each consumer).[16]

The nature of the free rider problem is revealed now by considering whether the efficient provision of the public good could be sustained by free market forces. Starting at the efficient allocation, if any one individual could reduce his expenditure on G by one unit of X, the level of G provided would fall by only one one-hundredth of a unit. At the efficient allocation, a one-unit reduction in

---

13 The role of legal liability in the allocation of resources will be discussed further elsewhere in this study.
14 On environmental externalities see Dewees et al. (1975), Friedlander (1978), and Baumol and Oates (1975); on locational externalities see Frankena and Scheffman (1980).
15 For a more thorough discussion of public goods see Orr (1976).
16 See Orr (1976).

G combined with a one-unit increase in X would, by definition of efficiency, leave him equally well-off. Consequently, he could increase his well-being by reducing his expenditure on G by one unit of X. Since all consumers find themselves in a similar situation, free market forces would result in a reduction in G below the efficient level, thus creating a market failure.

Although the province of Ontario is engaged in the public provision of many goods and services, many of these goods and services do not have public good characteristics (e.g., Ontario Hydro). Furthermore, the types of public goods provided by the province are generally not *pure* public goods. Public roads, for example, have public good characteristics, but since they are subject to congestion in use, they are not *pure* public goods. Average benefits decline with the number of users because of congestion. Such *impure* public goods create extra difficulties, since efficient provision of these goods requires not only a determination of the efficient supply but also policies to influence usage. Finally, some of the common publicly supplied goods may have no significant public good attributes at all, that is, they may be publicly provided *private* goods. (It has been argued by Stiglitz, 1977, for example, that public education is such a good.)

The provincial government has a major role in the provision of three types of goods and services with possible public good characteristics: non-local public goods (provincial parks, etc.), interurban transportation networks and major servicing schemes, and education. The role of the province in providing the first two types of goods is discussed in Frankena and Scheffman (1980). A discussion of public education is outside the terms of reference of this study. Finally, some mainly social phenomena may have public good characteristics, for example, 'public morality' or 'public health,' which may also have externality characteristics. Thus, government intervention in areas of public morality, etc., *may* have some economic justification based on public goods or externalities arguments.

Uncertainty

In the classic statement of the economic theorem, which shows that idealized competitive markets allocate resources efficiently, all agents are assumed to possess certain, accurate information about matters that concern them. Thus, all relevant prices and aspects of product quality are assumed known with certainty, and uncertain events such as product failure and accidents are assumed away. Since many important features of economic life are obviously uncertain, the classic statement of the efficiency theorem left little scope for analysing problems in which uncertainty was a featured participant.

However, modern restatements of the efficiency theorem and a burgeoning literature on the economics of uncertainty have shed considerable light on the efficiency properties of the market allocation of uncertainty. For example,

Arrow (1964) showed that in the standard model of an idealized economy without transactions or market set-up costs, a market economy could allocate uncertainty efficiently if the number of markets was expanded to include a contingent market for each uncertain outcome. As an illustration of this scheme, consider an economy in which the only source of uncertainty is the average temperature, and variations in the average temperature have important effects on some economic variables (e.g., the size of the harvest). The idealized market economy could allocate this uncertainty efficiently if the markets were expanded to include a market for each good contingent on the average temperature. One mechanism would have buyers and sellers of apples contract *ex ante* to deliver or take delivery of apples at a given (market-determined) price, contingent on the average temperature being, say, 20°C. If any other average temperature occurred, the contracts contingent on that temperature would be void.

Naturally the existence of transactions and market set-up costs precludes such a complete set of markets, and as with externalities, uncertainty can be viewed as a potential source of market failure because of a possible insufficiency of markets. However, it is clear that market economies have developed a myriad of institutions which serve as substitutes for formal contingent markets in the allocation of uncertainty.[17] Asset markets, commodities markets, insurance, and private contracts are just some of the devices by which our economy allocates uncertainty. Such arrangements exist, rather than formal contingent markets, probably because they economize on transactions or other costs.

Transactions, negotiations, and contractual enforcement costs obviously prevent a 'real world' economy from providing a complete set of substitutes for a complete system of contingent markets. A case for government intervention *may* be made on these grounds if the government can economize on these costs more efficiently than the private economy. In fact, the existence of government could be explained on these economic grounds – the superior ability of such an organization to economize on certain transactions and other costs.

For the purposes of this study we are more concerned with the problem that existing institutions may not allocate uncertainty efficiently. Leaving aside the problem of a possible insufficiency of markets, inefficiencies arise from two sources: (a) imperfect information, and (b) moral hazard.

(a) Imperfect information
Informational imperfections impair efficiency, because they result in economic agents making 'incorrect' choices relative to what they would choose if they were

17 Arrow (1964) showed that a complete set of contingent markets was formally equivalent to a certain system of securities markets.

perfectly informed. There are two types of problems here: (1) different agents have different information, that is, informational asymmetries; and (2) the market does not provide the efficient level of information – a form of the 'free-rider' problem.

1. *Informational asymmetries* A very substantial literature examining the allocative effects of informational asymmetries has developed in recent years. Two basic types of models have been examined: models in which sellers have information buyers don't have and models in which buyers have information sellers don't have. Purported examples of markets in which sellers have better information than buyers are: used cars (the seller knows more about the characteristics of the car than the buyer) and labour markets (labourers may have better information about their industriousness and perhaps their skills than employers do). Purported examples of markets in which buyers have better information than sellers are insurance markets (buyers may have better information than insurance companies do about their individual risks) and education (buyers may have better information about their industriousness and skills than college admittance boards do).

For expositional purposes let us consider a simple model of asymmetrical information adapted from Akerlof (1970), termed the 'lemons' model. Consider an economy with four consumers. Three of the consumers, numbered by $i = 1,2,3$, own used cars and agent number 4 does not own a used car. The used cars differ in quality, and assume that quality can be measured by an index x, $0 \leq x \leq 1$. Let x_i be the quality of the used car owned by 'Mr i.' Then, let us assume that

$$x_1 = 0, \quad x_2 - 1/2, \quad x_3 - 1. \tag{6}$$

Suppose the three used-car owners are identical in tastes, and each values a used car of quality x as $\$1000x$. Suppose Mr 4, who doesn't own a used car, values a single used car of quality x as $\$1\,100x$, but that he has no use for two used cars. Suppose further that Mr 4 is *risk neutral* (i.e., he is willing to take a chance on a fair bet), so if he knows the *average* quality of used cars offered for sale is $\bar{x}$, he is willing to spend up to $\$1100\bar{x}$ for (any) one of them. We shall assume that he knows the average quality of cars offered for sale (from collecting information from sources such as *Consumer Reports*, which reports on the average quality of used cars of various makes and years), but not the quality of individual cars. Therefore, his demand price function can be written

$$p \leq \$1\,100\bar{x}, \tag{7}$$

where p is the price he is willing to pay and x is the average quality of cars offered for sale.

Now let us consider the 'supply' of used cars. Given their common valuation of used cars, Mr 1 is willing to sell for any positive price, Mr 2 is willing to sell at any price exceeding \$500, etc. Therefore, the market supply function which gives the *average* quality of cars offered for sale as a function of price is

$$\bar{x} = \begin{cases} 0, & \text{if } p < \$500 \text{ (Mr 1's car offered for sale)}, \\ \frac{1}{4}, & \text{if } 500 \leq p < 1000 \text{ (Mr 1's and Mr 2's cars offered for sale)}, \quad (8) \\ \frac{3}{4}, & \text{if } 1000 \leq p \text{ (all cars offered for sale)}. \end{cases}$$

Comparing (7) and (8), it is easily seen that there is only one common solution for $(\bar{x}, p)$: that is, (0,0). However, this equilibrium clearly is not efficient. For example, Mr 4 could pay $\$1050x_i$ to either Mr 2 or Mr 3, and either transaction would make *both* participants better off than the market solution without making anyone else worse off.

The reader can probably easily construct his own example of an insurance market in which prospective buyers differ with respect to risk, but the fact that sellers can't differentiate buyers with respect to risk prevents the market from achieving an efficient allocation. (See Akerlof, 1970 and Rothschild and Stiglitz, 1976.) The problem resulting from buyers' being unable to differentiate sellers or vice versa is usually termed the problem of *adverse selection*. Adverse selection occurs when the market mechanism sorts out the 'wrong' participants in a potential transaction (e.g., only the used cars valued by the owners at less than the market price will be offered for sale; or only the sufficiently 'risky' people will buy an insurance policy at a given price).

The private economy is obviously not unaware of the problem of adverse selection. Life insurance companies usually require physical examinations and medical histories. Automobile insurance companies require a past driving record and other information. A used-car purchaser can generally have a car inspected by a mechanic. These are obvious examples of the market's attempt to remedy adverse selection problems. In stable market situations (where, for example, the same producer is selling approximately the same good over time) agents will learn, a fact which will diminish the informational asymmetries over time. Furthermore, to the extent that producer reputation is valued in a market, a deterrent to the lemons problem exists. This is one of the benefits of the system of property rights which allows brand names and trade marks. Thus, it clearly cannot generally be claimed that the 'quality' of consumer goods produced can necessarily be expected to be inefficiently low because of the 'lemons' problem. However, the market generally cannot be expected to cure completely problems of adverse selection because of the costs of collecting information. Since the government would generally face similar costs, problems arising from adverse selection are uncertain candidates for effective government action. The problem of adverse selection will be taken up again in the following chapter.

2. *The efficient production and dissemination of information* Another potential market failure arises because private markets may devote insufficient resources to the production and dissemination of information. The source of this potential market failure is the free-rider problem. As an illustration of the problem, consider the preceding used-car example. Suppose that there are now *two* identical potential car buyers, Mr 4 and Mr 5, who value a car of quality level x at 1100x$. Suppose further that there is some other enterprising soul in the economy, Mr 6, who decides to set up a used-car quality information service. This service will inspect the used cars available for sale and sell the results of the inspections to the used-car customers.

Assume that the costs of inspecting the three cars are $125. The maximum value of the information to *one* of the potential car buyers is $100 (if Mr 5 or 6 purchases Mr 3's car for $1000). Therefore, the information must be sold to *both* potential buyers in order for the information service to at least break even. But if Mr 6 sells the information to Mr 4 first, the information may become known to Mr 5, who will then no longer pay for the information. Mr 6, if he looks ahead to this problem, will see that it is not profitable to collect the information. But it *is* efficient for the information to be collected. The costs of information collection are $125 and the benefits are $150 (with the information Mr 4 can buy Mr 3's car for $1000, and Mr 5 can buy Mr 2's car for $500). Although in this simple example the free-rider problem might be circumvented by a simultaneous sale of information to the two potential buyers, it is obvious that the free-rider problem may be significant in 'real world' situations. This may be a justification for government intervention by information provision in some circumstances.[18] It should be noted, however, that despite the free-rider problem, the market does provide a considerable amount of information (an obvious example is *Consumer Reports*).

(b) Moral hazard

A problem of *moral hazard* may arise in situations in which agents are able to affect the likelihood of uncertain events and the market cannot 'police' or price the agent's behaviour. As an illustration of the moral hazard problem, consider a model with 100 identical drivers. Suppose each driver has two modes of driving, safe and unsafe. If he drives safely, the probability of an accident is $1/100$, but if he drives unsafely, the probability of an accident is $1/10$. Suppose that there is only one kind of accident, and that such an accident creates damages of $1000. Finally, assume that a driver incurs additional costs (e.g., increased travel time) of $10 for driving safely.

18 The case for government intervention by information provision will be examined later in this chapter and in Chapters 3 and 5.

If all drivers drive safely, a risk-neutral insurance company can sell car insurance at about $10 per policy. (On average, 100 safe drivers will have one accident.) However, unsafe driving will require a premium of about $100 per policy. If the insurance company can't tell the difference between safe and unsafe drivers, no driver will individually have an incentive to drive safely, since such behaviour incurs additional costs. Therefore the 'equilibrium' in this model will be characterized by 100 unsafe drivers paying a premium of about $100 for car insurance. However, this equilibrium is clearly inefficient. If all drivers operate their vehicles safely, the social costs of safe driving are $1000 ($10 per driver in increased driving costs), but the expected social benefits are $9000 (resulting from the value of a reduction in the expected number of accidents from ten to one).

The problem of moral hazard is a form of externality – the source of the potential difficulty is the inability of the market to price some sorts of interactions; that is, there are involuntary transactions. In the preceding example the market was unable to price unsafe driving. Again, 'real world' markets recognize the problem of moral hazard and attempt to remedy it. Private contracts are used to enforce behavioural standards. Repairs made under warranty can require a suitable record of maintenance. An insurance policy can be cancelled. However, moral hazard may be a significant problem inhibiting the efficient level of warranty protection on consumer durables,[19] and some sorts of government policies may exacerbate the incentives for moral hazard.[20]

Distortionary government policies
Government policies can introduce distortions which are, themselves, a potential source of market failure. As a simple illustration, in the absence of other imperfections imposition of a tax on a competitive industry creates a wedge between social and private marginal costs, resulting in a market failure. It has been argued that the taxation of corporations distorts the private discount rate, which may distort the intertemporal allocation of resources. Obviously there are a myriad of government policies which affect the allocation of resources. For example, Frankena and Scheffman (1980) argue that many of the provincial policies in Ontario, although not specifically directed at influencing land use, have a major impact on the pattern and extent of land use in the province.

At this point we wish merely to reiterate our earlier point that regulatory actions often have important indirect effects. In the area of social regulation, some actions of the provincial government in one area can work against policy

---

19 This point will be discussed in Chapter 3.
20 This issue will be discussed in the next section when we examine the distortions created by government policies.

goals in other areas. As just one illustration, the provincial government is clearly interested in reducing the number of automobile accidents in the province. On the other hand, the province has a health insurance program (OHIP) which is subsidized in that users of health care facilities do not directly pay the full marginal costs of treatment (of course the 'average' taxpayer pays indirectly, through his payment of taxes). This is an example of an externality created by government policy. (Notice also that this problem exacerbates the usual moral hazard problem in insurance markets.) In such a situation some drivers will probably drive less safely because the *apparent* costs of an accident (either direct or revealed implicitly in car insurance premiums) are lower than the social costs. Similarly, people in risky occupations – or indeed anyone – may act less prudently than is socially desirable. Therefore, if the provincial government is committed to OHIP in its present form, and if it is the case that the subsidization of OHIP does result in a marked increase in unsafe behaviour, a policy requiring safer cars, use of seat belts, etc., *may* be justified on efficiency grounds. Of course such a justification would have to be based on a calculation of the costs and benefits.

Conversely, actions of the provincial government in one area can work *for* policy goals in other areas. One recent example is the reduction in provincial speed limits, which was implemented to promote energy conservation but apparently had an initial impact of reducing highway accidents in the province.

Intertemporal efficiency

Each of the previously described potential sources of market failure, especially uncertainty, gains an added dimension when considered in an intertemporal context. Consider as an example the typical case of a substance which may be carcinogenic but whose toxicity cannot be determined without years of tests and whose effects on users will not be evident for several years. Will the private market make the 'right' (efficient) decision about whether or not to use the substance now? In making this decision, the market participants must trade off current benefits with potential future costs. Producers may not assess the trade-offs efficiently if they do not expect to bear the impact of any future costs. Although the drug manufacturer did have to bear the (assessed economic) costs of thalidomide, current producers of saccharin, for example, may justifiably feel immune from such actions. On the other hand, consumers *may* recognize future costs, but this is unlikely to be the case if they do not have accurate information or cannot 'process' it. If neither producers nor consumers appreciate the future costs of their current actions, a market failure will likely result.[21]

---

21 A discussion of what the government should do in such situations will be provided later in this chapter and elsewhere in this study.

INTERTEMPORAL EQUITY

In our discussion of economic methodology we explained that an idealized market economy allocates resources efficiently, but that the allocation attained by the market is only one of many efficient allocations. In a simple world in which equity and efficiency can be separated, if society is unhappy with the equity properties of the market allocation, the appropriate response is to alter the *distribution* of resources, leaving the market to allocate resources efficiently. There are two problems with this methodology. First, as we have already discussed at length, in the 'real world' equity and efficiency cannot always be taken to be independent concerns. A second problem arises when we consider the issue of *intertemporal equity*.

Intertemporal equity is a unique problem in that it involves agents (future generations) who have no direct voice in current market and policy decisions, many of which will affect them. For example, decisions of the current generation, which pollute the air and water, use up fossil fuels, risk the effects of radiation on genes, etc., have a potentially important effect on the well-being of future generations. Even if pollution is to be allocated *efficiently* by current society, the distribution of pollution over generations may be *inequitable* from society's point of view.

Of course the market does not ignore the future. It constantly makes decisions (e.g., investment) in which it is trading off current versus future benefits and costs. In the terminology of simple economic models, economists describe the intertemporal allocation of resources by the private economy as being governed by the *private discount rate*, which is the private market economy's intertemporal terms of trade ('the' interest rate serves this function in simple models). If the private market economy undervalues the well-being of future generations relative to society's criterion of fairness, this is described as a situation in which the private discount rate is larger than the social discount rate. In such a situation the private economy excessively discounts the value of investments which take a long time to pay off or the costs of current actions if the costs are incurred in the future. The private discount rate may also be distorted by market imperfections (e.g., taxes), which could lead to intertemporal inefficiencies.

Although the current generation is 'taking away' consumption from future generations by polluting the air and water, using up fossil fuels, etc., it is also 'giving' consumption to future generations in the form of building up the private and public capital stock and investing in research and development on projects that will benefit future generations. Public policy certainly recognizes the intergenerational equity problem. Public subsidization of research and development and attempts to control the rate of extraction of exhaustible resources are two obvious examples. Any redistributional policy is politically difficult, because some groups necessarily are made worse off (unlike efficiency-improving policies, which may in principle be designed so that no one is harmed). The political difficulties are exacerbated for implementing policies which attempt to redistribute from present to future generations, since the beneficiaries of such policies have no direct political 'clout.'

POLICY INSTRUMENTS

In the previous section we discussed the major potential sources of market failure. If the market is not able to remedy a source of market failure so that a market failure exists, there may be an efficiency augmenting government intervention. In this section we shall consider the basic potential instruments of government intervention in the area of social regulation.

Tax-subsidy schemes

Economists generally favour tax-subsidy schemes as a regulatory instrument, when feasible, over other forms of direct intervention. This is for two reasons. First, the levying of a tax or granting of a subsidy allows maximal latitude for the market in the allocation of resources, a task for which the market is generally aptly suited. Second, the informational requirements for designing an efficient policy are frequently less for a tax-subsidy scheme than for other forms of direct intervention.

As an example, let us consider a specific version of the power plant example discussed earlier. Suppose the production function for the power plant is

$$Q = F(K, L), \tag{9}$$

where Q is output of electricity, K represents use of capital, and L use of labour. We shall assume that the power plant is a perfectly competitive firm and the price of its output is P_Q, the rental rate on capital is R, and the wage rate is W. Suppose that only one party is affected by the emissions of the plant and that the 'production function' for emissions, E, is

$$E = G(K, L). \tag{10}$$

Finally, assume that the cost of emissions to the affected agent is constant, per unit of emissions, and let this cost be denoted P_E.

Efficiency requires that the social marginal cost of electricity production equal the price paid for electricity, and this efficient allocation can be found by choosing K and L to maximize

$$P_Q F(K, L) - RK - WL - P_E G(K, L), \tag{11}$$

i.e., maximize net *social* benefits. Notice that to produce this efficient allocation the government need merely tax the power plant on its production of emissions at a tax rate of P_E per unit of emissions. The alternative government policy would be to set a standard for the level of emissions E. The difficulty involved with such a policy is that to set the efficient standard the government must solve (11) for the optimal level of E.[22]

Clearly, in this example the tax scheme is a much simpler policy, and although the simplicity of the example overstates the difference in informational requirements of the two types of policies for most 'real world' problems, it should be clear why tax-subsidy schemes, if feasible, are often preferable. Tax-subsidy schemes are commonly used social regulatory instruments. Two obvious examples are taxes on alcoholic beverages and tobacco. However, for political, equity, and sometimes efficiency reasons, social regulation often uses other instruments. This fact is one of the issues of major concern to economists interested in social regulation, since much of the recent social regulatory activity of governments has involved a direct interference with the market. However, in some cases direct interference is probably the efficient policy.

As one example, let us consider highway safety. The province is clearly interested in reducing the number and severity of accidents, and to this end it has enacted three types of policies: (1) laws governing driving; (2) automobile safety standards (vehicles must pass a safety inspection in order to be licensed after sale); and (3) behavioural standards (occupants must wear seat-belts). The law is one method by which society attempts to allocate externalities. In principle, properly designed driving laws which would specify a system of fines for unsafe driving (including driving an unsafe vehicle) and perhaps fines for being involved in an accident could achieve the social safety objective. Such a system of fines (which is, in effect, a tax scheme) could force reimbursement of innocent victims of accidents, and penalize accidents, per se (i.e., no fault penalties), in order to remedy the possible disincentives for safety created by OHIP. Why would this not be a preferable policy? The problem here is that the efficient tax would be required to distinguish 'wrongdoers' from others, and this decision cannot generally be made without recourse to the courts – an expensive procedure. Setting explicit standards (on safety of vehicles, use of seat-belts) *may*, therefore, be more efficient than a tax scheme in this case.

---

22 Of course any explicit standard can be attained by an appropriate tax scheme. For example, saccharin could be banned by levying a large enough tax; however, this would be just an indirect method of setting a standard.

Thus, tax-subsidy schemes are probably not always preferable to other forms of intervention, even on efficiency grounds. None the less, the economic literature has developed a very strong case for the use of tax-subsidy schemes in some area of social regulation, particularly environmental regulation.[23]

Setting standards

Perhaps the typical visible social regulatory activity involves the setting of standards. The common types of standards include those for production processes (interpreted here in a general sense, including, for example, educational requirements for doctors), those for 'quality' of goods and services, safety, and behaviour. Before examining the case for setting standards, we want to distinguish between two basic types – design standards and performance standards.

(a) Design versus performance standards

In most cases social regulation arises from a concern with the *performance* of goods, services, or individuals, rather than a direct concern with product or service *design* or with the particular behaviour of individuals, except insofar as they have certain effects. As an illustration, society's concern about children's clothing or toys is presumably a concern with the safety of these products, not with the design and materials used in the products per se. On efficiency grounds, if possible, regulatory instruments ought to be directed at the perceived problem. For example, we would argue that if reduced gasoline use is desired, a policy which raises the price of gasoline is more efficient than a policy which taxes large cars.

Since society generally is basically concerned with performance rather than design, policies should be directed, if possible, to influencing performance rather than directly influencing design. This is because the pressure in the market to minimize costs will generally find the most efficient method of achieving a given performance objective. Consider again a policy designed to reduce the emissions from a smoke-stack to some given level. Ignoring the fact that a tax scheme may be the best instrument in this case, consider the setting of standards. Two sorts of standards could be set; the first would require that the level of emissions be reduced to the desired goal; the second would require a specific method of reducing emissions. For the second policy to be as efficient as the first, the policy-makers must be able to ascertain the most efficient means of reaching the performance target.

However, it is not always possible to set performance standards, because performance cannot always be easily measured (safety standards for foods or

---

23 For further discussion of the use of taxes for environmental regulation see DeWees et al. (1975) and Baumol and Oates (1975).

drugs cannot be set without design standards governing use of materials and production processes), or because compliance with the performance standard is too costly to monitor.

The question as to when a standard-setting policy might be desirable is thoroughly discussed in the following two chapters, so that our discussion here will be brief. We consider standard-setting to be generally the least preferable form of government intervention because of the extent of its interference with the market's ability to allocate resources. However, in certain cases standard-setting may be the only feasible policy. Such a case could be a highly toxic known carcinogen. It is typical with carcinogens that they act slowly enough that it is difficult to assign 'blame' ex post for their consequences. In these circumstances producers may not exercise sufficient caution, and consumers may be unaware of the risks. The best policy for such a situation may be the setting of standards – either for use of the substance (as is done with asbestos), or perhaps a banning of the substance (such as PCBs).

We would like to stress the fact, however, that most problems, especially those involving carcinogens, are not clear cut. For example, it has not been conclusively proved that saccharin causes cancers in human beings, and the available evidence suggests that saccharin is at most a 'mild' carcinogen. Furthermore, saccharin is beneficial to people with weight problems and since cyclamates have also been banned, no suitable safe alternative for saccharin exists. Therefore we are not convinced that the federal government's recent ban of saccharin is justified, particularly since it does not appear that an adequate assessment of the costs and benefits of such a policy was conducted.

It is difficult to reconcile the federal government's policies concerning cigarettes and saccharin. Cigarettes are an apparent toxic human carcinogen, but the remedy chosen was the provision of the information (in the form of warning labels and extensive advertising). Furthermore, cigarettes have no known health-improving properties, and may have important negative third-party effects. In contrast, saccharin is not considered to be a toxic human carcinogen, it does have beneficial properties, and it has no third-party effects (other than on unborn children). Even a justification of the differential remedies based on an argument that children consume saccharin and they are too young to make the correct choices is on shaky ground, given the incidence of smoking among children. (Of course our comparison of these two policies may merely indicate that the cigarette policy is wrong.)

We are inclined to believe that in the saccharin case an information remedy would have been preferable to a ban. This, in fact, has been the policy implemented in the United States, where warning labels are required on products containing saccharin and the government has widely publicized the relevant health information. Naturally, a definitive conclusion on the appropriateness of the two policies would have to be based on a thorough assessment of the costs and benefits, and we advocate that policy formation be required to consider such assessments in the future.

Government production
One way for the government to engage in social regulation is to produce the targeted good or service itself. This approach is used in Ontario for electricity generation (Ontario Hydro) and is a method by which both rates and 'quality' of service can be regulated, which may be justified by natural monopoly arguments. As another example, the province has a monopoly on the retail off-sale distribution of liquor. The advantages and disadvantages of such a form of regulation lie in the fact that a government producer has different incentives than private producers have. This can be an advantage in that some socially undesirable incentives may be subverted. On the other hand, government producers are insulated from market pressures to attain (private) efficiency.

Since the province can tax liquor and regulate the hours of retail establishments, we are unconvinced about the desirability of the provincial operation of off-sale liquor outlets in the province, given the probable inefficiencies arising from government production. On the other hand, it may be desirable to have public operation of nuclear power plants, since political accountability may be a stronger deterrent to inefficient safety policies than the limited liability incurred by modern corporations. Naturally, determining the 'best' policy regarding nuclear electricity generation is a very complicated problem, for which we cannot hope to produce definitive answers here.

Legal remedies
One of the most important, but often unappreciated instruments of social regulation is the law, particularly laws governing contracts and torts.[24] Since a summary of the legal basis of social regulation in Canada and Ontario will be provided in Chapter 5, the use of the law as a social regulatory instrument will be discussed in the abstract here.

The law is a social institution which has a major role in the allocation of externalities and uncertainty.[25] Questions such as who should bear the costs of an automobile accident and what recourse the purchaser of a defective product should have, the answers to which are forms of social regulation, are dealt with

24 A tort is 'a wrongful act for which a civil action will lie, except one involving a breach of contract' (*Webster's 7th New Collegiate Dictionary*, 1970, G.&C. Merriam Co.).
25 Several papers discussing the allocative role of the legal system can be found in Manne (1975).

in tort and contract law. Contract law specifies the basis for recourse and the remedies in the event of breach of a contract. What constitutes a contract is defined very broadly by the law. Participants in any economic transaction are generally bound by *implicit* contracts, even if no formal written (or expressed) *explicit* contract is part of the transactions. For example, there is an implicit contract between the agents in a consumer good transaction that the good transacted is 'merchantable.'[26]

Liability under tort can be roughly defined as liability incurred because a 'wrong' was done, not because a contract was breached. For example, the participants in an automobile accident usually are not bound by any explicit or implicit contract, so that redress must be determined on the basis of an action in tort law. Tort law might be viewed as society's 'backstop' for dealing with externalities problems which have not been otherwise suitably remedied by contract or regulation. In the context of products liability (as opposed to personal liability) a successful tort action generally requires the proof or inference[27] of an act of negligence or omission on the part of the manufacturer, and for this reason tort law is a limited instrument.

From the point of view of economic efficiency, contract and tort law are important, because they divide the liability between agents in a 'transaction.' In a world without transactions or negotiations costs and in which performance under voluntary contracts does not require enforcement costs, the specific division of liability between agents in a transaction would have no effect on the efficiency of the transacted allocation. This result, known as the 'Coase Theorem'[28] is illustrated by the following example. Consider as the 'transaction,' an automobile accident, which is a good example of a 'transaction' involving an externality. Suppose society adopts a 'no-fault' liability rule for all automobile accidents (participants in an accident bear only their own costs). Such a policy, in itself, would probably not lead to an efficient allocation of resources. For example, owners of inexpensive cars might devote insufficient (on efficiency grounds) resources to averting accidents because to them cost of an accident would be low. Alternatively, owners of large 'armour plated' cars might not operate their vehicles with sufficient safety. However, if the no-fault rule leads to an inefficient allocation, by definition there are potential gains to be made by all participants in moving to an efficient allocation. In a world with no transactions, negotiations, or enforcement costs, drivers could reach such an allocation by private voluntary contracts. Thus, for example, drivers for whom accidents

26 Implicit contracts will be discussed further in Chapter 5.
27 The necessary basis of a successful tort action will be discussed further in Chapter 5.
28 See Coase (1960), Demsetz (1972), and Calabresi (1968).

are expensive could 'bribe' drivers with otherwise insufficient incentives for safety to drive more safely.

This example of voluntary contractual arrangements may seem far-fetched, and of course it is. 'Real world' transactions and negotiations costs would clearly preclude the web of voluntary contractual arrangements required for efficiency in this case. The lesson of this example is that the presence of significant transactions and negotiations costs and enforcement costs on voluntary contracts will often result in the division of liability determined by the law having an important impact on the efficiency of the allocation of resources. The importance of transactions, negotiations, and enforcement costs and therefore of the effect of the liability rule on efficiency will generally be greater, the larger the number of potential agents involved in the particular transaction are. For example, in a town with only two cars and two drivers we would expect that the allocative implications of the automobile accident liability rule would be markedly less than in Toronto.

Since the focus of the present study is social regulation in markets for consumer goods and services, our major interest here is how the law allocates liability for product or service failure.[29] On the basis of the preceding discussion we would expect that the division of liability for product failure between producer and consumer would generally be expected to have important efficiency effects. This issue will be thoroughly examined in the following chapter.

Information remedies

Our discussion of potential sources of market failure identified informational imperfections as a major source of concern. This argument will be reinforced by the analysis developed in the following chapter. In cases where informational imperfections are the problem, one obvious policy action is some form of information remedy (e.g., provision of information, forced disclosure, barring misleading information, or prescribing curatives for previous misleading information). One advantage of information remedies is that they leave maximum latitude for the market to allocate resources. As one illustration, in the used-car example described above, if the government could without cost obtain and disseminate information on the quality of the cars, the market failure could be simply remedied. The 'free rider' problem, also described above, which may inhibit the private incentives for information production and dissemination, is another argument for the role of government prescribed information remedies.[30]

---

29 The specifics of the Canadian law in this area will be taken up in Chapter 5.
30 The desirability of various forms of information remedies will be examined closely in Chapters 3 and 5.

THE DEMAND FOR SOCIAL REGULATION[31]

Several authors (Stigler, 1971, Posner, 1971, 1974, and Peltzman, 1976a) have argued that government intervention in the market allocation of resources is generally not motivated by a desire to increase the efficiency of resource allocation. Rather, they argue that such intervention is largely a device to redistribute resources to well defined constituencies which are then expected to return the favour in some manner, perhaps with votes. For example, pressure groups may trade votes or campaign financing in exchange for regulation which redistributes resources to them. Occupational licensing clearly redistributes income to current members of licensed occupations. Home-owners are generally the net beneficiaries of policy interventions in land and housing markets. Many people apparently believe that requiring safety equipment on cars makes the manufacturer 'pay' for the equipment. Unfortunately, unlike efficiency-augmenting policies, which at least have the potential to benefit everyone, policies which are primarily redistributive in nature necessarily make some groups worse off, often with an added cost of a reduction in efficiency.

Although this theory is overly simplistic in its view of the political process, it is patently clear that much of the social regulation in Canada is not directed to ameliorating market failures. As the analysis developed in this chapter has shown, whether or not a proposed or existing provincial policy can improve efficiency is generally ambiguous, and this ambiguity can be resolved only by an assessment of the costs and benefits of the policy. Furthermore, such assessments have not been appropriately used as an input in most policy discussions and decisions in the past.

A popular theory of traditional economic regulation (the regulation of rate-of-return, price, and quantity, such as the federal regulation of Bell Canada) argues that the regulators are prone to be 'captured' by those being regulated. This is because the regulatees are typically a small strong vocal constituency and rival constituencies are diffuse. However, much of social regulation is not adequately explained by the capture theory, although it could be argued the governments were captured by consumerist and environmental groups during the 1970s. Social regulation often is directed at a diffuse group (e.g., all emitters of effluents), so that there is typically not a small, strong, affected constituency. In addition, the beneficiaries are typically diffuse.

Finally, bureaucracy theories of regulation, which argue that the regulators have incentives to increase the scope of their powers and influence, are also of importance in understanding the roots of the demand for social regulation.

31 For a summary of theories of regulation see Wilson (1974).

Whatever the source and result of the demand for social regulation, the analysis we have developed in this chapter shows that intervention is not justified on *economic* grounds without a careful assessment of the costs and benefits of intervention and their distributions. Although policy decisions are not made solely on economic grounds, we have argued that such a cost-benefit calculation is an indispensable input into formulation of sensible public policy.

3

The economics of product reliability and warranties

INTRODUCTION

In the preceding chapter the various potential sources of market failure were enumerated and discussed. In assessing the likely importance of these imperfections in consumer goods markets it is useful to distinguish between three basic types of goods and services: *search goods*, *experience goods*, and *credence goods*. Search goods are those for which the consumer, through searching and information collection, can fully determine the 'quality' at the time of purchase. Most types of clothing are probably search goods. Experience goods are those for which the consumer can fully ascertain quality only after 'experiencing' (by consumption) the good. Most consumer durables are experience goods in that the consumer generally can ascertain the quality of the services which the product provides by using the product. In addition, the product may break. Credence goods are those for which the quality cannot be fully ascertained, even after consumption. For example, one is likely to be uncertain about the quality of a complicated medical treatment (was it necessary?, was it done correctly?) even after it has been administered.

The purpose of this chapter is to develop an analysis of markets for experience and, to some extent, credence goods. The central issue here is that for such goods and services consumers are by definition uncertain about product quality at the time of purchase – an obvious potential source of market failure. The conceptual focus of this chapter will be consumer durables markets, where uncertainty about product reliability is generally important. For example, the consumer cannot know with certainty whether the automobile, toaster, etc. which he purchases will function correctly. In such markets it is rational for the consumer to assume that the product is not 100 per cent reliable (i.e., not every unit produced can reasonably be expected to function perfectly) and product failure imposes significant costs on the purchaser, including perhaps the possibility of personal injury. Furthermore, it would generally be unreasonable to assume that consumers and producers possess the same information about product reliability, so that informational imperfections exist.

Producers presumably have the best information as to the *designed* reliability of their products, but casual observation of the functioning of consumer durables markets suggests that producers do not provide much of this information to consumers. One of the contributions of this chapter will be to provide an explanation for this phenomenon. On the other hand, consumers have better information on their pattern and use of maintenance of the product, which are factors that affect *realized* reliability.

Two critical attributes of product failure will be featured in our analysis: (1) product failure imposes costs on purchasers in the form of forgone product services and leisure, product repair costs, etc.; and (2) personal injury may result from product failure. Although our conceptual focus is on consumer durables markets, producer goods can easily be modelled within the basic structure we present, and consumer non-durables and services for which product failure is important (e.g., botulism in canned soup, faulty auto repair) also can be accommodated. Finally, our model can be used to analyse many markets in which the attribute of product quality about which consumers are uncertain is more subtle than simple reliability.

The model presented and the results derived or stated in the following sections of this chapter are based on the analysis developed in Scheffman and Appelbaum (1979). That analysis builds directly on a model first presented in Spence (1977), and some of the basic results we shall present here can be found in their original form there. Our discussion will be non-technical; readers interested in pursuing the technical details of the analysis are referred to the Scheffman-Appelbaum paper.

ASSUMPTIONS AND NOTATION

For expositional purposes the model presented here will be based on very restrictive assumptions. We caution the reader not to dismiss the results of our analysis on the basis of the restrictiveness of the assumptions. Most of the basic results presented here can be derived from a much less restrictive model. The sensitivity of the conclusions to modifications in the assumptions is discussed at the end of the chapter.

Consider a product that has the following characteristics: if it performs reliably, it functions perfectly for exactly one period; the alternative event to perfect functioning is that the product completely fails immediately after purchase. The consequences of product failure may impose costs on consumers, producers, or both. The division of these costs (i.e., the assignment of liability for product failure) between consumers and producers will be determined in the model.

It may facilitate the reader's intuition to think of the product as a toaster. The consumer faces uncertainty as to whether the toaster will break. In addition, there may be some risk that the toaster may break in a manner which causes personal injury. In such a market the manufacturer will furnish a warranty or guarantee with the product which protects the consumer against certain types of product breakdown for a limited time. On the other hand, a breakdown that causes personal injury will generally have to be dealt with in the courts. Our model will explain how the level of coverage is determined.

Why does the producer offer a warranty? Because consumers face uncertainty about product reliability, if they are risk averse they will be willing to purchase insurance against this risk at a premium over the expected costs of the risk. If producers are less risk averse, they will be willing to furnish such insurance. The other function of a warranty is that it may serve as a signal of product reliability, particularly when consumers do not have good information about reliability. Thus, a producer who has a more reliable product may find it in his interest to signal that his product is better by offering a better warranty than his competitors. On the other hand, it is possible that such signals could be used by producers to deceive consumers about product reliability. These aspects of warranties will be captured and explained by our model.

Producers
Producers are assumed to be identical. Let s be the probability that a given unit of the product *does not fail*. Then the *unit* cost of producing a product of reliability level s is assumed to be a constant, $c(s)$, where $c(s)$ is an increasing function of s, with increasing marginal cost of reliability. Producers can choose to offer a product warranty of the following kind: the producer pays the purchaser of a defective product $\$m$. The price charged for the product is denoted p. Producers are assumed to be *risk neutral*, and therefore their objective is to maximize expected profits.

Consumers
Consumers are assumed to be identical, and have an inelastic demand for one unit of the product. Letting y denote a consumer's income, the utility (i.e., index of well-being) derived by one of the identical consumers from spending p *on a unit that functions perfectly* will be denoted $u(y-p, 1)$, where the second argument of the function $u(\ )$ denotes the services provided by one unit of the

product. (From now on for notational simplicity this argument will be suppressed, so that $u(\ )$ will be written $u(y-p)$.)

Consumers know that the product either will function perfectly (for one period) or will fail, and the utility derived from spending p on a unit that fails will be denoted $v(y-p+m)$. Notice that the utility function in the case of failure ($v(\ )$) is written differently from the utility function in the case of no failure ($u(\ )$). This is because product failure causes harm. The harm may simply be the loss of the services of the product or the cost of repair. On the other hand, product failure may be accompanied by personal injury (e.g., a tire blows out, causing an accident). Thus $v(y-p+m)$ is the index of consumer well-being for net income $(y-p+m)$ after the consequences of the product failure. As a macabre example, if product breakdown could cause blindness, $v(y-p+m)$ would recognize the reduction in well-being resulting from blindness.

The typical case of product failure is not so complicated, since it would not be accompanied by personal injury. Products for which failure does not cause personal injury can be modelled in a more straightforward manner, since it is reasonable to assume that product failure imposes certain dollar costs on the purchaser. For example, if a toaster fails (in a manner which doesn't cause personal injury), the cost imposed on the purchaser is the cost of repairing the toaster. For such products the utility derived in the case of product failure can be written $u(y-p+m-L)$, where L is the dollar cost of product failure.

Consumers have perceptions about the likelihood of product failure (discussed fully below), which are summarized by r, their perception of the probability that the product won't fail (i.e., r is consumers' estimate of s). Therefore, the *expected utility*[1] derived by a consumer paying p for a product with warranty terms m is

(a) $ru(y-p) + (1-r)v(y-p+m)$,

or (1)

(b) $ru(y-p) + (1-r)u(y-p+m-L)$,

depending on the type of product.

In (1a), $u(y-p)$ is the utility derived from consuming a product which doesn't break, r is consumers' estimate of the probability that the product won't break, and $v(y-p+m)$ is the utility derived from a product that breaks if the warranty payment is m. For those readers unfamiliar with the concept of expected utility, consider the following example. Suppose a consumer has an income of $100, the price of the product is $10, and the warranty payment is $5. Suppose further that

---

1 See Baumol (1977), Hirshleifer (1976), and Hey (1979).

the consumer's estimate of $s(r)$ is 0.9. Then the consumer's expected utility from the product is $0.9u(90) + 0.1v(95)$, where presumably $v(95) < u(90)$. This expected utility is a weighted average of the two utilities, with the weight being the probability that the product doesn't break.[2]

We shall assume consumers are risk averse or risk neutral. If they are risk averse, by definition they are willing to pay a premium over expected costs to ensure themselves against a given risk. For example, consider a risk averse consumer who faces a risk of one chance in ten that he will lose $1000. His expected costs of the risk are $100, and since he is risk averse, he would be willing to pay more than $100 to insure himself against this risk. A risk neutral consumer would pay no more than $100 to insure himself against this risk. Consumers are clearly generally averse to risks which are significant relative to their wealth or income. This is demonstrated by the fact that they buy insurance against fire, theft, auto accidents, death, etc., and such insurance is actuarially 'unfair.' (The 'unfair' odds are what generate insurance company profits.) In terms of equation (1), the assumption of risk aversion or neutrality means that marginal utility (of u or v) of income is a non-increasing function of income.

Consumer perceptions

Where do consumer perceptions of product reliability, r, come from? Presumably r is derived from past experience, current information sources (e.g., *Consumer Reports*), and information provided directly or indirectly by producers. Initially we shall consider a static model, so that past consumer experience will not formally enter the structure of the model. (Later in the chapter a dynamic model in which past experience is featured as a critical component will be discussed.) Therefore, at this point we shall be concerned only with representing how consumer perceptions are affected by *current* producer actions. We shall focus on three categories of producer actions which may directly or indirectly affect consumer perceptions: (a) actual reliability of the product (s), (b) terms of the warranty (m), and, (c) advertising, packaging, labelling, and other methods by which a producer might directly influence consumer perceptions of the reliability of his product, which we shall summarize under the term '*advertising*.'

For some products a consumer can find direct evidence concerning product reliability (e.g., *Consumer Reports*, word-of-mouth), so we shall assume (as in Spence, 1977) that r is positively related to s. As we argued above, consumer perceptions are also likely to be influenced by the terms of the warranty offered

---

2 The Expected Utility Theorem shows that under certain plausible assumptions a consumer's preferences over risky alternatives can be written as an expected utility function. See Baumol (1977).

(in our model, m), since consumers may use the warranty as a signal of product quality. Although plausible arguments can be made either way, we shall assume that a better warranty *increases* a consumer's perception of reliability, ceteris paribus. Therefore, we assume that r is positively related to m. In fact, one of the results of our analysis is that for products for which consumers do not have much direct evidence of reliability (i.e., s does not have much effect on r) and thus the importance of the warranty as a signal of reliability is enhanced, better warranties will, in fact, be associated with more reliable products, ceteris paribus. Therefore, at least under these conditions, it is rational for consumers to use warranties as a positive signal of product reliability.

(a) 'Advertising'
We summarize all methods by which a producer can directly influence consumers' perceptions of reliability under the term 'advertising.' Such advertising will be modelled in a very simple way. The expenditure on advertising is assumed to be subject to neither economies nor diseconomies of scale, so that in order to change *each* of n purchaser's perceptions of reliability (r) by ϵ, the producer must spend $\$n\delta$ on resources devoted to advertising, where δ is independent of n. One 'story' consistent with this assumption is that all advertising takes the form of labels on the box containing the product.

We shall distinguish two types of advertising: (i) *informative advertising*, where an expenditure of $\$A$ per customer *reduces* the divergence between r and s, ceteris paribus, and (ii) *misleading advertising*, where an expenditure of $\$a$ per customer *increases* the divergence between r and s, ceteris paribus. Notice that one of the advantages of this simple model is that informative and misleading advertising can be easily defined. The reader can probably think of 'real life' experiences with each type of advertising.

Therefore, we summarize our assumptions about consumers' perceptions of product reliability:

$$r = r(s, m, A, a), \tag{2}$$

where r is positively related to s and m, an increase in A reduces $|r - s|$, and an increase in a increases $|r - s|$.

Producer profits
For given (p, s, m, A, a), expected profits per unit sold are

$$p - c(s) - (1 - s)m - A - a, \tag{3}$$

where p is the price per unit, $c(s) + A + a$ are the direct costs per unit, and $(1 - s)m$ is the expected warranty costs per unit. If each producer sells a large number of units, (3) will approximate actual realized profits per unit. Since we have assumed producers are expected profit maximizers, they will seek to maximize (3).

COMPETITIVE MARKET: PRODUCT BREAKDOWN CANNOT CAUSE
PERSONAL INJURY

In this section we shall examine the properties of the market allocation of product reliability and risk-bearing under the assumption that there is free entry by producers. In addition, we shall concentrate on product types for which product failure does not result in personal injury (i.e., we assume $v(y-p+m)$ can be written $u(y-p+m-L)$). With free entry and risk neutral producers, *in equilibrium* expected profits will be driven to zero; so

$$p = c(s) + (1-s)m + A + a. \tag{4}$$

Furthermore, the competition of free entry ensures that the market allocation (p, s, m, A, a) is 'best' as evaluated by the (identical) consumers, given (4) (otherwise a firm could make positive expected profits by offering a different (p, s, m, A, a)). Since consumer preferences are given by (1b) the equilibrium can be described mathematically as the maximization of (1b) subject to (4).[3]

Summarizing the model and the equilibrium, there are many identical consumers who have imprecise (common) estimates of product reliability which are influenced by actual product reliability, the terms of the warranty offered, and advertising. There are several identical risk neutral producers who will compete for sales, attempting to maximize expected profits. As in any simple perfectly competitive model, equilibrium requires zero (expected) profits, so that producers compete through changing price, reliability, warranty terms, and advertising to exploit profitable opportunities, which are defined by what consumers are willing to pay for a product with a certain set of characteristics (s, m, A, a) and the costs of providing those attributes. Therefore the forces of competition will lead to a product with characteristics which consumers most prefer, given that producers must break even.[4]

In what follows we shall summarize and discuss the implications of this model. The formal analysis can be found in Scheffman and Appelbaum (1979).

Implications of the equilibrium
(a) The warranty coverage (m) offered in equilibrium is the same as that which would result from the offer of coverage by a risk neutral competitive insurance industry (which knew s).

---

3 See Scheffman and Appelbaum (1979).
4 'Normal' profits are included in $c(s)$.

Thus, the fact that the producers have better information than consumers and offer the warranty coverage is not, itself, a source of concern. The forces of competition lead producers to compete in the warranty coverage they offer.

(b) Sign $(m - L) = $ sign $(s - r)$, that is, consumers are under-, exactly, or over-[5]-insured by the warranty in equilibrium as they over-, correctly, or underestimate product reliability, respectively.

To see why this result obtains, consider a simplified version of the model with no advertising, risk neutral consumers, and where r is not affected by m. Consider an equilibrium with $r > s$. Suppose producers are offering a warranty $\bar{m} > 0$. To break even they will have to charge a price for the product of $p = c(s) + (1 - s)\bar{m}$. Since consumers are risk neutral, the value placed on the warranty itself is at most $(1 - r)\bar{m}$ (their expected costs of product failure), which is less than $(1 - s)\bar{m}$ (since $r > s$). Therefore if a producer reduced his warranty coverage to zero ($\bar{m} = 0$), he could reduce his price to $c(s)$. Since consumers placed less value on the warranty $((1 - r)\bar{m})$ than the amount of the price fall $((1 - s)\bar{m})$, they would prefer the zero warranty situation. In this simple example competition would drive warranty coverage to zero.

In the general model with risk averse consumers, advertising, and m having an effect on r, the qualitative result still obtains – warranty coverage will be less than L in equilibrium if $r > s$. Therefore one reason why we observe less than 'full' warranty coverage for most products may be that consumers overestimate product reliability. However, there may be other reasons for this (e.g., moral hazard), which we shall discuss below.

Many consumerists seem to argue that warranties are given merely at the whim of producers, with consumers having no voice or choice. This sort of argument is nonsense. Consumers influence the provision of warranty protection through their market votes. Producers clearly recognize the importance (or lack of it) that consumers attach to warranties, as evidenced by any number of examples of product promotion which stress warranty coverage.

It is important to realize that the lack of full warranty protection arises because the level of protection offered is what consumers cast their market votes for, given their perceptions of reliability. Of course consumers would rather have full warranty protection, ceteris paribus, but to offer such protection producers would have to raise their price, and the new combination of reliability and warranty protection at the new price would not be as attractive to consumers. In this sense producers are not 'ripping off' consumers; they are simply responding

---

5 In most circumstances we would expect that $m > L$ would be ruled out by moral hazard, which has not been incorporated in the model here. However, we do observe products with 'double-your-money-back' guarantees. Moral hazard will be discussed later in this chapter.

to market votes. In general, the lack of full warranty protection arises from three sources: (i) asymmetric information, (ii) moral hazard, and (iii) producer risk aversion. The importance of the latter two sources will be discussed below.

(c) If consumer perceptions are not influenced by the current level of reliability (r not a function of s), better products (larger s) are positively correlated with better warranties.

This is an important result, since it shows that in cases where there is little direct information about reliability it is rational for consumers to take the warranty as a (positive) signal of reliability. The intuition for the result is straightforward. A producer of a more reliable product can offer the same warranty as the producer of a less reliable product at a lower cost, since his expected costs ($(1 - s)m$) will be lower.

(d) Producers will not use informative advertising.

This is a very striking result which is independent of the usual 'free rider' arguments. Even the existence of perfect competition and free entry in the model does not provide incentives for the direct provision of information. The problem here is that consumers are not willing to pay for information, at least not indirectly through their market votes. Therefore producers have no incentive to provide such information. Since (e) is a further and related surprise, we shall postpone discussion until after (e).

(e) Producers may use misleading advertising.

Thus, in our model, consumers through their market votes provide no incentives for producers to provide correct information and may provide incentives for producers to deceive them!

To understand (d) and (e) it must first be realized that even in this simple model, consumers are purchasing a complex product, comprised of the physical product itself, the warranty protection offered, and the 'aura' of reliability (affected by (s, m, A, a)). The more reliable the consumer believes the product is, the lower will be his demand for insurance against product failure and the higher will be his valuation of the product for any level of warranty protection, ceteris paribus. Consider the possible actions by a producer if his customers overestimate the reliability of his product. If the consumer overestimates reliability, the producer can incur costs to remedy this misperception by advertising. However, besides these costs the producer will now have to offer greater warranty protection or lower his price to make a sale to the newly informed consumer. On the other hand, if the producer incurs costs to further distort the consumer's perceptions and this action is successful, the consumer will now be willing to pay a higher price for the same actual level of reliability and warranty coverage.

False or deceptive advertising is illegal under both federal and provincial statutes (see Chapter 5), so there are legal disincentives to deception. Furthermore, our model gives *producer reputation* no role, and reputation, if important, also provides disincentives to deception, an issue which we will return to below. None the less, a lot of advertising we observe is clearly directed to enhancing consumers' perceptions of product reliability (although such advertising need not be deceptive if in the absence of the advertising, consumers underestimate reliability).

Of more importance, in our view, than the fact that producers may deceive their customers, is our conclusion that producers will not have an incentive to provide (truthful) information to their customers. Although the result is also likely to be tempered if producer reputation is important, it is clear that producers often have significant information about product reliability which they do not make available to producers. Recent examples such as the Firestone 500 and Ford Pinto cases provide supporting evidence for this assertion, but such dramatic examples are not needed to make the point. A more pedestrian illustration is that home appliance (e.g., freezers, refrigerators) manufacturers have generally not provided information on the cost of running their products, even though they have this information or could obtain it very easily (uncertain operating costs could easily be incorporated in our model in a manner analogous to uncertain reliability). Our model captures the disincentives for producers to provide such information.

COMPETITIVE MODEL: PRODUCT FAILURE CAUSES PERSONAL INJURY

For products where the costs of product failure are not easily quantifiable; that is, where the product failure may result in personal injury, the utility function in the event of product failure must be written $v(y - p + m)$. Therefore a competitive equilibrium with free entry can be characterized mathematically as the maximization of (1a) subject to (3); that is, the market allocation is best for consumers (in terms of criterion (1a)), given producers break even.

Implications of the equilibrium

In most respects the implications of the equlibrium conditions are similar to those of the simpler preceding model. However, the meaning of 'full' warranty coverage is now ambiguous. One natural definition of under, over, or full coverage is $u(y - p) <, >, = v(y - p + m)$, respectively. With this definition under certain assumptions[6] a result similar to (a) above obtains. The main difference

6 If sign $(u - v) = -$sign $(u' - v')$, which is a sort of generalized concavity condition. Unfortunately, it does not seem possible to get intuition about whether this is a plausible condition.

from the preceding model is that informative advertising may be profitable for producers. Thus, even in the absence of possible legal recourse by the consumer, products for which failure may result in personal injury are accompanied by stronger incentives for producers to provide accurate information. None the less, producers may (as above) instead have incentives to deceive.

MONOPOLY

What if the industry is not competitive? To investigate the implications of an imperfectly competitive market structure, suppose for simplicity that there is a single monopoly producer who faces no threat of entry. Let $\hat{U}$ be the utility level attained by consumers if they cannot consume the product. A monopolist will maximize his expected profits, that is, choose p, s, m, A, a so as to maximize

$$p - c(s) - (1 - s)m - A - a. \tag{6}$$

But he can't charge a price which would reduce consumers' expected utility (1) below $\hat{U}$.[7]

Implications of the monopoly equilibrium
The implications of the monopoly equilibrium are identical with those of the competitive equilibrium described in the two preceding sections. Therefore the relationship between the extent of warranty coverage and consumer perceptions of reliability and the incentives for informative and deceptive advertising are not affected by market structure. This is because it is a matter of indifference to the monopolist whether he offers the warranty or it is offered by a competitive risk neutral insurance industry. He can fully extract his monopoly rents through his control of p and s.

Furthermore, the product attributes (s, m, A, a) in the monopoly equilibrium may be identical with what would result from a competitive industry, although in this case the price charged by the monopolist would be higher. Therefore, as in our discussion of the implications of market structure in Chapter 2, market structure does not have an a priori predictable effect on product reliability and the extent of warranty coverage.

There is a strong strand of thought in the consumerist literature, and indeed in contracts case law,[8] that transactions between producers and consumers are characterized by 'unequal bargaining power,' making such transactions unfair to consumers. Although on economic grounds the exercise of market power

---

7 The equilibrium conditions are derived in Scheffman and Appelbaum (1979).
8 Where warranties are often viewed as 'contracts of adhesion.'

may be viewed as unfair (since consumers' utility level is reduced), and will generally lead to inefficient allocations, it does not necessarily result in 'too little' warranty coverage. Furthermore, the notion that consumers are completely at the mercy of manipulative or arbitrary producers for obtaining warranty protection is clearly wrong. Producers are restricted by consumers' demands, that is, what they are willing to pay. Finally, very few, if any markets could be characterized as monopolies.

To the extent that producers in concentrated industries act non-competitively, it is usually through a restraint of price competition and is usually characterized by competition through product differentiation. Warranty coverage is clearly used on occasion as an important component of product differentiation. Two examples are American Motors's promotion of its 'full' warranty on its cars and Proctor-Silex's touting of its uniform warranty coverage over its whole range of consumer appliances (one year – repair or replacement). Thus, imperfect competition could *improve* the variety of warranties and extent of their coverage (relative to a competitive market), if one takes the commonly held view that imperfect competition leads to 'excessive' product differentiation. However, such an allocation would be inefficient.

EFFICIENCY

We have discussed the basic properties of the market determination of product reliability, warranty coverage, and advertising. Now we shall examine the efficiency of the market-determined allocation. However, the existence of both uncertainty and informational asymmetries in our model makes the concept of efficiency itself ambiguous. There are at least three criteria by which the efficiency of the market allocation could be measured: (1) consumers' ex ante well-being (given by (1)), (2) the ex post well-being of a consumer who purchases a non-defective unit ($u(y-p)$)), and (3) the ex post well-being of a consumer who purchases a defective unit ($v(y-p+m)$)).

We urge the reader to study the following discussion of concepts of efficiency, because it is at the core of understanding both the source of concern with the market allocation and the efficacy of possible remedies.

Ex ante efficiency
By ex ante efficiency we mean that the market allocation is best for consumers in terms of their ex ante well-being (as measured by (1)). By definition, the free entry competitive allocation maximizes consumers' ex ante criterion of well-being ((1)), subject to producers' breaking even; that is, competitive pressures lead producers to provide the combination of reliability, warranty coverage, and

advertising which consumers desire (in terms of ex ante market votes), consistent with zero expected profits. Therefore, the free entry competitive equilibrium is, by definition, ex ante efficient. Although consumers may be unhappy with their choice ex post, it would be patently wrong (at least where deceptive advertising is not used) to argue that they have been 'ripped-off' by producers, since the producers have provided them with exactly what they *thought* they wanted. A producer who tried to give the consumers a product and warranty which were 'best' for them (whatever that might mean) instead of what they wanted would be penalized, at least in the short run. Although the equilibrium is efficient in an ex ante sense, one feels uncomfortable with an allocation based on misinformed preferences. Thus, we shall now consider concepts of ex post efficiency.

Ex post efficiency
Although there is no ambiguity in the concept of ex ante efficiency, ex post efficiency has no obvious a priori definition. Although all consumers in our model are identical, ex ante, they are heterogeneous, ex post, since some will have purchased 'good' units, while others will have purchased units that fail. Denote those who purchase good units as being in the G group, and those who purchase units that fail as in the F group.

The Pareto methodology discussed in Chapter 2 suggests that an efficient allocation should be defined as one for which the well-being of consumers in group F cannot be improved without reducing the well-being of at least some consumers in the G group. However, use of this criterion is problematic in this case, since it cannot be known ex ante which group a consumer will be in ex post, or how many consumers will be in each group (which will be determined by s, which is one of the parameters chosen in the efficient allocation). Therefore, some explicit value judgments must be made about trade-offs between the well-being of group F and group G. Since there are only two types of consumers ex post, there are two obvious candidates: (1) a *common law criterion* (full compensation for product failure), in which there is no trade-off allowed between the well-being of the two groups; and (2) an *average man criterion* (average ex post well-being), in which tradeoffs between the two groups, as determined by averaging, are allowed.

(a) Common law criterion
One of the dominant strands of thought in the common law would require full compensation for product failure. In terms of our model this approach would require that all consumers (i.e., purchasers of both defective and non-defective products) be equally well off, ex post. For goods for which no personal injury is involved this requirement is easily understood. It simply requires that $m = L$. However, when personal injury is involved in product failure, full compensation

is more difficult to define. In terms of our model what is required is that m be such that $u(y-p)=v(y-p+m-L)$. Of course equalization of ex post well-being is not a complete criterion for efficiency. The natural definition of efficiency consistent with the common law is that ex post well-being is maximized, given that the ex post well-being of members of groups F and G is equalized. We shall term this definition of efficiency the 'common law criterion.'

1. *Products for which no personal injury is involved.* For this sort of product, equalization of ex post well-being clearly requires $m=L$, which determines m. Now the efficient level of reliability must be determined. The cost of producing a unit of reliability level s is $c(s)$. The expected costs of product failure of a unit of reliability levels are $(1-s)L$. An increase in s increases production costs by increasing $c(s)$ and reduces the expected costs of product failure by reducing $(1-s)L$. Efficiency will require that s be such that a small increase in s increases $c(s)$ by the same amount that it reduces $(1-s)L$. At any other s total unit costs to society, $c(s)+(1-s)L$, can be made smaller. Therefore, efficiency requires that s be such that the marginal production costs of reliability $(c'(s))$ equal the marginal benefit in reduced expected costs of product failure, that is,

$$c'(s)=L, \tag{7}$$

where $c'(s)$ is the marginal production costs of reliability and L is the marginal benefit in reduced expected costs of product failure $(-d(1-s)L/ds)$.

It should not be surprising that efficiency does not generally require perfect reliability ($s=1$). Production of 'reliability' uses scarce resources, and for efficiency these costs must be balanced against the benefits of the resources in alternative uses.

Therefore the common law criterion requires full warranty protection, $m=L$, and reliability determined as the solution of $c'(s)=L$. The market allocation will not satisfy this criterion unless consumer perceptions are accurate ($r=s$).

2. *Products for which failure causes personal injury.* For this sort of product the common law criterion requires $u(y-p)=v(y-p+m)$. If m is such that this criterion is met, the expected unit social costs of product failure are $(1-s)m$. Therefore, as in the preceding argument, s should be chosen so that the marginal production costs of reliability equal the marginal benefit in reduced expected costs of product failure, that is,

$$c'(s)=m. \tag{8}$$

Mathematically, the common law efficient allocation is the solution for s and m of the two equations

(a) $u(y-c(s)-(1-s)m)=v(y-c(s)-(1-s)m+m)$,

(b) $c'(s)=m$.
$$\tag{9}$$

If we ask now whether the competitive market allocation will be common law efficient, the answer is generally no, even if consumer perceptions are accurate $(r=s)$. This is because even if consumer perceptions are accurate, the market allocation will not generally equalize ex post well-being.

(b) Average man criterion
Appealing to the law of large numbers, if s is the level of reliability produced, approximately s per cent of consumers will purchase functioning units and $(1-s)$ per cent will purchase defective units. Therefore the *average* ex post well-being, or alternatively, the ex post well-being of the 'average man,' will be

$$su(y-p)+(1-s)v(y-p+m).^9 \qquad (10)$$

The average man criterion requires that s and m be chosen so as to maximize average ex post well-being, that is, to maximize (10). In terms of our earlier discussion, s per cent of the consumers are in the G group and they receive ex post utility of $u(y-p)$; $(1-s)$ per cent are in the F group and they receive ex post utility of $v(y-p+m)$. This criterion does not generally require that the well-being of the two groups is equalized.

1. *Products for which no personal injury is involved.* If personal injury is not involved, $v(y-p+m)=u(y-p+m-L)$, and (10) becomes

$$su(y-p) + (1-s) u(y-p+m-L). \qquad (11)$$

Now, notice that if we require full compensation $(m=L)$, (11) becomes $su(y-p)$ $+(1-s)u(y-p)$, which is equal to $u(y-p)$. Therefore if $m=L$, s should be chosen to minimize social unit costs $=p=c(s)+(1-s)L$, which by the argument of the preceding section requires $c'(s)=L$. It is straightforward to demonstrate mathematically that this allocation is average-man-criterion efficient. Therefore the average-man-criterion requires

(a) $m=L$, $\qquad (12)$
(b) $c'(s)=L$.

Therefore the average-man-criterion efficient allocation is identical with the common law criterion efficient allocation (for products not involving personal injury). This is a comforting result, in that at least for products for which personal injury is not an important component of product failure, the choice of efficiency criterion is irrelevant to the characteristics of the efficient allocation. Furthermore, for such products the competitive allocation will be efficient by either criterion if consumer perceptions are accurate $(r=s)$.

9 An alternative interpretation of (10) is the expected utility of a perfectly informed consumer.

2. *Products for which failure causes personal injury.* For products for which failure causes personal injury the common law criterion and the average man criterion are not generally equivalent. This result obtains because the average man criterion will not usually lead to an equalization of utility levels. The competitive market allocation will not usually satisfy either criterion, even if consumer perceptions are accurate.

Summary of efficiency implications of competitive allocation

The competitive allocation will, by definition, be ex ante efficient. However, one is uncomfortable with this notion of efficiency, especially if consumers have incorrect information which leads to misperceptions about product reliability and distorted market votes. For products for which product failure is not accompanied by personal injury, our two proposed definitions of ex post efficiency lead to the same allocation. The competitive allocation will, in this case, be efficient if consumer perceptions are accurate. For products for which product failure is accompanied by personal injury, the two ex post efficiency criteria differ, and the competitive allocation will not generally be efficient by either criterion, even if consumer perceptions are accurate.

It is important to note that market determined levels of reliability and warranty coverage are not necessarily lower than the efficient (in either sense) levels! For example, if perceptions are not affected by current reliability (r not a function of s) and personal injury is not involved, it can be shown that the market determined levels of s and m are *higher* than the efficient levels if consumers underestimate reliability ($r < s$).

POSSIBLE REGULATORY ACTIONS

The discussion of the previous section showed that although the market allocation will be ex ante efficient, ex post efficiency will not usually be attained. As we shall point out below, regulation in such a situation is especially problematic, since forced deviations from the market allocation will affect *both* consumers and producers adversely, when valued in terms of their ex ante criteria. In this section we shall provide an abstract evaluation of the major policy instruments in terms of the model presented in this chapter. In Chapter 5 we shall summarize the legality of possible regulatory actions and in Chapters 5 and 6 we shall place the abstract arguments of this chapter in a more realistic context.

Imposition of producer liability

In a world in which the legal system operates without frictions or transactions costs, simple imposition of full liability on producers for the costs of product failure (i.e., making producers responsible for warranty coverage that ensures $u=v$) will result in a market allocation that achieves common law efficiency. This is because the pressures of competition will lead producers to produce the best combination of s and m, consistent with the requirement that $u=v$. This allocation will also satisfy the average man criterion for products for which failure does not involve personal injury. However, 'real world' complications temper the strength of this conclusion for three reasons: (1) Imposition of full producer warranty creates possible *moral hazard* problems, since such liability reduces the incentives for consumers to engage in the efficient level of care and maintenance. This problem is recognized by the law, in that a producer-defendant in a product failure case may be able to win by establishing sufficient carelessness on the part of the consumer-plaintiff. (2) The legal system is far from frictionless and the costs of using it are generally high, so that especially for products for which failure results in only moderate costs, attempted redress through the courts is unlikely to be effective. (3) Explicit or implicit *limited* liability of producers may temper the incentives for efficient risk avoidance by producers.

For product failures which result in significant personal injury one may be uncomfortable trading off the well-being of injured with non-injured parties. If that is the case, one would be more comfortable with the common law criterion, and so recourse to the courts is probably the best feasible regulatory system. Of course it would be beneficial to have a less frictional legal system, but it is beyond the scope of this study to suggest possible institutional changes in the legal system. The legal system has some latitude for dealing with the limited liability problem through imposition of criminal penalties in some cases, but this problem should also be given further study by legal experts.

Recourse to the courts is not a reasonable remedy for a broken toaster. In principle, full liability could be imposed on producers for such cases by mandating warranties, but we would argue against such a policy. First, if the only source of inefficiency is consumer misperceptions, the market may eventually solve the problem, since we would assume that consumers do learn. Secondly, if consumer misperceptions are the only problem, it may be more efficient to 'cure' the misperceptions.

A third problem with mandated warranties is the fact that since the unregulated market allocation is ex ante efficient (i.e., it is perceived as best for consumers and producers given the information they have), forced deviations from this allocation create incentives for both consumers and producers to evade the regulations. One method by which the market can circumvent a mandated warranty is for producers to adjust the quality of service given under the warranty. As an illustration, one possible explanation for the seeming variation in warranty service performance by automobile dealers is that this is an example of a market with a mandated (by the manufacturer) warranty. This mandated warranty may not be optimal, ex ante, for all consumers and dealers. Thus we have the apparent phenomenon of 'low overhead,' low price, low service quality (?) dealers, and high price, high service quality (?) dealers. Therefore a policy which mandates warranties may not be effective without *enforcement costs*. Finally, attempting to define product failure (as opposed to normal wear, consumer negligence, etc.) at all, let alone in a manner which deals effectively with moral hazard, is a very formidable task.

The average man criterion for efficiency cannot be met by simple imposition of producer liability for product failures involving personal injury. This result is derived in Spence (1977), where it is argued that efficiency can be achieved only by an imposition of a *two*-part liability on producers. In this scheme producers must make a liability payment to the consumer *and* to the government in cases of product failure. However, the practical usefulness of this policy prescription is tempered by the difficulty that would be encountered in attempting to calculate the optimal liability schedules in any particular case.

The role of producer liability will be discussed further in Chapter 5.

Direct regulation of product reliability

(a) The type of regulation
The direct regulation of product reliability is a commonly discussed remedy for perceived deficiencies in the market determined level of reliability. Such regulations will be of two basic types: *design standards* and *performance standards*. Design and materials standards specify product characteristics, while performance standards specify product performance. Since it is presumably a concern with product performance (reliability) which gives rise to a desire for remedial action, performance standards are generally the preferred remedy. Besides being more cumbersome, trying to control performance by the indirect means of regulating product design is likely to be inefficient. This is because the market will, through competitive pressures and the incentive to minimize costs, generally find the most efficient design which satisfies a given product performance standard. The regulator, however, often has neither the incentive nor the expertise to specify efficient design.

Nevertheless, design standards may be preferable for products for which performance standards cannot be set, because, for example, performance cannot be measured (e.g., prescription drugs and food additives).

(b) Properties of efficient regulation
Because products have at least *two* important characteristics – reliability and warranty coverage – use of the single policy instrument of reliability regulation

will not generally be able to achieve full efficiency. The problem here is that full efficiency (in either sense) specifies the level of both reliability and warranty coverage, but the specification of only the reliability level will generally lead the market to choose an inefficient level of warranty coverage. Thus only *second best* efficiency can generally be attained by direct regulation of product reliability.

Finally, recall from our earlier discussion that the market determined level of reliability is not necessarily *below* the first-best efficient level of reliability; this situation may also occur for second-best reliability. Thus, it is possible that the second-best policy for a particular case could require *lowering* the level of reliability, rather than setting a minimum level of reliability!

1. *Common law criterion.* To satisfy the common law criterion, consumers must be equally well off, ex post. Therefore the second best common law efficient policy for regulating reliability requires: (a) setting s so that the market provides full warranty coverage ($u = v$), or (b) requiring perfect reliability, that is, setting $s = 1$. If both policies are feasible, the one which results in highest utility is chosen. It should be clear that the regulation of reliability is particularly inappropriate (at least as a piecemeal policy) if the policy-maker has a common law criterion. Setting $s = 1$ is not likely to be possible and a policy which attempts to set m indirectly by setting s is absurd as long as the policy-maker can directly set m. Finally, a second-best situation in which only reliability standards can be set is likely to make the common law criterion (second best) Pareto inefficient. This is because it will often be possible to make *all* consumers better off than the second-best common law criterion (but not *equally* well off). None the less, real world considerations may make the direct regulation of reliability desirable. We shall discuss this point further below.

2. *Average man criterion.* The second-best efficient policy (in the average man sense) of directly regulating reliability is to set s at the level which maximizes average utility, given that the market determines warranty coverage. Since in our model this is a simple maximization problem, the properties of such a policy are easily derived. The second-best specification of s will not generally coincide with the first-best efficient s. This is because the policy-maker must take into account how the market's choice of warranty coverage and price will react to a reliability standard. The second-best efficient s will generally be difficult to calculate.

(c) Situations in which direct regulation of reliability may be desirable

Although in general only second-best efficiency can be attained by reliability regulation, such regulation may be desirable if product failure results in significant economic or human costs and: (i) moral hazard or externalities are important (e.g., automobile safety standards *may* be justified on the grounds that drivers do not consider the *social* cost of accidents in the calculations determining their demand for safety); or (ii) if recourse to the courts is likely to be ineffective. Legal redress may be ineffective if it is very difficult to establish liability (e.g., in the case of a slow acting or widely used carcinogen), or if corporate limited liability or other restraints on liability weaken the incentives for adequate risk avoidance by producers. One possible example of the latter problem is nuclear power plants. However, the *apparent* limits to liability are weakened in some situations because of the possibility of imposition of *criminal* penalties, but this could happen only if *negligence* is proved.[10]

As with the imposition of producer liability, the direct regulation of reliability may be complicated by the fact that the unregulated market allocation is ex ante efficient, so that there are incentives for the market to attempt to evade the regulation. For example, consumers can evidently benefit in terms of increased power and mileage by removing the catalytic converters and other pollution control devices on their cars.

Finally, it should be noted that industry and trade associations often seek to control product characteristics through self-regulation by adopting voluntary product guidelines. In addition, there are several testing agencies in Canada (e.g., Canadian Standards Association), which test products for manufacturers to determine whether they meet criteria set by the CSA, by the manufacturers, or by government. Such self-regulation may be beneficial in that product 'quality' is controlled and often certified in a manner which provides consumers information (e.g., that a product meets the CSA standards). However, such self-regulation can be used to restrict competition. That issue will be considered extensively in Chapter 4.

Information remedies
There are two basic types of information remedies possible: (1) prohibiting misleading information and (2) providing consumers with accurate information. Our simple model predicts that only misleading advertising will be used by producers. Although this result is tempered by a recognition that factors such as producer reputation have no role in our model, none the less misleading advertising is still likely to arise on occasion. Both the federal and provincial governments have powers to regulate false, misleading, or deceptive advertising (discussed fully in Chapter 5), so that there are apparent remedies for this problem. Of course, establishing that advertising is false, misleading, or deceptive is a formidable task in practice.

---

10 For a recent example of an attempt to bring criminal action in a case of product defect in the United States – the Ford Pinto case in Indiana – see 'Ford goes to trial' (1980). Ford was found not guilty in the case.

Our model also shows that there may be insufficient incentives for producers to provide purchasers with information, so government inducements to provide information may sometimes be desirable. Regulations such as 'truth in lending' and health warnings on cigarette packages are examples of such actions. There are two basic types of information provision policies. First, direct disclosure by producers can be required. Second, the government can provide information. In practice, information provision policies have generally been combinations of these two basic types of policies. (For example, the health hazard problem with cigarettes was dealt with by both forced disclosure through labelling and a myriad of public announcements.)

When consumer misperceptions are a major potential source of inefficiency, the provision of information is an attractive policy remedy, since it makes maximum use of private incentives. Of the three policy instruments we have discussed, it is the only one that does not create ex ante incentives to subvert the regulation. However, three aspects of information provision policies must be considered in any decision to implement such a policy. First, since information will be provided through regulation of producer behaviour, or directly by the government, consumers are likely to bear at least some of the costs of information provision, through taxes or in the form of higher prices. Thus, as with any policy, the costs and benefits must be considered. The second important aspect of information provision is that even if consumers are given usable, accurate information, they may not fully respond to it. In terms of our simple model, even if the government knows s and makes this information available to consumers, their perceptions (r) will adjust, but probably not fully (i.e., $r \neq s$), because this information is only one source from among many which they may use to form their perceptions.

The last important aspect of information provision is that some types of product information may be too technical to be usable by consumers. However, we believe that this argument has been excessively and sometimes inappropriately used as a justification for using policies other than information provision. For example, although mandatory use of seat belts may be justified on other grounds, we are unconvinced by arguments which claim that drivers do not correctly perceive the risks of driving without seat belts.[11] As another example, we argued in Chapter 2 that information remedies may have been preferable to banning saccharin.

Finally, it is worth pointing out that the market does attempt to respond to a demand for better information by consumers. Better business bureaus and

11 However, they may miscalculate the costs of accidents because of subsidized hospitalization.

periodicals like *Consumer Reports* are perhaps the two best-known private sources of information on product and service quality and reliability. In addition, there are several other sources of information relevant to particular markets. One instance is that automobile clubs in many cities attempt to gather information on the reliability of automobile repair firms. In larger cities a prospective house purchaser can hire an 'expert' house inspection service. Naturally, such private responses to demand for information work best when the 'free rider' problems usually associated with information dissemination can be ameliorated by collective action (such as automobile clubs' auto repair programs), or by the particularity of the product (such as the house purchase case).

LONG-RUN MARKET PERFORMANCE

Definition and properties of a long-run equilibrium
If consumers misperceive product reliability, they presumably eventually learn of their mistake and adjust their perceptions. Thus the market will continue to adjust over time (to these changes in perceptions) as long as consumer perceptions are inaccurate. We shall define a *long-run equilibrium* to be an equilibrium in which consumer perceptions are accurate ($r = s$).

It is easily seen that for products not involving safety hazards such a long-run equilibrium is efficient (in both the common law and average man senses) and that advertising is not profitable.[12] However, such a long-run equilibrium generally will not be efficient in either sense and advertising may continue for products for which safety hazards are important. Therefore, there are three policy issues arising from our discussion of long-run equilibrium: (1) will the market attain the long-run equilibrium? (2) are there policies which would facilitate the attainment of long-run equilibrium? and (3) what, if anything, should be done about the inefficiency of even the long-run equilibrium for products for which safety hazards are important?

The first two of these issues will be directly addressed in the following section. With respect to the third issue, if we view the common law criterion as the appropriate definition of efficiency, recourse to the courts seems the best policy for attaining efficiency for products involving safety hazards. (However, recall our qualifications to this prescription, discussed earlier.) Attainment of the average man efficient allocation would require a fundamental change in liability law.

12 If perceptions are accurate (1b) becomes $su(y - p) + (1 - s) u(y - p + m - L)$, which is the average man criterion. For products not involving personal injury the common law and average man criteria are equivalent. See above 52–5.

Will the long-run equilibrium be attained?
In Scheffman and Appelbaum (1979), the model thus far described is amended
to incorporate consumer learning. It is assumed that consumers learn from the
past in that the actual reliability of the product sold during the previous period is
known with certainty. In that model consumers' current perceptions of product
reliability are assumed to adjust to past information ($r_{t-1} - s_{t-1}$), changes in the
terms of the warranty offered ($m_t - m_{t-1}$), and to current advertising.

The Scheffman-Appelbaum model assumes that the market reaches an equilibrium (as described above) in each period and that consumers learn over time in
the manner we have just described. It is shown that if the market starts out 'near'
to the long-run equilibrium, the long-run equilibrium will be attained if consumers adjust to past information quickly enough and if they respond sufficiently
to the warranty signal. This is a weak result, in that attainment of the long-run
equilibrium is by no means assured. The possibility that the market may not
attain the long-run equilibrium strengthens the possible case for information
remedies. However, the cases in which non-attainment of long-run equilibrium
is most critical in terms of consumers' ex post dissatisfaction (products with
significant costs, such as new automobiles) often provide incentives for private
market information remedies (e.g., *Consumer Reports*) and strengthen the
importance of producer reputation.

DISCUSSION OF THE ASSUMPTIONS OF THE MODEL

Let us begin our discussion of the assumptions of the model by enumerating the
basic assumptions: (1) consumers are identical in tastes and perceptions, (2)
producers are identical, (3) producers are risk neutral, (4) producers know the
level of produced reliability (*s*), and (5) one 'period' model. Now let us consider
the implications of modifying these assumptions.

Heterogeneous consumers
If consumers are heterogeneous, even defining the appropriate efficiency criterion becomes more complicated. Abstracting from this problem, as is pointed out
in Spence (1977), when consumers differ in tastes and perceptions two potential
efficiency problems arise: (1) the market may provide the 'wrong' menu of
products and warranties, and (2) consumers may purchase the 'wrong' product
from the menu offered by the market. Besides the reasons already elaborated for
the market providing the wrong product, *moral hazard* presents an additional
problem with heterogeneous consumers, because if consumers differ, they probably differ with respect to the amount of product care and maintenance they
provide. Since warranty protection is a form of insurance, we have the usual

problem of *adverse selection* (discussed in Chapter 2), arising from the fact that consumers differ in risk, but producers can't differentiate them. This problem can be partially remedied by imposing maintenance compliance standards as a condition for warranty coverage (such as the requirements found in most new car warranties). Offering different product types and optional warranty coverage may also facilitate the 'sorting' of consumers by producers.

The possibility that consumers may purchase the wrong product is more difficult to deal with. Common law efficiency (defined here as identical consumers being treated identically ex post) requires full warranty protection, but if all products provide full warranty protection, consumers will all buy the cheapest product. However, this solution isn't efficient if the loss incured from product failure differs significantly over consumers. Spence (1977) proposes a theoretical solution to this problem, but admits that the solution is not of practical relevance. If the average man criterion is chosen, Spence (1977) has shown that the market will solve the problem (for goods not involving safety hazards) if consumers are well informed about product reliability. Such a situation again suggests a role for information provision.

Heterogeneous producers

If producers are heterogeneous and consumers cannot differentiate them sufficiently, we have a possibility of the 'lemons' problem, discussed in Chapter 2. With heterogeneous consumers and producers, monopolistic competition may be a more likely market structure than perfect competition. This situation is very difficult to model adequately, so that we must fall back on our competition-monopoly comparison for intuition. That comparison suggests that market structure itself is probably not an important source of inefficiency of the allocation of reliability and warranty coverage.[13]

Risk averse producers

If producers are risk averse, the market will usually not provide full warranty protection, even if consumers have correct perceptions. The more risk averse producers are, the higher will be the costs (in terms of higher prices, excessively high reliability) that consumers will bear as a result of a policy which mandates full warranty coverage. However, the private economy may find more efficient methods of risk pooling (e.g., through private insurance). If producers are small, with limited abilities to bear risk, risk-pooling through an industry association is

---

13 One additional facet is created with heterogeneous consumers. A monopolist may be able to 'price' discriminate over consumers by offering a variety of warranty coverage. The effect of such discrimination on efficiency is ambiguous.

an attractive remedy. (For example, partly in response to pressure by the provincial government, the travel agents in Ontario insure customers through their industry association.) Such a scheme is possibly more efficient than private insurance, since an industry association probably has better information and expertise which allow it to police its members' actions more effectively. However, industry associations with effective policing and co-ordination powers may also be able to co-ordinate non-competitive or anti-competitive behaviour (such as prohibition of price advertising).

Imperfectly informed producers
Our assumption that producers know the level of reliability of their product will generally not fully coincide with reality, but it is important only if producers are risk averse. If producers are risk neutral, price will equal expected (production and warranty) costs in equilibrium, so that our previous analysis goes through unchanged. If producers are risk averse and uncertain about the reliability of their products, the problems that may arise are simply complications of the problems that may arise if they are risk neutral.

If producers are risk averse, we would expect that warranties on new products, for which failure may be costly, would offer less coverage than warranties on established products. An example of this phenomenon may be the trend in automobile warranties over the past decade. The five-year warranties offered early in the decade have been supplanted by one-year warranties, at least for the 'big three' automobile manufacturers. This reduction in warranty coverage has coincided with major engineering changes arising from environmental and economy regulations. The manufacturers have now had considerable experience with much of the new engineering (e.g., catalytic converters, low compression engines), and we have recently seen the appearance of (optional) three-year warranties.

Multi-period model
The inherently difficult problem of defining product failure was apparently side-stepped in our model by assuming that the product lasts for one 'period,' and if it fails, it fails totally. However, it is fairly easy to generalize the model to incorporate a more realistic modelling of product failure. For example, we could have a multi-period model with the probability of different degrees of product failure being defined for each period. Such a model could also easily include depreciation of the product over time.

With risk neutral producers and risk averse, perfectly informed producers, the market would provide full warranty protection over the life (possibly infinite) of the product, and the common law criterion would require this for efficiency. However, moral hazard becomes increasingly important over time, as the effect of product misuse and inadequate maintenance accumulates. Thus, it is clear why we don't observe 'lifetime' warranties for most products and that efficiency, however defined, will not require such warranty coverage. None the less, there remains the question as to how product defects which appear outside the period of warranty coverage should be treated. This question has been given added prominence in recent years because of cases such as the 'Firestone 500 Radial' and 'Ford Pinto' cases.[14] The legal basis for private redress in the courts for product defects occurring outside the warranty period and for government-mandated recalls or government-mandated, product defect information provision is fully discussed in Chapter 5.

Summary
Changing any of the five basic assumptions would make our model much more complicated. However, the basic qualitative conclusions of the model will be generally unaffected by modifications of the assumptions.

EXTENSIONS OF THE MODEL

The model we have developed here could be extended fairly easily to consider general problems of uncertain product quality. For example, for simplicity assume that the consumer knows that a product may be one of two 'qualities,'[15] but he is unsure as to which. let $u(y-p)$ be the utility he derives if it is of one quality and $v(y-p)$ if it is of the other quality. Let s be his estimate of the probability that it is of the first quality. Then we have a model similar to the one of this chapter. Producers may be led to provide 'quality warranties' ('double-your money back,' 'satisfaction guaranteed,' trial periods, pro-rata refunds), which is not an uncommon phenomenon. The concept of advertising in the model (advertising which influences s but not u or v) is somewhat different from the usual perception of advertising in consumer goods markets. However, especially in food and other moderate-cost consumer non-durables where the producer is trying to get customers to switch to his product, this concept of advertising may be plausible. For example, a consumer considering the purchase of a previously untried generic cola beverage may think: 'It may be as good as Coke or it may only be as good as previously tried generics.'

14 See 'Ford goes to trial' (1980).
15 The model can be easily extended to more than two events or qualities.

FINAL COMMENTS

The reader is reminded that the purpose of this chapter was to develop an abstract analysis of the problem of uncertain product quality, particularly product reliability. In Chapters 5 and 6 this analysis will be applied to specific regulations in Canada and Ontario.

4

The regulation of quality by licensing and certification

INTRODUCTION

The purpose of this chapter is to develop an analysis of a certain kind of social regulation – regulation that attempts to improve the 'quality' of goods or services by controlling the quality of some of the inputs used in their production. Such regulation is a type of design (rather than performance) standard[1] and it is commonly used in a variety of areas. Two examples are standards for the quality of inputs used in the production of many foods and drugs, and occupational licensing and certification programs; the latter example is the main impetus for the analysis developed in this chapter, because the province of Ontario has an extensive program of occupational licensing and certification (described in Chapter 6). Therefore, we shall describe the market being analysed as the market for 'professional services' (hair-cutting, automobile repair, optometry, dentury, etc.). However, it should become apparent that the analysis is generally valid for any sort of market which is regulated by the setting of standards for inputs used in the production process.

Professional services have the characteristics of experience goods in that the quality of the service generally cannot be fully determined by the purchaser at the time of purchase. Quality is revealed only after the service has been consumed. In addition, for many types of professional services quality cannot be completely ascertained even after consumption. For example, one is likely to be unsure about the quality of a medical treatment even after it has been administered. In this respect professional services are credence goods.

---

1 See our discussion of design standards in Chapter 2.

The market for professional services is therefore similar in many respects to the market for other experience or credence goods and some of the issues involved are therefore captured by the analysis developed in the preceding chapter. The purchase of professional services is usually infrequent and the complex nature of such services is better understood by the professional than the consumer. Therefore such markets will be typically characterized by consumers facing uncertainty about the quality of services provided, and practitioners will generally have better information than consumers about such quality. Since these aspects of the market are easily addressed by the model developed in Chapter 3, we shall not consider them further here.

In this chapter our analysis will be directed to the common type of regulation found in markets for professional services – licensing and certification. A compulsory certification program requires that all practitioners meet certain educational and experience standards. A licensing program generally requires such certification and limits entry through control of entry to required education (as with doctors) or experience (as with apprenticeship programs). A voluntary certification program simply certifies practitioners who have met certain educational or experience standards, but does not preclude those who do not meet the standards from being practitioners.

A concern with the quality of service is presumably a major motivation for such regulation.[2] In this chapter we shall analyse the effects of such regulation, in particular, whether such regulation can be expected to increase the quality of service. Since the implications of consumer uncertainty about service quality are thoroughly examined in Chapter 3, we shall not emphasize those issues here. The model presented and the results derived or stated in the following sections of this chapter are based on the analysis developed in Appelbaum and Scheffman (1979). Besides developing a general analysis of regulation such as occupational licensing, the last section of this chapter will present some evidence on the market for dental services which gives some empirical support to the theoretical predictions of our model.

POSSIBLE PROBLEMS IN THE MARKET FOR PROFESSIONAL SERVICES

Several features of the markets for professional services make it likely that important potential sources of market failure may be present. Professional services are very often complex in nature, making it very difficult for a consumer

---

2 In Chapter 6 we shall see that concern with quality of service is not a major factor behind the system of occupational licensing and certification in Ontario.

to decide what type of service and how much of it he should buy. Furthermore, the quality of the service, once obtained, may be difficult and costly to evaluate. In fact, very often the reason an individual turns to a professional in the first place is that he has insufficient knowledge and cannot judge for himself.

As we have already noted, some of these problems are similar to those considered in Chapter 3. Owing to imperfect information and to high learning costs consumers may not be fully or correctly informed. Furthermore, the suppliers usually have better information than the consumers. Thus, for the reasons discussed in Chapter 3 the incentives for producers to provide 'correct' information may be limited. Furthermore, the market may not provide efficient remedies for faulty service.

An additional important potential source of market failure in markets for professional services is the existence of certain forms of externalities. For example, seemingly free hospital facilities available to the doctor may lead to excessive use of these facilities, especially when consumers have medical insurance and do not directly face the costs of treatment. As was pointed out in Chapter 2, existence of a universal social medical insurance scheme such as OHIP may introduce a moral hazard problem through its effect on the incentives for care and self-maintenance. Finally, the costs of a faulty brake job or of a mistreatment of a contagious disease may be higher than those facing the individuals obtaining 'treatment,' so the quality of service demanded may be too low.

We see that the special nature of the market for professional services gives added importance to certain potential sources of market failure. Therefore, such markets may misallocate resources by providing the wrong quantity and quality of services. Informational imperfections may result in the wrong quality and type of services being consumed, and the jointness in the provision of services may result in the wrong amount of services being purchased.

The joint provision of diagnosis and treatment
Professional services are usually purchased infrequently, thus making the acquisition and verification of information very costly. Furthermore, these services normally involve the application of some general knowledge or rules to the personal circumstances of the individual, again making it difficult to acquire and verify information. Consequently, the consumer turns to the professional as an agent for whom information and knowledge can be purchased to help in his decision. In fact, the relationship between the consumer and the professional is somewhat unique. The professional usually plays a dual role in that he is both the agent and the principal. As an agent the professional typically provides two services: diagnosis and recommendation of treatment (for example, a doctor will

diagnose the illness and then recommend a treatment). As a principal the professional provides the treatment. The nature of the market introduces three potential problem areas: the quality of the diagnosis, the quality of the treatment, and the possibility of excessive diagnosis or treatment.

Consider the diagnosis service. Almost any diagnosis will involve some uncertainty; in other words, there is always some probability that the diagnosis will be wrong. A consumer may, therefore, have a very hard time evaluating the quality of the diagnosis. In such a situation the 'lemons' problem (discussed in Chapter 2) may arise, and so the market allocation may be characterized by a lower level of quality of diagnosis than would result if there were perfect information.

Similarly, the consumer may find it difficult to evaluate the quality of the treatment, both because of the limitations on his knowledge and ability to judge and because his evaluation will depend on information about the problem which was provided by the professional himself. Furthermore, it is generally difficult to obtain any information before the treatment is actually purchased and tried out and even if the problem whose cure was sought has disappeared, it still is difficult to assess whether or not excessive (or too many treatments) were used. Again, as long as the consumer cannot fully and correctly evaluate the quality of the treatment, there may be an incentive for the professional to provide the 'wrong' (in terms of efficiency) quality treatment.

Finally, the dual role played by most professionals introduces incentives to over-diagnose and to recommend unnecessary treatments. Since the professional acts as both agent and principal, he can create a higher demand for his services as a principal by providing information that suits him best, that is, by recommending excessive treatment. This is in fact a moral-hazard-like problem which may lead to the 'wrong' amount and type of services being traded in the market. The problem of the possible excessive recommendation of treatment is a direct result of the dual role of the professional and is independent of the quality of service provided. Even if the quality of services provided by the professional were efficient, there still may be an incentive for him to recommend excessive treatment.

Given the obvious potential sources of market failure present in such an arrangement, why is it that we observe such a dual role played by many professionals? To the extent that private markets can appropriate efficiency gains, the existence of such an institutional arrangement may indicate that it is the most efficient way of combining the various services provided by professionals. It seems clear that in many cases there are very strong economies in combining services. For example, it is presumably more efficient, ceteris paribus, to have the same mechanic who opened the transmission and detected the problem do the necessary work. In other cases (e.g., most medical services) it is even impossible to buy a treatment without a diagnosis from the same provider. Thus, to avoid over-diagnosis one would have to buy it twice.

OCCUPATIONAL LICENSING[3]

The preceding section established the existence of various potential sources of market failure in markets for professional services. Therefore some sort of intervention may sometimes be desirable (efficient). One possible form of regulation which is commonly observed is occupational licensing. The standard argument for such intervention is the insurance of output quality, and such an objective may be justified on efficiency grounds. However this type of regulation typically sets standards for the 'quality' of the practitioners and is evidently intended to act as a screening device, weeding out the unqualified practitioners and thus increasing the average quality of the practising ones. The poorly informed consumer is therefore less likely to commit errors by choosing practitioners who turn out to be incompetent.

This type of argument has long been questioned by many observers, who have argued that there are incentives other than a concern with the quality of service (mainly the self-interest of the professional groups) which often motivate the introduction of such restrictions. The fact that in many cases quality or qualification standards are set by the profession itself, that entry restrictions are usually imposed, and that members of the profession typically do not have to be re-examined for licences to be renewed would indicate that the protection of the public is not necessarily the main impetus for professional regulation.[4]

In what follows we develop a model of a market for professional services and examine the effects of various professional qualifications restrictions. In particular, we show that the introduction of occupational licensing will not necessarily improve the quality of services being provided, and moreover, it may even lower it. The introduction of such restrictions will, however, increase the welfare of (some of) the profession's members (usually the practising ones), which suggests that the self-interest motive is strong.

---

3 In what follows, the regulation we shall model is actually compulsory certifications. The further restriction of entry by licensing easily could be included in the analysis, and the results of such restriction will be obvious.

4 In Chapter 6 we shall see that concern with protection of the public is not a major impetus for occupational licensing in Ontario.

THE MODEL[5]

Consider a market for professional services in which heterogeneous services of different qualities are provided by individual suppliers. The suppliers are characterized by their ability, qualifications, productivity, and tastes.

Let n^j be the number of times a specific service is provided by the jth supplier. For example, it can represent the number of treatments of a certain type provided by a doctor or dentist, the number of cars certified by a mechanic, or the number of haircuts done by a barber. Of course, in some cases the service provided by a professional is very complex and requires a more detailed description. To capture this complexity we allow for differences in the quality of the services provided.

The *quality of the service* is assumed to be a function of the *quality of the provider* of the service, that is, his human capital (education, training, experience, etc.), ability and technology, *and* the amount of time he spends per unit of service provided (e.g., the time a dentist spends per treatment). Thus we write

$$S^j = f^j(t^j, k^j), \tag{1}$$

where S^j is the measure of the quality of the service provided by the jth supplier, t^j the length of time that he spends providing the (unit) service, k^j the measure of his human capital (e.g., years of training) and f^j is his production function for quality which is assumed to be increasing in t^j and k^j.

The various professionals may differ in terms of their technology, inherent ability (or productivity), human capital, or time spent per unit service, and therefore they may differ in the quality of the service they provide. It is important to notice that we have to distinguish between the quality or qualifications of the professional (measured by k^j) and the quality of the service which he provides (measured by S^j). The latter depends on the former but also on the time input (t^j).[6] Thus, for example, even if $k^j > k^i$ (the jth supplier is more qualified) it is still possible to have $S^i > S^j$ if $t^i > t^j$.

Let the demand function facing the jth supplier be given by

$$p^j = D^j(n^j, S^j, N),[7] \tag{2}$$

---

5 The model presented here is a simplified version of one developed in Appelbaum and Scheffman (1979).
6 Inputs other than time could be easily incorporated into the model. See below.
7 These demand functions could arise from consumers' misperceptions about S^j. The model presented here is of monopolistically competitive professionals. Below we shall consider a model with perfectly competitive professionals.

where N is the number of suppliers in the market and p^j is the price consumers will be willing to pay for n^j services if the quality of services provided is S^j. It would be expected that consumers' demand for the services of a particular supplier would depend on the total number of suppliers. In particular we assume that the demand facing supplier j is a decreasing function of the total number of suppliers. (D^j is a decreasing function of N.) Presumably, the price consumers are willing to pay is an increasing function of the quality of service, and a decreasing function of the number of times the service is provided (i.e., the demand curve of the jth supplier is downward sloping).

Next we must model suppliers' supply decisions. Taking the standard simple economic model of the supply of labour,[8] we assume that supplier j's well-being depends on his income (which he can use to spend on goods and services) and on his consumption of leisure time. Therefore, we shall write the utility function of professional j as:

$$U^j = U^j(Y^j, L^j), \tag{3}$$

Where Y^j is his income and L^j the amount of leisure time. U^j is assumed to be an increasing function of Y^j and L^j (i.e., well-being increases with income and with more leisure time).

Supplier j's income is generated by selling his services. Given (2) we can write his income as

$$Y^j = n^j D^j(n^j, S^j, k^j) - rk^j, \tag{4}$$

where r is the (full) user's cost of human capital (r, for example, is the cost of increasing his human capital by one unit). Let R be the maximum number of hours of leisure available. Then (3) can be written

$$U^j = U^j(n^j D^j(n^j, S^j, k^j) - rk^j, R - n^j t^j), \tag{5}$$

where $S^j = f^j(t^j, k^j)$.

Now supplier j's choice of k^j, n^j, and t^j can be described as the values of those variables which maximize (5); that is, he chooses his level of human capital, number of treatments, and time per treatment so as to maximize his well-being, given his production function for service quality (1) and his demand function (2).

In addition, we want to allow for the possibility that some sorts of regulatory actions may cause some suppliers to abandon their practices. Let $\bar{U}^j$ be the highest level of well-being that a supplier can attain in the best alternative occupation. Then the main choice of k^j, n^j, and t^j requires that the utility level reached is at least $\bar{U}^j$, that is,

8 See Hirshleifer (1976).

$$U^j \geqq U^j. \tag{6}$$

Let U^{*j} be the maximized level of well-being of supplier j, and k^{*j}, n^{*j}, t^{*j} be the optimal choices of k^j, n^j, and t^j. If $U^{*j} < U^j$ then supplier j leaves the industry.

As new individuals enter the profession, the demand curve facing each existing supplier (given by (2)) will shift to the left (assuming no change in total demand) because of the effect of an increase in N. This increased competition will naturally reduce the well-being of current suppliers. With free, unregulated entry, new individuals will enter the profession until the marginal supplier derives only marginal returns, that is, for this individual, say the kth, $U^{*k} = U^k$. Entry will stop when no one outside the profession can enter it and attain a sufficiently high level of well-being (U^j). The equilibrium in this market will be characterized by a variety of 'quality' (k^j) of practitioners providing a variety of 'quality' of services (S^j) at a variety of prices. Such variety is, of course, typical in markets for professional services.

REGULATION OF QUALIFICATIONS

Suppose that a regulation specifying minimum standards for qualifications (which we shall call occupational licensing) is introduced in order to protect the imperfectly informed consumer[9] and to guarantee some acceptable service quality by raising the average and minimum level of quality of service. Let us then consider the effects of such occupational licensing and see whether this type of regulation in fact will increase the average and minimum quality of service provided. Occupational licensing implies higher entry costs, and therefore it should lead to a decrease in the number of suppliers in the market. It might be expected that the higher entry or opportunity costs will increase the average quality of those remaining in the market, because the less efficient and less productive suppliers will no longer find it profitable to operate.

As a particular type of occupational licensing, consider a requirement that the human capital of suppliers must be no less than a certain level. Within our simple model this is a reasonable representation of the educational or training requirements typical in most forms of occupational licensing, where no one without a particular training or with less than a certain number of years at school is allowed to provide a particular service. In the context of dental services the restriction could be that only those with a degree in dentistry will be allowed to fill teeth, place crows, etc.

Restrictions of this nature can be introduced into our model by the imposition of a constraint of the form

9 The demand functions (1) may arise from imperfect perceptions.

$$k^j \geq k \quad \text{all } j. \tag{7}$$

That is, no individual can supply this service unless he satisfies condition (7), which specifies a minimum requirement for 'human capital.' Clearly, for (7) to be useful it must be effective for at least some suppliers; that is, at least for some the optimal choice of k^j is lower than k.

Now let us consider the effect of this regulation on supplier j. Let U^1_j be the level of well-being attained by supplier j after the imposition of this regulation. If $U^1_j < U^j$, he will now leave the industry (e.g., if the regulation requires that he have an additional year of education, he may decide that it is not worth meeting this requirement). If $k^*_j > k$, that is, if supplier j already exceeded the regulated minimum, the regulation has no direct effect on him. However, the regulation is likely to effect N (the total number of suppliers) and therefore the demand for his services (2). Therefore, the regulation will have an indirect effect on supplier j, even if $k^*_j > k$.

Now suppose that for supplier j, $k^{*j} < k$, that is, he is not currently meeting the regulatory constraint. In order to stay in the industry he will now have to expand resources to increase k^j to k. This will result in $U^1_j < U^*_j$, that is, the introduction of the regulation reduces his well-being. Therefore, for some individuals, the higher standards requirement will lead to a reduction in the possible utility that they can derive by operating in the industry. If this reduction is large enough, they will leave the industry. In particular, (marginal) individuals for whom $U^1_j < U^j$, will leave the industry.

Thus as k increases, some professionals will leave, thus increasing the average quality (measured by k^j) of all those remaining in the industry. This result however, does not necessarily imply that the average quality of the *service* provided will increase. To see whether in fact this change occurs, it is also necessary to determine how the regulation affects the amount of time[10] spent per unit of service. Furthermore, since the total number of suppliers, will be affected by the regulation, the demand curves facing all of those remaining in the industry will shift. In particular, as k increases, the demand curves of the remaining suppliers will shift to the right (because of the reduced number of practising professionals in the market). This will affect the behaviour of all existing suppliers, even those for whom the qualifications constraint was ineffective.

THE EFFECTS OF LICENSING[11]

Let us assume that a regulation prescribing that the minimum level of k by k is enacted. First, we shall consider the effect of this regulation on an individual

---

10 Or other inputs, in a more general model.
11 The results discussed here are derived in Appelbaum and Scheffman (1979).

supplier, *assuming his demand curve remains unchanged*. The behaviour of the individuals for whom the regulation is ineffective (i.e., $k^{*j} \geq k$) will be unchanged (given we are assuming their demand curves are unchanged). Therefore, let us look at those for whom the regulation is effective (i.e., $k^{*j} < k$). For these individuals the introduction of the regulation will reduce their well being. The marginal ones (i.e., those for which $U^{*j} = U^j$) will leave the industry, whereas some of the infra-marginal producers (i.e., those for which $U^{*j} > U^j$) may remain in practice, but with a lower level of utility. Such producers will now be required to increase k^j from k^{*j} to k. This move will reduce their income (by $r(k - k^{*j})$), which will affect their choice of n^j and t^j, for the same reason that a reduction in a consumer's income will affect his consumption choices.

There are two effects here. First, a reduction in income will affect the supplier's labour-leisure choice. For example, a reduction in income may increase the total number of hours he works, in order to make up for the fall in income. The second effect is that by increasing k^j from k^{*j} to k, he presumably becomes more productive, that is, he can provide a higher quality service than before, even spending the same amount of time per service provided. (Recall in (1) that f^j is an increasing function of k^j.)

To examine the effect of the regulation on the quality of service, recall the quality-of-service production function (1). The quality of service provided will increase, for a given t^j, because of the increase in k^j from k^{j*} to k. But since the increase in k^j both increases the quality of service and reduces income, ceteris paribus, the effect on t^j is ambiguous. it is not surprising that the net effect of the regulation may be to decrease t^j.[12] However, it is shown in Appelbaum and Scheffman (1979) that t^j may be reduced so much that S^j, the quality of service provided by the jth supplier, is reduced! For example, requiring a doctor to have an additional year's education results in his 'loading up' on patients to make up for the loss in income from the additional year's education.

Thus, we conclude that the imposition of higher standards will not necessarily improve the quality of the service provided by the infra-marginal producers (given a fixed number of suppliers), and *the minimum level of quality supplied may not be increased by the regulation*. This conclusion, of course, implies that the *average* quality of service provided will not necessarily increase. What is the reason for this seeming paradox? The required increase in k would increase the quality of service provided by the marginal producer, ceteris paribus. However, the regulation affects the producer's use of *other* inputs (in this model, time). It is not surprising that the increased k-requirement is likely to reduce the time spent per unit of service. It may reduce this input so much that the quality of service falls. Of course, in that case the price per unit of service will also fall. The

---

12 In a more general model the use of other inputs would also be affected.

likelihood that the quality of service will fall depends on the extent to which the producer is willing to trade income for leisure and the 'productivity' of k.[13]

Next, let us consider the effects of an increase in the required k, now allowing for the fact that the number of professionals and thus the demand curves will also change. Again some (the marginal) producers will leave the industry and others will remain. The demand for those remaining in the industry will be increased because of the reduction in the number of competitors. This means that consumers will now be willing to pay a higher price for the same quality of service or alternatively, will be willing to pay a comparable price for a somewhat lower quality of service. It should be clear that the demand shift effect does not reduce the ambiguity of the effect of the regulation on the quality of service. For example, a supplier for which $k^{*j}>k$, could reduce the quality of service, and have more leisure and / or income because of the demand shift effect. Therefore, the effect of the regulation on the quality of service provided by any supplier is ambiguous. As shown in Appelbaum and Scheffman the final effect depends on: (1) the marginal productivity of k, that is, is human capital important in the production of quality? (2) the substitution possibility between human capital and other inputs, that is, how easy is it to adjust with respect to other margins? (3) market effect on the demand curve and thus on the shadow price of time.

Since it has been shown that these forms of regulation do not necessarily achieve their declared objectives, it is interesting to examine alternative motivations for such policies. To do so let us consider the effect of an increase in k on the welfare of the practising professionals.

Consider first those for whom the regulation is ineffective (i.e., $k^{*j}>k$). The only effect of the regulation on these suppliers is that because the regulation reduces the number of suppliers (reduces N), their demand curve shifts out. This clearly makes them better off, so that suppliers for whom the regulation is ineffective always gain from the regulation. As we pointed out above, some of those suppliers for whom the regulation is effective ($k^{*j}>k$) are necessarily made worse off by the regulation.

It is clear therefore that it is in the interest of at least some suppliers in any profession to impose higher qualification standards, regardless of the effect on service quality. Furthermore, in any profession in which the number of individuals for whom the constraint is ineffective is large relative to the rest, or if that group has more political power, we would expect pressure from the profession for the introduction of such policies. The claim that it is not necessarily the quality consideration that is the real objective may be supported by the fact that in most cases such policies include some form of 'grandfather clause,' and that in general they do not involve continuous testing. In terms of our model such a

13 See Appelbaum and Scheffman (1979).

clause implies that for a certain subset of individuals (normally those already in practice) the constraint is ineffective. In other words, the only new professionals have to meet the new and higher standards; those already in practice are exempt and do not have to keep renewing their licences.[14]

MANY INPUTS

So far it has been assumed that there are only two inputs in the quality production function. However, the model can be easily generalized so that it includes additional inputs. For example, the providers of services may be able to hire various labour and physical capital services and thus increase the quality. The model was generalized in this manner in Appelbaum and Scheffman (1979). The basic results, that regulation of the quality of the supplier has an ambiguous effect on the quality of the service and such regulation benefits infra-marginal suppliers, can be shown to be valid in the general model.

TECHNOLOGY REGULATION

Another possible form of regulation is the imposition of restrictions on the technology that may be used in the production of the service, for example, requirements that specify that the service must be produced in a particular manner. Some aspects of building codes are, in essence, this sort of regulation. In this section we investigate whether it is possible to increase the quality of the output by constraining the technology. In principle, at least, the analysis is similar to that outlined above. With no regulation producers will choose technologies depending on their demand functions and their (own) efficiency. In other words producers choose inputs, technology, output quantity, and output quality. Suppose we rank technologies according to an increasing order of minimum quality provided (regardless of inputs used). Then it is clear that banning the lower tail of the technology distribution will have an effect similar to the cutting off of the lower tail of the human capital distribution. In other words, some will be forced to leave the industry and the remainder will alter all their choices, including choice of technology and inputs. From the discussion of the effects of a human capital constraint it is obvious, therefore, that while the minimum quality of technology will be raised, what will happen to the quality of output is not at all clear. Individuals who are using high quality technologies and who are unaffected by the restriction will, as a result of the change in the number of firms in the industry, change the technology they use and the inputs used, so that it is in

14 See our discussion of occupational licensing in Ontario in Chapter 6.

general impossible to say whether the quality of their output will increase. Individuals who are affected by the restriction will now use not only a higher quality technology but also different inputs, so again it is impossible to say whether the quality of their output will increase. Therefore, such a policy will not necessarily increase the average quality of service provided.

EFFECTS OF INCREASED COMPETITION

Let us consider now the effects of increased price competition among suppliers, which may arise as a result of an increase in the amount of information available to the consumer about the various suppliers and the nature of their services (resulting, perhaps, from a government imposed information remedy). The effect of such an increase in information would be higher cross-elasticities of demand among professionals, which would tend to make the demand functions facing individual professionals more elastic.

In Appelbaum and Scheffman (1979) the effects of such increased competition are analysed by assuming that the suppliers' demand curves (2) are linear; that is,

$$p^j = f^j(t^j, k^j) + A + Bn^j, \tag{9}$$

where A and B are constants. The slope of the demand curve is determined by B. If we model increased competitiveness by an increase in B (which implies a flattening of the demand curve), it can be shown that increased competitiveness increases the minimum quality of service provided in the market. Therefore, information remedies which would lead to increased competition owing to better consumer information may be effective in increasing the quality of service. However, the effect of increased competitiveness on infra-marginal suppliers is ambiguous.

PERFECT COMPETITION

The model presented above was monopolistically competitive in that each individual supplier had some degree of monopoly power (i.e., faced a downward sloping demand curve). In such a model it is very difficult to 'close' the model, that is, to examine directly the effects on the demand side, particularly the welfare of consumers. In this section we present a somewhat modified version of the model presented above. We consider a perfectly competitive market for professional services, which in many ways is very similar to the model presented in the previous chapter.

Consider a market for professional services in which heterogeneous suppliers provide their services. We assume that there are many suppliers, so that no individual supplier can exercise monopoly power. The suppliers are different in terms of their ability, technology, and human capital. Each supplier j provides one unit of service of quality S^j. The quality of services provided is taken to depend on the inputs used in the production of quality. In particular, we assume that the quality of (a unit) service is a function of the supplier's human capital k^j, time spend per unit service provided t^j and other inputs x^j. The production technology itself, that is, the function which transforms inputs into quality may also differ, reflecting inherent differences among suppliers, say in terms of their ability and productivity.

The quality production function of the jth supplier is therefore written as

$$S^j = f^j(t^j, k^j, x^j) \quad \text{all } j, \tag{10}$$

where f^j is assumed to be increasing in t^j, k^j, and x^j (i.e., all inputs are productive). For simplicity we assume that the distribution of human capital and the other characteristics of the suppliers are given.[15] Thus, in the 'short run' suppliers have a given stock of human capital which cannot be varied.

We assume that there are N identical consumers who have an inelastic demand for one unit of service. The consumers' utility function is given by

$$u = u(y - p, S), \tag{11}$$

where y is income, p the price of the unit service and u is a non-decreasing concave function in net income $(y - p)$ and service quality (S). In what follows we shall describe the implications of such a model. The interested reader is referred to Appelbaum and Scheffman (1979) for the details of the analysis.

We shall assume that consumers have perfect information about the quality of services provided. With free entry by producers, as in the model of Chapter 3, an equilibrium will require that all consumers receive the same utility and that this utility level is maximized, given the technological constraints facing producers. However, since the producers differ, the quality of service and price charged will generally differ among producers, even though consumers are identical. Thus, the equilibrium will be characterized by the N most efficient producers each providing one unit of service, with the quality of service and price charged generally differing by producer, but the utility derived by any consumer purchasing the service from any producer will be identical.

Suppose now that an attempt is made to raise the average quality of services provided by introducing constraints on human capital. More specifically,

---

15 This assumption is relaxed in Appelbaum and Scheffman (1979).

suppose authorities introduce a regulation requiring a certain minimum level of human capital, for example, that certain training is necessary before a person will be allowed to provide the service. Since such a constraint (if it is effective) cuts off part of the lower tail of the distribution of human capital, it leads to an increase in the average quality of the suppliers. But does it increase the quality of service? Let us examine the effects of such regulation.

Suppose a restriction is imposed requiring that

$$k^j \geq k \quad \text{all } j. \tag{12}$$

In other words, no one with human capital lower than k is allowed to operate. The direct effect of this restriction is to exclude those suppliers who do not meet the new requirement. Let the number of suppliers who do satisfy the constraint be L, where $L < N$ (for the constraint to be effective). Then it is clear that less than N consumers will be able to obtain the service.[16]

In equilibrium $N - L$ of the consumers will not be able to purchase the service. Therefore, in equilibrium, since all consumers must attain identical levels, the utility level of those consumers who are able to purchase the service will be identical to the utility level of consumers who aren't able to purchase the service. The effect of such a regulation therefore reduces the welfare of consumers.[17] In addition, the quality of services provided in the market does not necessarily improve (see Appelbaum and Scheffman, 1979). There are two interpretations of this result. First, if consumers are perfectly informed, the market – being perfectly competitive – would have allocated resources efficiently in the absence of intervention, and so it is not surprising that the government intervention distorted the allocation and reduced efficiency. On the other hand, suppose that consumers do not perceive the quality of services correctly, so that the utility function in (10) is based on incorrect perceptions. In such a case the government intervention reduces perceived utility, but the intervention may increase the efficiency of resource allocation. Since this issue was considered extensively in Chapter 3, we shall not pursue it here.

Although the competitive model presented here is very simple, the conclusion that input standards will not necessarily raise either the quality of services or consumer welfare in competitive markets is generally valid (see Appelbaum and Scheffman, 1979). However, as before, such regulations generally benefit some of the producers.

---

16 Recall that consumers have an inelastic demand for one unit and suppliers can provide only one unit.

17 This result does not depend on the inelastic demand assumption.

Of course, this result is not conclusive. Occupational licensing and similar types of regulation *may* increase quality of service, but they may not. In evaluating the desirability of such regulation we must start with the potential sources of market failure. Is there reason to believe that the quality of service provided in the market is too low (by *efficiency* standards)? Then we must examine the costs and benefits of a proposed action to determine its desirability.

The basic lesson of our analysis is that if the government wants to raise the quality of service in a given industry, an occupational licensing program will have to be carefully designed in order to achieve this result. Furthermore, to the extent that the source of the problem is inadequate consumer information, information remedies may be preferable. One such remedy is to encourage or provide a rating of suppliers (i.e., a rating of the quality of the *service* they provide). For example, automobile clubs in major cities often provide ratings of automobile mechanics through designation of 'approved' mechanics.

EMPIRICAL EVIDENCE: THE QUALITY OF DENTAL SERVICES

The model developed above demonstrated that the quality of the services provided by professionals will not necessarily increase if input standards are imposed. In this section we provide some empirical evidence to support our conclusions. In particular, we apply our model to the market for dental services and provide evidence suggesting that for some of the dental services studied the introduction of qualification constraints in fact lowers the quality of services provided.

In dentistry, as in many other professions, only individuals with certain qualifications (licences) can perform certain tasks. In fact, we observe a hierarchy, where those at the top usually determine the tasks that may be performed by those junior to them. At the top we have the dentists, followed by dental nurses, dental hygienists, and various types of dental assistants. The differences among these categories are in their training and qualifications or, in the language of our model, in terms of their human capital.

The usual and commonly accepted argument for the introduction of a legal (or professional) delegation of permissible tasks is, of course, the quality argument. Thus, we face a situation similar to the one discussed in our theoretical model – qualifications constraints in terms of human capital requirements are introduced in order to improve the quality of dental services provided and thereby protect the consumer.

The empirical evidence presented here arises from two studies comparing the quality of dental services provided by dental auxiliaries with those provided by dentists, in two separate programs, one in Saskatchewan and the other in

Ontario. The results are given in Ambrose et al. (1976) and Hord et al. (1978). These programs allowed dental auxiliaries to perform tasks which previously were restricted, by regulation, to dentists. Ambrose et al. (1976) and Hord et al. (1978) provide evidence on the effect of this restriction on the quality of service provided. In both programs the evaluation of the quality of the services was done by a group of experts, all of whom were dentists. Moreover, the services considered were more than just simple tasks and in fact included some tasks that most people believe, or were led to believe, can be performed only by dentists (e.g., place crowns).

Two main problems arise when we try to examine the effects of qualification constraints, or occupational licensing on quality. First of all, we face the difficult problem of defining and measuring quality. By its nature this problem has no exact solution and all we can hope for is a satisfactory approximation. Second, even if we solve the identification and measurement of quality problem, we still have to be able to obtain information on the quality of services before and after professional standards have been introduced, or alternatively, on the quality of services provided by regulated and unregulated individuals (who provide the same service).

Since the tasks that may be performed by dental auxiliaries are restricted by law and exclude many tasks that are reserved for dentists, it is necessary to find a framework within which tasks are comparable. In both studies the comparison of the quality of services was made possible because one involved an experiment undertaken by the Dental Association of Ontario and the other a policy implemented by the Saskatchewan government. Thus, in both cases dental auxiliaries were legally allowed to perform tasks that normally are excluded.

With respect to the definition and measurement of quality, the experts in the two studies define a set of criteria for the different services (see Tables 1–3, taken from Ambrose et al., 1976, Hord et al., 1978) and determine how well these criteria are being met on a scale of one to three. The overall quality is then taken as the average of the different criteria performances. Thus, the studies recognize the fact that quality is a complex and multi-dimensional concept and take into account those aspects considered to be important.

Considering the results of the Saskatchewan study first, we see from Tables 4–7 that the quality of amalgam restorations placed by dental nurses was found to be significantly higher than those placed by dentists. This conclusion applies to one-surface as well as to multi-surface fillings and to both deciduous and permanent teeth.

Tables 8–11 give the results on the quality of stainless steel crowns placed by dentists and dental nurses. The results indicate no significant differences in the quality of this particular service. The study also reports on the quality of

TABLE 1

Saskatchewan dental plan, post-treatment restorative quality evaluation project

Amalgam restoration – criteria to be evaluated	
Anatomy	The remaining tooth structure should serve as the guide for anatomical form. The marginal ridge and related fossa should approximate the antomy of the natural tooth. The outline form should reflect current concepts of tooth preservation and exhibit reasonable principles of extension for prevention.
Proximal contour	It should closely reproduce the original contour of the proximal surface. This will be influenced by the matrix band techniques employed by the operator.
Interproximal contacts	This should be firm enough to prevent food impaction and allow dental floss to pass with a definite 'snap'. The location and area of the proximal contact will be determined by the anatomy of the tooth and arch alignment.
Margins	These should blend with the adjacent enamel so that the margins are imperceptible or slightly detectable to the time of an explorer passed over the junction between enamel and restoration. No overhand should be apparent at the gingival margin.
Occlusion	The intensity of contact for a restored tooth during occlusion should be the same as for the other teeth. The restoration should not interfere with or prevent the functioning of any other teeth.
Surface consistency	The accessible, completed surfaces should be (1) free from scratches, pitting and any gross irregularities, (2) smooth in appearance, and (3) preferably have a satin or lustrous finish.

radiographs taken by dental assistants. Unfortunately, it was impossible to obtain comparable information for dentists. Table 12 does show, however, that the quality of radiographs taken by the dental auxiliary was fairly high.

Tables 13–16 give the results of the Ontario study. Again from Tables 13 and 14 we find that the quality of amalgam restorations placed by dental auxiliaries is significantly higher than those placed by dentists. Tables 15 and 16 show a slightly higher quality (although not very significant) of resin restorations placed by dental auxiliaries compared with those placed by dentists.

The results presented in both the Saskatchewan and Ontario studies, therefore, lead to the same conclusion, namely, the higher qualification (more human capital) of the dentists does not imply higher quality of services provided by them. In fact, if there are differences in quality of services, the results indicate that in the cases studied, it is the dentists who provide lower quality services.

TABLE 2

Saskatchewan dental plan, post-treatment restorative quality evaluation project

Stainless steel crowns – criteria to be evaluated	
Margin extension	The margin of the preformed stainless steel crown should extend to just (i.e., up to 1 mm) below the free margin of the gingiva on all four surfaces. The contouring of the crown margin must be such that it is not underextended (particularly on the vestibular surfaces) nor overextended so as to damage the eputhelal attachment.
Margin adaptation	The crown margins must be adapted as closely to the tooth as possible. In most instances, this requires proper crimping of the original margins. Gross spaces between crown margin and tooth should not be apparent.
Occlusion	The crown margins must be properly seated and the occlusal surface should be in proper contact with the opposing teeth. The height of the occlusal surface of the crown should not have a flat, squashed appearance nor should intrusion of an opposing tooth be visible.
Tissue health	The gingival tissue surrounding the crown should demonstrate normal colour and architecture. Swollen, edematous tissue from overextended or rough irritating margins is unsatisfactory. Care should be taken to distinguish this cause of irritation from that caused by retained cement as the latter condition would be correctable.

In view of the model presented above, these results are not surprising. We showed that qualifications constraints will not necessarily increase service quality and may even decrease it. The constraints imposed in the case of the dentists increase their opportunity cost of time and thus reduce their per unit time input, which in turn lowers the quality of their service. The dentists themselves may be more qualified, but in view of their opportunity costs, it appears that they cannot 'afford' to provide higher quality service.

Naturally, there are inherent biases in studies of this type. The dental auxiliaries knew that their work was going to be evaluated, which increased their incentive to maintain quality. In addition, the pay structure encouraged them to spend more time per treatment. None the less, the Saskatchewan program reduced the cost of the services to consumers. Therefore the two studies undeniably demonstrate that dental auxiliaries can satisfactorily perform tasks which are currently restricted to dentists, and at a lower cost to consumers. An obvious solution is to allow dental auxiliaries to perform these tasks under the supervision of dentists. Such a system would presumably reduce consumer costs without a sacrifice in service quality. An alternative solution, which would offer the greatest cost-saving to consumers, would be to allow dental auxiliaries to

TABLE 3

Saskatchewan dental plan, post-treatment restorative quality evaluation project

Radiographs – criteria to be evaluated	
Radiographs should be scored as acceptable unless their diagnostic value is significantly reduced because of one or more of the following:	
Overexposed	The film appears too dark, hindering accurate reading of anatomical and diseased structures.
Underexposed	The film appears too light, hindering accurate reading of anatomical and diseased structures.
Poor contrast	The range of light density of the film is too narrow, so that radiolucent structures may not be accurately differentiated from radiopaque structures. Pulp chambers and periodontal ligament spaces are not clearly visible.
Overlap	This is considered a significant problem when more than 1/2 the interproximal enamel layer on approximating teeth is superimposed on the film.
Cone cut	Should be considered a diagnostic problem only when critical structures are involved. On bitewing films, critical structures would include the interproximal surfaces from the distal of the deciduous canines to the mesial of the first permanent molars if these are present. On periapical films, the full length of the teeth should be visible.
Image off film	This would be the case if the film is not cone cut and yet critical structures, as defined above, are not present on the film.

perform the services on their own, that is, without the supervision of dentists. However, it is unlikely that dental associations would find such a system acceptable, particularly in light of their current struggle with the denturists.

OTHER FORMS OF REGULATION

As was discussed above, an unregulated market for professional services may not function efficiently, and various market failures may result. In some cases such market failures may be remedied by some form of regulation. Our analysis of the effects of occupational licensing concluded that it may not yield the desired results. Occupational licensing attempts to regulate output quality by regulating input quality, and as we saw, it is questionable whether this form of regulation can be successful.

Even if occupational licensing were successful (in raising quality of service), it could have substantial social costs, since it would eliminate the market for low quality services. Clearly, not all consumers of all types of services necessarily

TABLE 4

Quality of amalgam restorations placed by Saskatchewan dentists and dental nurses – deciduous teeth, one-surface fillings

Amalgam quality level	Percentage distribution	
	Dentists $n = 191$	Dental nurses $n = 352$
1.00–1.49	22.5	3.7
1.50–2.50	61.2	44.7
2.51–3.00	16.3	51.6
Mean quality level	1.86	2.48
Significance test	$t = 13.0$	$p < 0.001$

TABLE 5

Quality of amalgam restorations placed by Saskatchewan dentists and dental nurses – deciduous teeth, multi-surface fillings

Amalgam quality level	Percentage distribution	
	Dentists $n = 290$	Dental nurses $n = 706$
1.00–1.49	23.1	5.6
1.50–2.50	61.7	49.5
2.51–3.00	15.2	44.9
Mean quality level	1.89	2.37
Significance test	$t = 13.2$	$p < 0.001$

want to purchase high quality services, given the price they would have to pay. In general, professionals provide a very wide range of services which require a wide range of qualifications. Some tasks are very simple and can be performed by virtually anybody, whereas others are complex and require additional training. Occupational licensing, however, grants one single licence to perform all tasks within the profession, whether simple or complicated. This is clearly an inefficient scheme, since for some tasks (the complex ones) the skills of the professional will be too low and for others (the simple ones) they will be too high.

To resolve this problem it may be possible to use a finer and more specific definition of tasks with many corresponding licences. However, aside from the

TABLE 6

Quality of amalgam restorations placed by Saskatchewan dentists and dental nurses – permanent teeth, one-surface fillings

	Percentage distribution	
Amalgam quality level	Dentists $n = 107$	Dental nurses $n = 358$
1.00–1.49	13.5	1.2
1.50–2.50	65.4	49.1
2.51–3.00	21.5	49.7
Mean quality level	2.02	2.49
Significance test	$t = 9.02$	$p < 0.001$

TABLE 7

Quality of amalgam restorations placed by Saskatchewan dentists and dental nurses – permanent teeth, multi-surface fillings

	Percentage distribution	
Amalgam quality level	Dentists $n = 16$	Dental nurses $n = 87$
1.00–1.49	18.8	0.0
1.50–2.50	59.7	53.0
2.51–3.00	21.5	47.0
Mean quality level	1.89	2.50
Significance test	$t = 5.18$	$p < 0.001$

TABLE 8

Margin extension in ninety-seven stainless steel crowns placed by dentists and dental nurses

	Per cent			
	Superior	Acceptable	Unsatisfactory	N
Dentist	42.1	13.2	44.7	38
Dental nurse	52.5	18.6	28.8	59

Chi-square = 2.61, 2 df, not significant

TABLE 9

Margin adaptation in ninety-seven stainless steel crowns placed by dentists and dental nurses

	Per cent			
	Superior	Acceptable	Unsatisfactory	N
Dentist	34.2	28.9	36.8	38
Dental nurse	32.2	35.6	32.2	59

Chi-square = 0.48, 2 df, not significant

TABLE 10

Occlusion in eighty-six stainless steel crowns placed by dentists and dental nurses

	Per cent			
	Superior	Acceptable	Unsatisfactory	N
Dentist	47.1	47.1	5.9	34
Dental nurse	46.2	46.2	7.7	52

Chi-square = 0.96, 2 df, not significant

TABLE 11

Tissue health in ninety-six stainless steel crowns placed by dentists and dental nurses

	Per cent			
	Superior	Acceptable	Unsatisfactory	N
Dentist	42.1	42.1	15.8	38
Dental nurse	37.9	44.8	17.2	58

Chi-square = 0.17, 2 df, not significant

fact that the licensing scheme may not achieve its aims, there will be very high administrative costs, and competent and well diversified individuals may incur high costs in obtaining the many licences.

An effective alternative could be a form of voluntary certification of individuals. Such certification would not give exclusive rights to practise but simply a right to a title. This type of certification acts as an identification mechanism. It points out those individuals with a certain training, again assuming some direct relationship between training and output quality, and leaves it up to the

TABLE 12

X-ray films – acceptability of films taken by the Saskatchewan dental team

Type of protection	Number of sets assessed	Per cent acceptable
Bitewing	289	81.3
Periapical	181	94.5

TABLE 13

Quality of amalgam restorations placed by dentist

Restoration component	Number of restorations	Restoration quality (per cent)			
		Excellent	Good	Satisfactory	Unsatisfactory
Anatomy	69	13.8	52.2	34.1	0.0
Contour	69	20.3	63.0	16.7	0.0
Contact	48	13.5	60.4	20.8	5.2
Margins	69	19.6	55.8	21.7	2.9
Occlusion	8	6.3	87.5	6.3	0.0
Consistency	69	21.0	65.9	12.3	0.7
Average	1.93	17.6	60.1	20.8	1.5

consumer to choose whose services he wishes to obtain. In this respect certification is an information remedy.

Voluntary certification may be more attractive than licensing, since, while identifying high quality professionals, it leaves the choice to the consumer. It does not eliminate the market for lower quality services. Simple tasks can be obtained from uncertified suppliers and more complicated ones from certified suppliers. However, if 'bad' service imposes large costs (e.g., as with defective surgery), such certifications may not be sufficient. The argument here is the same as that elaborated in Chapter 3.

While the voluntary certification approach is more attractive than licensing in many respects, it suffers from the same main weakness, namely, it assumes that output quality can be affected directly by regulating input quality. As we have seen, this is not necessarily the case; thus voluntary certification may fail to achieve its aim.

Rather than regulate inputs, it may be possible and desirable to regulate output directly. Output regulation requires the setting of performance standards

TABLE 14

Quality of amalgam restorations placed by hygienist

Restoration component	Number of restorations	Restoration quality (per cent)			
		Excellent	Good	Satisfactory	Unsatisfactory
Anatomy	110	30.9	55.9	13.2	0.0
Contour	135	38.9	48.5	12.6	0.0
Contact	100	20.5	64.5	14.0	1.0
Margins	135	44.4	48.9	6.8	0.4
Occlusion	22	34.1	59.1	6.8	0.0
Consistency	135	45.2	51.9	2.6	0.4
Post-operative Lavage	10	65.0	25.0	10.0	0.0
Average	2.27	37.4	53.0	9.3	0.3

TABLE 15

Quality of resin restorations placed by dentist

Restoration component	Number of restorations	Restoration quality (per cent)		
		Excellent	Good	Satisfactory
Anatomy	11	36.4	45.5	18.2
Contour	11	22.7	59.1	18.2
Contact	7	28.6	50.0	21.4
Margins	11	22.7	40.9	36.4
Occlusion	2	50.0	50.0	0.0
Consistency	11	27.3	63.6	9.1
Shade	11	27.3	68.2	4.5
Average	2.06	28.1	54.7	17.2

and a monitoring or enforcement mechanism. Anybody is allowed to provide the service but a monitoring system exists which can impose penalties on those who provide services below the specified standard. For example, occasional and random checks could be used to ensure the satisfaction of the required standards. A monitoring scheme, therefore, acts as a mechanism for the enforcement of the required standards in the provision of diagnosis and treatment services, but also as deterrence mechanisms controlling the recommendation and supply

TABLE 16

Quality of resin restorations placed by hygienist

Restoration component	Number of restorations	Restoration quality (per cent)		
		Excellent	Good	Satisfactory
Anatomy	22	31.8	65.9	2.3
Contour	22	29.5	56.8	13.6
Contact	20	17.5	72.5	10.0
Margins	22	15.9	70.5	13.6
Occlusion	4	37.5	62.5	0.0
Consistency	20	32.5	65.0	2.5
Shade	19	42.1	50.0	7.8
Average	2.19	28.3	63.3	8.1

of unnecessary treatments. Thus, it affects all three main problems in the market for professional services: quality of diagnosis, quality of treatment, and unnecessary treatment.

Output regulation does, of course, have its own weaknesses, primarily the difficulty in setting and determining the required standards. The output of the professional is multi-dimensional and very difficult to measure, let alone determine its quality. While this problem is indeed troublesome, it may not be more difficult than the problems that arise in the determination of the quality of the inputs. Furthermore, the agency that sets the standards is usually well qualified to do so and normally represents members of the profession who have the information about the prevailing standards in the profession.

Finally, as in Chapter 3, we would stress the usefulness of information remedies as a curative for many of the problems arising in markets for professional services. Such remedies can take many forms. One example is the collection and dissemination of information by automobile clubs about the quality of automobile repair.

5

Social regulation and the Canadian legal system: an economic view

INTRODUCTION

In this chapter we shall present a brief overview of the legal basis of social regulation in Canada and Ontario. Since we are economists not legal scholars, the material presented here should not be taken as definitive on fine legal points.[1] Our intention is to set out the economic implications of the law, broadly defined. The institutional focus of this study is social regulation in Ontario, and so the featured element of this legal overview will be an examination of the division of powers and responsibilities between the federal and provincial governments in the area of social regulation.

We are concerned with two basic questions: (1) what powers does each level of government have in the area of social regulation?, and (2) is this division of powers efficient? We shall argue in this chapter that the division of powers between the federal and provincial levels makes it difficult to enact certain types of social regulation effectively. In our view, in some cases this is a benefit and in others it is a cost. Given prominence in our discussion will be: (1) the difficulty of enacting product standards and a strict product liability policy on a national level; (2) the difficulty of enacting certain types of information remedies on a national level (e.g., 'corrective' advertising); and (3) the ability of the provinces to use social regulation as an instrument to promote regional objectives.

In the first part of this study the standard economic protocol for evaluating the economic case for social regulation was presented, and the major economic arguments for social regulation were developed. This methodology will be used in this chapter, since our main concern here will be the economic effects of

1 Readers interested in pursuing the legal aspects of our discussion are referred to Hogg (1977), Lederman (1965), Romero (1975), and other entries in the bibliography.

existing and proposed legislation, and the (economically) optimal division of powers between the federal and provincial governments.

In the next section an overview of the division of powers between the federal and provincial levels as defined by the British North America Act and subsequent case law will be presented. Then, the specific area of the regulation of advertising will be addressed. That discussion will be followed by a summary of the basic legal remedies available for dealing with the problem of product failure. The chapter will end with a critical economic summary of the legal basis of social regulation in Canada and Ontario.

THE BNA ACT[2]

The main component of the Canadian constitution is the British North American Act (BNA Act). This document (and the case law pertaining to it) defines the division of legislative powers between the federal and provincial governments. The main sections setting out the delineation of powers between the two levels of government are sections 91 and 92. The federal level is given 'exclusive' power to legislate 'in relation to the matters coming within the classes of subject' listed in section 91, and the provinces are given 'exclusive' power with respect to the subjects listed in section 92.

As a result of the exclusive nature of the legislative power held by each level, the failure of one level to legislate to the full limit within its power does not enable the other level to act. However, the apparent exclusivity of sections 91 and 92 does not preclude similar laws from being enacted by both levels of government. This apparent contradiction is explained by the *aspect doctrine* which had played a key role in the court's interpretation of the constitution.

As an example, consider a law which prohibits painting obscenities on fences, walls, etc. Such a law could be categorized as pertaining to neighbourhood amenities and thus be a law falling in the context of property and civil rights. Under such an interpretation the law would be within provincial authority under section 92(13). On the other hand, the law could be categorized as pertaining to social evil and therefore within the criminal law power of the federal level under section 91(27). Thus, such a law has different *aspects* which might allow it to fall under either federal or provincial authority, or both. The power to legislate on a particular subject from a particular aspect remains exclusive, but any given law may have a double aspect, so that the power to pass the law may become *concurrent*.

2 For a description of the BNA Act see Hogg (1977).

The aspect doctrine can also be used to explain why a statute may be upheld if it is required to make some validly enacted legislation functional, even if part of the statute, on its own, would be invalid.[3] For example, the custody of children is generally a matter falling within property and civil rights and therefore is under provincial jurisdiction. However, it has been held that the federal Divorce Act's provisions dealing with the custody of children are valid.

Whenever both levels can enact laws on the same subject matter, there is a possibility of conflict between the different laws. The *doctrine of paramountry* provides that in such cases the federal law prevails and the provincial law is rendered inoperative while the federal law exists. However, the courts have been increasingly reluctant to find conflict between federal and provincial laws.

Although the tendency has been to allow *concurrent* legislation, there are also doctrines which prevent total concurrency. The leading concept is that of *mutual modification*, which means that sections 91 and 92 must be read together in order to limit overlap to the extent possible, and to prevent one level from totally dominating the other. This doctrine has been of central importance in the judicial interpretation of section 91(2), the federal trade and commerce power, which has been given a very narrow interpretation. (This issue will be discussed in the next section.)

Therefore, the BNA Act is generally comprehensive enough to allow at least one level of government to legislate in virtually all potential areas of social regulation. However, effective regulation usually requires co-ordination between federal and provincial authorities, always a potentially complicated situation. Furthermore, the division of authority of the two levels may frustrate the process of obtaining private redress in the courts.

Federal powers under the BNA Act
In section 91 of the BNA Act the parliament of Canada is given the power 'to make Laws for the Peace, Order and Good Government of Canada in relation to All Matters not coming within the Classes of Subjects by this Act assigned exclusively to the legislatures of the Provinces.' In addition 'for greater certainty,' section 91 specifies thirty-one specific areas over which parliament has exclusive powers. They include the power to regulate trade and commerce and the power to legislate with respect to criminal law; these powers plus the 'peace, order, and good government' (p.o.g.g.) powers (defined below) provide the main basis for federal activity in the area of social regulation.

---

3 A review of the basic doctrines used by the courts in reviewing the constitutional validity of legislation can be found in Lederman (1965).

(a) The trade and commerce power
Although the power to regulate trade and commerce, as stated in section 91, suggests a major role for the federal government in the area of social regulation, early decisions by the Privy Council severely restricted this power, evidently in order to protect the provincial jurisdiction over property and civil rights. These decisions resulted in a trade and commerce power which encompassed interprovincial trade, foreign trade and the 'general regulation of trade affecting the whole Dominion' (*Citizens Insurance Co. v. Parsons* (1881), 7 AC 96 (PC)). In addition, until recently the courts have generally taken a very narrow view of interprovincial or foreign trade. As one illustration, in 1937 the Privy Council held that a federal act which provided for the establishment of a body of marketing products whose main market was outside the province of production was invalid, since some transactions which could be completed within the province would be affected (*A. G.B.C. v. A.G. Canada* (1937), AC 377 (PC)). Clearly, such an interpretation of the trade and commerce power left little scope for effective use of this power over interprovincial trade.

In the past twenty-five years, however, the courts have taken a less restrictive view of interprovincial trade and foreign trade. In 1959 a federal marketing statute designed to regulate interprovincial and export trade was upheld, even though the statute could incidentally regulate the purely intraprovincial activities of a local producer (*R. v. Klassen* (1959), 20 DLR (2nd) (Man. CA)). This trend in the interpretation of the law was reinforced in 1971, when the Supreme Court unanimously upheld a federal regulation which prohibited transportation or sale of imported oil west of the Ottawa Valley (*Caloil Inc. v. A.G. of Canada* (1971), SCR 543). However, the extent of the federal government's trade and commerce power to regulate products consumed locally is still uncertain. None the less, when we discuss provincial powers we shall see that co-ordination of federal and provincial legislation has allowed extensive regulation of trade and commerce.

As noted above, an early action by Privy Council included the 'general regulation of trade affecting the whole Dominion' as part of the trade and commerce power. However, the meaning of this phase is still ambiguous, although it has thus far been interpreted very narrowly. As one illustration, this power cannot generally be invoked to regulate a trade, an occupation, or an industry within a province, even though the industry or trade may be engaged in throughout the country and may be of considerable importance to the country as a whole. (An attempt to regulate federally interprovincial insurance companies was stricken down in 1916 (*A.G. of Canada v. A.G. of Alberta* (1916), AC 588).

'General regulation of trade affecting the whole Dominion' has been used mainly to create national *trade marks*, which are symbols identifying compliance with federal quality standards. However, this power does not generally include the ability to require compliance with trade mark standards, if a producer does not choose to use the trade mark.

Despite the ambiguity of the federal trade and commerce power, this power forms an important basis for much of the federal legislation in the area of social regulation. Examples of such legislation are the Motor Vehicle Safety Act (RSC 1970 (1st supp.), c.26), the Canada Agricultural Products Standards Act (RSC 1970, c.A-7), and the National Trademarks and True Labelling Act (RSC 1970, c.N-16). The Motor Vehicle Safety Act is a good illustration of limits of the trade and commerce power. This act creates a national trade mark which specifies certain safety standards which must be met for a new motor vehicle in order for a manufacturer to display the trade mark. In addition, export, delivery for export, or the transport for sale from one province to another of a (new) motor vehicle manufactured in Canada which fails to meet the safety standards is an offence. The act does *not*, however, require *all* vehicles made or sold in Canada to meet the standards set.

In summary, the federal government's trade and commerce power probably cannot be used to set standards for all products manufactured and sold in Canada. However, it can generally set quality standards for goods which have entered into the flow of interprovincial or foreign trade. it can also create federal trade marks for goods and impose conditions on their use.

(b) The criminal law power[4]

The criminal law power has been defined very broadly by the courts. Roughly speaking, federal legislation has been upheld under the criminal law power if non-compliance is prohibited with penal consequences and if the court has not been convinced that the legislation's real and primary purpose was a direct legislative intervention into areas reserved for provincial jurisdiction.[5] Examples of federal laws regulating economic activity which have been upheld under the criminal law power include prohibitions of price discrimination, laws governing resale price maintenance, anti-combines laws, the regulation of hazardous products, and regulations governing the packaging and labelling of consumer products.

---

4 The discussion in this section draws heavily from Hatfield (1977).
5 See Lord Atkin in *Proprietary Articles Trade Assn. v. A.G. Can* ((1931) AC 310 (PC)), and in *A.G.B.C. v. A.G. Canada* ((1937) AC 368 (PC)), Mr Justice Rand in *Reference re Validity* of section 5 of the Dairy Industry Act ((1949) SCR 1), and Chief Justice Laskin in *Morgentaler v. The Queen* ((1975) SCR 616). For a general discussion see Hatfield (1977).

The use of the criminal law power to protect the health and safety of the public is perhaps the most visible social regulatory activity of the federal government. Examples of legislation of this kind are: the Hazardous Products Act (RSC 1970, c.H-3), the Explosives Act (RSC 1970, c.E-15), the Radiation Emitting Devices Act (RSC 1970, c.34 (1st supp.)), the Food and Drug Act (RSC 1970, c.F-27), and the Consumer Packaging and Labelling Act (1970–71–72 (Can.), c.41).

The Hazardous Products Act is a good illustration of such legislation. Under this statute hazardous products are divided into two categories, defined by a two-part schedule. The importation, advertising, and sale of products listed in part I of the schedule is completely prohibited. The importation, advertising, or sale of products listed in part II is prohibited except as authorized in regulations passed under the act.

A new product can be added to the schedule by Order-in-Council if it (1) is or contains a poisonous, toxic, inflammable, explosive, or corrosive product or substance, or a product or substance of a similar nature which is or is likely to be a danger to health or safety of the public; or (2) is designed for household, garden, or personal use, or for use in sports or recreational activities, or is used as life-saving equipment, or as a toy, plaything, or equipment for children and is, or is likely to be, a danger to the health or safety of the public, because of its design, construction, or contents. Under the act products can be banned, or their use restricted, or warning labels can be required.

Several regulations have been promulgated under the Act. Examples of a few are: requiring warnings labels on antifreeze containers, specifying maximal lead omission standards for kettles, and specifying technical standards for play-pens and children's car seats. Enforcement of the act is through penal sanctions. Violation of the statute is a criminal offence and conviction makes the violator liable for a fine of up to $1000 and up to two years' imprisonment.

The Hazardous Products Act was recently upheld as a legitimate exercise of the power of parliament to pass legislation in relation to criminal law, which merely affects property and civil rights (*R. v. Cosman's Furniture* (1977), 1 WWR 81 (Man. CA)). The court noted in its decision that the purposes of the act were clearly to protect the health and security of Canadians.

The Food and Drug Act regulates the advertising, importation, and sale of certain foods, drugs, cosmetics, and medical devices. It is administered by the department of national health and welfare and by the department of consumer and corporate affairs. Among other things, the act prohibits the sale or importation of food which contains poisonous substances. Deception in labelling, advertising, or selling is prohibited, the labelling and packaging of foods and drugs is regulated.

The Hazardous Products Act and the Food and Drug Act indicate that the federal government has considerable authority, under the criminal law power, to regulate products that may adversely affect the health and safety of the public. One example of current interest is the ban of saccharin, discussed in Chapter 2. However, establishing such legislation within the criminal law (as opposed to civil law) may have certain disadvantages. This issue will be discussed in detail later in this chapter, where the appropriateness of civil or criminal recourse is considered.

Finally, a good illustration of the federal government's attempt to 'stretch' its criminal law power is the Consumer Packaging and Labelling Act. This statute, administered by the department of consumer and corporate affairs, regulates the packaging and labelling of prepackaged products. Products are defined as articles that are or may be the subject of trade or commerce, excluding land. Commercial goods, goods for export, and consumer textile goods are exempted. The regulations stipulate the required contents of labels and control the sizes of prepackaged products. For example, as of 30 September 1978 refrigerators that are or could be the subject of trade and commerce have had to carry an energy consumption label setting out the kilowatt hours per month of energy consumption as tested by methods approved by the Canadian Standards Association. Dealers (defined to include retailers, manufacturers, processors, importers, packers, and sellers) who sell, import, or advertise any prepackaged produce that does not meet the requirements of the Act commit an offence for which they can be fined or imprisoned.

The ability to 'stretch' the criminal law power in this manner was recently challenged in a case before the Supreme Court (*Labatt's v. A.G. Canada* (1980), not yet published). In that case Labatt's argued essentially that the criminal law power must be limited in this area to health and safety issues (rather than extended to an authority over the labelling of beer). The Supreme Court ruled in favour of Labatt's. The effect of this ruling on other existing federal regulation is unclear at this point.

(c) The 'peace, order, and good government' power[6]
The courts have apparently interpreted the p.o.g.g. powers of section 91 of the BNA Act as giving the federal government authority in two areas: (1) subjects which are not enumerated in section 92 and which by their nature are of national concern – such as aeronautics and radio and television; and (2) all subject matters needed to deal with an emergency. Within the context of social regulation, the most important area of federal authority derived from the p.o.g.g.

6 For a more complete discussion see Lederman (1975) and Hogg (1977).

power is federal control of radio and television broadcasting. This authority includes the power to regulate programming content and advertising. The regulation of advertising will be discussed later in this chapter.

Provincial power under the BNA Act
In section 92 of the BNA Act the provinces are given exclusive power to legislate with regard to matters coming within sixteen enumerated classes of subjects. The classes most relevant to social regulation are as follows.

92(8)   Municipal Institutions in the Province.
92(9)   Shop, Saloon, Tavern, Auctioneer, and other licenses in order to the raising of a revenue for Provincial, Local or Municipal purposes.
92(13) Property and Civil Rights in the Province.
92(15) The Imposition of Punishment by Fine, Penalty, or Imprisonment for enforcing any Law of the Province made in relation to any Matter coming within any of the Classes of Subjects enumerated in this Section.
92(16) Generally all Matters of a merely local or private nature in the Province.

The issue of central importance to our current discussion is to what extent a province can engage in social regulation; of greatest relevance in this context are sections 93(13) and 92(16), which are usually grouped together by the courts and treated almost as residual powers. The courts have granted a very broad although largely unspecified meaning to the term 'property and civil rights.' In practice, therefore (although the courts have consistently stated that the federal level has residuary power), the federal power generally is limited to the power to legislate in relation to the matters falling within the classes expressly enumerated in section 91.[7] In other words, only the matters falling within section 91 are subtracted from matters falling within section 92. It is almost as if the provinces were given all residual power and the enumerated classes of subjects listed in section 91 were subtractions from this provincial power.

Thus, the provincial governments have considerable authority in the area of social regulation, the main limit on this authority being the extent to which provincial legislation affects interprovincial or foreign trade. The exact scope of this limit is still ambiguous. However, a 1971 Supreme Court decision (*A.G. of Manitoba v. Manitoba Egg and Poultry Association* (1971), SCR 689) suggested

7 See Smith (1927), whose analysis is still basically valid, although the scope of the federal power has been increasingly widened by the enlargement of several key powers enumerated in section 9.

that the regulation of pricing and standards of goods produced for export outside the province would not be upheld. Furthermore, it was also indicated in this decision that a province could not subject goods to a general regulatory scheme upon entry into the province; but this decision does not preclude imported goods from being subject to the same controls in retail distribution to consumers as applied to similar goods produced in the province.

The purpose of the legislation also appears to be important. If it can be shown that the purpose of the provincial legislation is to control the importation of products, it will likely be held to be an invalid exercise of provincial authority over interprovincial or foreign trade.

The regulation of professions and trades with the province is almost exclusively with the property and civil rights of the provinces.[8] Since the provincial regulation of professions and trades in Ontario will be discussed in Chapter 6, we shall not address it further here.

Because of the property and civil rights power, the provinces can regulate business and selling practices, terms of contracts, and warranties, and they can require warranties on goods in intraprovincial trade. These areas of regulation will be considered below, when we discuss the regulation of advertising and the contractual rights and forms of redress available to consumers.

The Ontario New Home Warranties Plan Act (SO 1976, c.52) is illustrative of the extent of provincial powers to require warranty coverage. This plan applies to single-family dwellings, one-owner duplexes, and condominiums. Every builder or vendor of a new home must warrant that the home is constructed in a workmanlike fashion, is free from defects in material, is fit for habitation, is constructed in accordance with the Ontario Building Code, and is free from major structural defects. The warranties offer protection for five years, and cannot be waived. The act is administered by a non-profit corporation called the HUDAC New Home Warranty program. A representative of the ministry of consumer and commercial relations and representatives of the building industry and consumer groups comprise the corporation's board of directors.

A person who has a cause of action in damages against a vendor for breach of warranty, failure to perform the contract, or for a major structural defect is entitled to be compensated from the guarantee fund. The fund is financed by fees required of builders on the construction of new homes. All vendors or builders of new homes must be registered under the act.

---

8 However, it has recently been held that the Combines Investigation Act applies to lawyers in British Columbia (*Jobur v. Law Society of BC* (BCSC, unreported as yet)).

This act shows that the provincial law has scope to be quite creative in this area, in that the major industry organization (HUDAC) is given significant responsibility for administering the program. The Travel Industry Act, which requires performance bonds and provides consumers with compensation from an industry collected and administered fund, is another such example.

The Ontario Building Code Act, 1974 (SO 1974, c. 74) is an excellent illustration of the extent to which the provinces can regulate intraprovincial trade. The code and its regulations specify a very comprehensive set of uniform standards for the construction industry. Very detailed materials and design standards for various types of construction are specified. The act is administered by the Building Code branch of the ministry of consumer and commercial relations, but municipalities are given the responsibility for enforcement and inspection.

(a) Methods of federal-provincial co-operation
Since it frequently will be impossible to identify whether goods are being produced or manufactured for the local or interprovincial and foreign markets, effective setting of standards will generally require federal-provincial co-operation. Much of the provincial legislation in Ontario which sets standards for goods basically requires that the goods meet the federal standards. For example, Ontario's Highway Traffic Act (RSO 1970, c.202, as amended) prohibits the sale of new motor vehicles which do not conform to the (federal) Motor Vehicle Safety Act. Similarly, the Ontario Upholstered and Stuffed Articles Act (RSO 1970, c.474, as amended) basically 'piggybacks' on federal statutes in this area.

There are several methods by which the federal and provincial governments can co-operate in creating effective legislation. However, the direct delegation of legislative authority from one level to another has been held unconstitutional (e.g., *A. G. of Nova Scotia v. A. G. of Canada* (Nova Scotia Interdelegation) (1951) SCR 31). Despite this prohibition, each level can delegate its legislative authority to its executive branch, to administrative authorities, etc. One illustration is that municipalities are creatures of the province and have as much legislative authority as the province decides to delegate. Of course, a province can delegate only the powers it has under the BNA Act.

Although the direct delegation of legislative authority from one level to another has not been upheld in the courts, it has been held constitutionally valid for one level of government to delegate its legislative authority to an administrative agency created by the other. One level can also incorporate the other's legislation by reference (as in the Ontario Highway Traffic Act example, described above). These two techniques can be utilized, in effect, to delegate legislative authority for a particular subject matter to the other level. For example, parliament can authorize a provincial board to license public carriers engaged in interprovincial travel and stipulate that the board is to license such operations in accordance with provincial legislation which presently exists or as altered by the province in the future. This technique has been utilized not only where one level does not want to exercise its constitutional powers (as in the case of licensing of interprovincial carriers), but also to regulate effectively a particular activity in conjunction with the other level. An example of such co-ordination of regulation is the marketing of many agricultural products.[9] Case law up to the 1950s indicated that the control of the marketing of products headed for interprovincial and export trade has to be exercised by parliament under its 'trade and commerce' power, but that products headed for intraprovincial trade could be regulated only by a provincial marketing scheme. Since it was frequently impossible to determine if a particular item would eventually be exported or used locally, no government could effectively set up a marketing scheme without the close co-operation of the other. The solution was to set up one marketing board with delegated authority from both levels of government.

Another way in which provincial and federal levels of government can co-operate is by reaching agreement on the division of an area of overlapping jurisdiction (a *concurrent field*) before legislation is passed. This type of arrangement has been worked out in areas such as agriculture, where by section 95 of the BNA Act the federal and provincial governments share concurrent power. The departments of agriculture of the two levels of government have been able to develop working arrangements whereby they divide the field and provide different programs and services to Canadian farmers. Similarly, the governments have reached various forms of taxation agreements.

The adoption of conditional legislation whereby a certain conduct or practice is not prohibited if it is permitted or sanctioned by the other level of government is another legislative device which can be used in concurrent fields. This device has been used in the new sections of the *Combines Investigation Act* (RSC 1970, c.C-23, as amended by SC 1974–75–76, c.76) dealing with pyramid selling and referral selling.

Yet another method of co-ordination is that one level can simply ensure that its legislation meshes with that of the other, so that a particular activity is rationally regulated. An example is the setting of standards for agricultural products sold to consumers in Ontario. Under the Canada Agricultural Standards Act the Governor-General-in-Council (in effect, the cabinet) has made

9 As of 1 September 1970 fifty-nine provincial marketing boards had their provincial powers extended into interprovincial and export trade by virtue of delegated authority under the federal Agricultural Products Marketing Act (RSC 1970, c.A-7). See Safarian (1974) and Romero (1975).

regulations establishing standards for agricultural products and prohibiting the sale of such products under certain grade names unless the products meet the standards set. In addition, the regulations prohibit the interprovincial or export sale of agricultural products unless the product bears the grade name and meets the standard. The (Ontario) Farm Products Grades and Sales Act (RSO 1970, c.161) and the regulations passed under it require grades on farm produce sold in Ontario, and the grading system adopts the federally set standards. The result is that a retailer in Ontario must use the Canadian grade system and the produce sold must meet the federal standard. If no grade is used, the Ontario legislation is violated. If a grade is used but the product does not meet the standard, then the federal legislation is violated. Although no overt agreement between the two levels need be involved in such a scheme, regulation of an activity which neither level has jurisdiction to regulate completely is a good example of effective co-operation.

Thus, we see that there are several means by which the two levels of government can co-ordinate their legislation. Much of the social regulation legislated by the provincial government in Ontario is co-ordinated with the federal government by one or more of the methods we have described.

It is clear that the provinces have extensive powers to regulate intraprovincial trade, which include the ability to set product standards and require warranties. However, to the extent that the courts hold the federal authority in this area to health and safety issues, the setting of national standards for products or warranties will at least require federal-provincial co-operation. Such co-ordination may be more difficult to effect than in the past, given the current climate of intense federal-provincial rivalry.

REGULATION OF ADVERTISING

In the model developed in Chapter 3 the importance of information remedies (prohibiting misleading advertising, requiring informative advertising, or other methods of information provision) as curatives for inefficiencies was stressed. In this section we shall examine the legal basis for federal and provincial regulation of advertising.

Federal regulation
The federal level's ability to regulate advertising is derived mainly from its criminal law power. In addition, the 'peace, order, and good government' power gives the federal government jurisdiction over radio and television broadcasting, which includes the power to regulate advertising through these media. Because these media are closely regulated in other respects (e.g., their existence depends

on government licensing), significant control over advertising can be exercised by the government and CRTC simply by 'moral suasion,' without formal regulation or legislation. Advertising on these media is explicitly regulated by the Broadcasting Act (RSC 1970, c.B-11).

The two major statutes derived from the criminal power regulating advertising are the Combines Investigation Act and the Food and Drug Act. The provisions of the Combines Investigation Act dealing with advertising define advertising very broadly, and misleading advertising of the type we were concerned with in Chapter 3 is restricted by section 36 (1)(b).[10] However, the powers to regulate advertising provided by the Combines Investigation Act have certain weaknesses. First, the combines branch has no direct power of enforcement. It can only investigate and recommend that the department of justice commence prosecution under section 15 of the act. For example, in principle, cessation of ongoing misleading or false advertising can be forced only by a formal court order which is obtainable only upon successful completion of criminal proceedings launched under the act.

A second possible weakness of the act lies in the type of remedy the courts can impose. Because the act is based on the criminal power, violation is punished by fine or penal sanctions.[11] Section 31.1 enables any person who has suffered loss or damage from a violation of the act to sue for damages in the federal courts. However this provision is considered to be of doubtful constitutionality by some legal experts.[12] This issue will be considered further below.

Finally, one remedy which might be beneficial for dealing with some cases of false or misleading advertising would be to require the violator to use corrective advertising. This sort of remedy has been used in the United States recently. (For example, Bristol Myers was required to insert disclaimers in its advertising of Listerine about previous claims about the effectiveness of the product for preventing colds, and Warner-Lambert was required to advertise disclaimers about previous claims about STP that the product reduced oil usage.) For cases in which false or misleading advertising has a lingering, cumulative effect, such a remedy is attractive. However, it is unclear whether the federal government could impose such a remedy.

The federal government has considerably greater power to require 'informative advertising' for products which have significant health and safety connotations. For example, the Food and Drug Act governs the labelling, packaging,

10 The section dealing with advertising is given in an appendix at the end of the chapter.
11 The problems of controlling misleading advertising by criminal actions are outlined in Trebilcock et al. (1976).
12 See Hatfield (1977), Hogg and Grover (1976), and Grange (1975).

and advertising of food and drugs. Advertising (other than radio and television) of food is within the jurisdiction of the Bureau of Consumer Affairs of the department of consumer and corporate affairs. Advertising (other than television and radio) relating to drugs is within the jurisdiction of the department of national health and welfare.

The Hazardous Products Act prohibits the advertisement (and sale or importation) of products listed in its schedule I. Products listed in schedule II may be advertised (or sold or imported) only as authorized by the regulations. A common use of this power is the requirement of warning or use labels on products such as antifreeze.

The Motor Vehicle Safety Act requires the manufacturer, distributor, or importer of a vehicle for which safety standards have been set under section 4 or section 7 to give notice to the dealer, the current owner, and the minister of any known defect in the construction, design, or functioning of that vehicle which affects or is likely to affect the safe operation of that vehicle (section 8(1)). This notice must contain a description of the defect, evaluation of the safety risk related to the defect, and a statement of the means taken to correct it (section 8(2)). Furthermore, the minister can order newspaper publication of the defect (SC 1976–77, ch. 19, s. 3). The manufacturer must forward full particulars of this defect to the minister or other similar official responsible for motor vehicle administration in each province (section 8(3)), and he must submit quarterly reports to the minister relating to the defect (section 8(4), amended by SC 1976–77, ch. 19, s. 3). In practice, the requirements of notice of defects have resulted in voluntary recalls by manufacturers and dealers. Notice, however, that federal authority in such areas is generally based on the criminal law power, so that it is doubtful that a federal regulation requiring notice of *non-safety related defects* would be upheld. We shall return to this issue below.

As a final example, the Consumer Packaging and Labelling Act regulates the packaging and labelling of prepackaged products. Dealers who sell, import, or advertise any prepackaged product that does not meet the requirements of the act commit an offence punishable by fine or imprisonment. However, as mentioned above, in a recent case before the Supreme Court Labatt's was upheld in a challenge of the constitutional validity of the act, arguing essentially that criminal power must be limited in this area to issues explicitly concerned with health and safety.

To the extent that the federal authority to require 'informative advertising' is restricted to health and safety issues (an issue which will be partially resolved by the Labatt's case), the ability of the federal level to deal with informational imperfections of all kinds is limited. For example, in the United States the federal government, believing that consumers could generally not understand the terms of warranties offered on consumer products, enacted legislation (the 'Magnuson-Moss' Act) which regulated the language used in and the terms of some warranties. Although this particular legislation may have serious defects (e.g., it may have *reduced* the warranty coverage offered for some products), a case might be made that warranties should be required to be 'comprehensible.' However, it is unclear whether the federal government in Canada could enact appropriate legislation. Such legislation is within the purview of provincial authority, but it might be more efficient in some cases to have a national regulation, an issue we shall return to.

In summary, although the federal government does have substantial powers to regulate advertising, these powers are evidently limited both in the range of products which can be required to provide 'informative advertising,' and in the type of remedies that can be prescribed for dealing with imperfect information and misleading and false advertising.

Provincial regulation

Under its power to legislate with respect to matters involving property and civil rights a province can regulate the commercial conduct of persons engaged in the sale of goods within a province. A province can therefore validly regulate the advertising practices of such individuals. Recently, the Supreme Court has held that provincial power to regulate advertising includes the ability to prohibit certain ads on television stations within the province. In this case (*A.G. of Quebec v. Kellogg's Co. of Canada Ltd. et al.* (1978), 19 NR 271 (SCC)) a Quebec law which prohibits companies from directing advertising to children was upheld. Thus, television and radio advertising appears to be a concurrent field.

The two major pieces of legislation regulating advertising in Ontario are the Consumer Protection Act (RSO 1970, c. 82) and the Business Practices Act (SO 1974, c. 131). The Consumer Protection Act provides for the disclosure of the cost of borrowing in credit transactions, and allows the Consumer Advisory Services Bureau of the ministry of consumer and commercial relations to order immediate cessation of false, misleading, or deceptive advertising by sellers of consumer goods. In addition, the Business Practices Act (also administered by the Consumer Advisory Services Bureau of CCR) prohibits 'unfair practices,' most of which could be included under a general concept of 'misleading advertising' (in the sense used in Chapter 3). One illustration of a prohibited unfair practice is 'a representation that the goods or services have sponsorship, approval, performance characteristics, accessories, uses, ingredients, benefits or quantities they do not have' (section 2 (a)(i)).

The main enforcement vehicle for the Business Practices Act is the power given to the ministry of consumer and commercial relations to control, *without judicial intervention*, the prohibited unfair practices. The ministry may order a person to refrain from engaging in a specified act or practice, provided notice and the reasons for the order are furnished (section 6). An order under section 6 is subject to a right of hearing. If no hearing is requested within fifteen days, the order takes effect. Using section 7, the ministry can make an order have immediate effect. Where a hearing is requested after a section 7 order, the order expires fifteen days after such a request, unless the hearing intervenes.

The act also makes provision for assurances of voluntary compliance between the ministry and the 'defendant,' which has the status of an order, and therefore breach of such an agreement entails penalties. Thus, the province can effect a cessation of false, misleading, or deceptive advertising fairly quickly. Although an agent subjected to ministry action always has the ability to seek final redress in the courts, the combination of ministry orders, voluntary compliance, and the possibility of obtaining an injunction against the practice during litigation allows the province to achieve a prompt cessation of the practice.

The powers of the province to regulate advertising in some industries is very extensive, as evidenced by the control of advertising in the alcoholic beverages manufacturing and retailing industry in Ontario. Advertising by (retail) licensees and manufacturers in all forms of media must be approved by the Liquor Licence Board. Thus, the provinces have considerable powers to regulate advertising. It is probably within the power of the provinces to require *corrective* advertising (as a remedy for the earlier use of false, misleading, or deceptive advertising), but such a remedy would probably require new legislation, unless it was achieved by voluntary compliance.

Non-governmental regulation

It is worth noting that there is some self-policing of advertising by the advertising industry and the business community. The two major organizations involved are the Canadian Advertising Advisory Board and the Better Business Bureaus. Their stated objective is to obtain compliance with a minimum standard of advertising ethics and thus make unnecessary further government regulation over commercial advertising. Not surprisingly, such self-policing is generally able to deal with only blatant examples of false, misleading, or deceptive advertising.

REMEDIES FOR PRODUCT FAILURE

In Chapter 2 and especially in Chapter 3 we stressed that the division of liability between producers and consumers in cases of product failure was important for the determination of the market allocation of reliability and risk pooling. In this section we shall summarize the legal remedies available to consumers for seeking redress in the case of product failure.

Federal remedies

As we have seen, the ability of the federal government to legislate in the area of product failure problems is derived largely from its criminal law power. Therefore, its ability directly to provide civil remedies (such as restitution to consumers) without recourse to *criminal* action is questionable.[13] As mentioned earlier, the Combines Investigation Act specifies in section 31.1 that a person who has suffered loss or damage as a result of the failure of any person to comply with the act has the ability to sue for damages in the federal courts. In principle, this legislation might allow a consumer redress for product failure in a case where the product reliability was misrepresented. However, since the Combines Investigation Act is derived from the criminal power, the constitutional validity of this provision of a civil remedy has been questioned by some legal experts (see Hatfield, 1977, Hogg and Grover, 1976, and Grange, 1975).

While there is some doubt whether parliament can provide for a civil remedy for breach of a statutory duty contained in legislation based on the criminal law power, failure to comply with federally established standards (such as a national trade mark) could be a factor in the determination as to whether the defendant had been negligent (see, e.g., *Direct Lbi. Co. v. Western Plywood Co.* (1962), SCR 649).

Because of the limitations of the trade and commerce power (described above) the federal level cannot legislate comprehensively concerning the civil liability of manufacturers, on the basis of this power.

Provincial remedies

Because of their property and civil rights power the provinces can legislate on contracts and torts (a tort is a 'wrongful act for which a civil action will lie, except one involving a breach of contract'), which form the basis for legal redress for product failure.

(a) Contractual remedies

1. *Breach of contract.* The rights of the seller and purchaser in a typical consumer sale are governed by contract law and provincial legislation. In

13 The courts have been willing to accept a wide range of sanctions as valid incidents of a criminal law, including an order prohibiting recurrence of the criminal conduct (*Goodyear Tire and Rubber Co. v. The Queen* (1956) SCR 303) and an order compensating the victim of the offence (*Re Torek* (1974), 2 OR (2nd) (Ont. HC)). But these sanctions were imposed as part of *criminal* proceedings.

Ontario the two basic statutes are the Sale of Goods Act (RSO 1970, c.421) and the Consumer Protection Act (RSO 1970, c.82).

Section 2 of the Sale of Goods Act describes a contract of sale of goods as 'a contract whereby the seller transfers or agrees to transfer the property in the goods to the buyer for a money consideration, called the price.' Any transaction falling within this definition (which includes almost all common consumer *goods* (but not services) transactions) is governed by the act.

Contract law distinguishes between *warranties* and *conditions* within the terms of a contract. Conditions are those terms of a contract which are regarded as essential to the purpose of the contract. Breach of an explicit condition of the contract gives the other party a choice of *repudiating* the contract, that is, returning the goods and refusing to pay the price in a sale, or damages. A warranty is a term which is collateral to the main purpose of the contract and its breach permits the disadvantaged party only to sue for damages. The warranties and conditions codified in the Ontario Sale of Goods Act[14] are:

Implied warranties:
1. The buyer is to have quiet possession of the goods.
2. The goods are to be free of encumbrances.

Implied conditions:[15]
3. The seller has the right to sell the goods.
4. The seller will have the right to sell the goods at the time the property in the goods is transferred.
5. The goods will correspond with the description in sales by description.
6. The goods will correspond with the sample in a sale by sample.
7. The goods are of merchantable quality.
8. The goods are fit for a particular purpose, if the buyer either expressly or impliedly lets the seller know the particular purpose for which the goods are required and indicates that he is relying on the seller's skill and judgment, and the goods are those normally supplied in the seller's course of business.

The act regulates the remedy available for redressing a breach of a condition or warranty. The law has generally taken the view that repudiation is a somewhat drastic remedy, since among other reasons it may be highly disruptive of smooth commercial transactions. Section 12(3), which governs *consumer sales*,

14 The Act does not govern sale of consumer *services*.
15 We shall see below that if a consumer has accepted the goods in a consumer sale, the implied conditions essentially become implied warranties.

provides that where the goods which are the subject of the contract *have been accepted* by the buyer, the breach of any condition to be fulfilled by the seller can be treated only as a breach of warranty. This provision precludes the buyer repudiating the contract in virtually all consumer sales.

The two implied conditions that are the predominant concern of the consumer are the condition that the goods are fit for the purpose for which they were purchased, where the buyer implicitly or expressly informs the seller of this purpose, and the condition that the goods are of merchantable quality. Merchantability is an ambiguous concept, but in general it has come to mean that the goods sold are: (1) fit for the ordinary purposes to which such items are normally put; (2) free from defects interfering with such use; (3) salable in the marketplace designated; and (4) genuine according to name and description. Thus (except for the problem of privity, described below), consumers have considerable scope for redress for product defects and faulty workmanship.

Under common law parties may generally contract howsoever they please, and this right is preserved under section 53 of the act, which enables the parties to a contract of sale expressly to agree to exclude terms implied by the Act. However, the Ontario Consumer Protection Act (RSO 1970, c.82) prohibits the seller, under section 44a, in the case of a consumer sale, from contracting out of the conditions and warranties in the Sale of Goods Act. Section 44 defines a 'consumer sale' as 'a contract for the sale of goods made in the ordinary course of business to a purchaser for his consumption or use ...' From an economic point of view this legislation is equivalent to mandating warranties (within minimal terms specified by the conditions and warranties of the Sale of Goods Act), and for the reasons elaborated in Chapter 3 it is not necessarily desirable. This issue will be addressed below in our economic evaluation of the legal system.

Statutory provisions which govern the quality of goods, without specifying that these are to be statutory or implied warranties, may indirectly aid the purchaser in a breach of contract action. For example, a vehicle which does not meet the safety standards set by either provincial or federal law is likely to be considered unmerchantable or unfit for the purpose for which it was intended to be used (see *Henzel v. Brussels Motors Ltd.* 1973), 1 OR 339 (Cty. Ct.)).

2. *Privity of contract.* Privity of contract refers to the relationship which exists between the parties to the contract. The rights and obligations under the contract govern only the parties to the contract, so that a typical consumer good contract of sale binds the retailer and the purchaser only. Thus a purchaser's only recourse under contract law for defective goods is against the seller, not against the manufacturer. (In a typical case the manufacturer may join the seller as a third party to the action, because of the manufacturer's obligation to

indemnify the retailer, arising out of their contract.) The limitation of rights and obligations to exclude the supplier and manufacturer is referred to as vertical privity.

Another dimension of privity of contract, horizontal privity, refers to the limitation of rights under contract to exclude redress by or for persons who may use or be affected by the goods but who are not parties to the contract. For example, if a parent buys a product for his child's use which is defective and causes the child harm, the parent cannot sue the retailer in contract because the parent (being the relevant party in the contract) has not suffered the damage. Furthermore, the child cannot sue in contract because he was not a party to the contract. The only course of action available would lie in negligence.[16]

There are further procedural difficulties with respect to the doctrine of privity. If the consumer has moved a substantial distance from the original place of purchase, a legal action in the place of purchase will be expensive and inconvenient. If the cause of the breakdown of goods is disputed, the buyer will not have the right to obtain discovery of documents from the manufacturer or to examine its officers. Yet the manufacturer, rather than the retailer, is likely to be in possession of all the pertinent facts. The retailer who is the defendant in the consumer's suit is forced to go to the expense and trouble of formally joining the person next in the distributive chain as a third party. If the consumer has delayed his action against the retailer, the retailer may find that the prescriptive period has lapsed and that it is too late for him to issue a third party notice.

The Canadian common law has made little headway in the task of remedying the difficulties arising out of the concept of privity. In *General Motors of Canada v. Kravitz* (1979), 1 CPSG 25,0216) the Supreme Court of Canada held the manufacturer liable for a breach of warranty implied under the Quebec Civil Code. However, this decision has little applicability to common law provinces such as Ontario.

The English courts have developed the concept of 'collateral warranties.' This doctrine makes the manufacturer liable for breach of an express warranty made by the manufacturer if the warranty is intended to induce the buyer to order the manufacturer's product from another person. In a decision of the Supreme Court of Ontario ((1979), CPSG 25,015 (Ont. HC)) this doctrine was used to find a manufacturer of farm machinery liable in contract to the buyer of defective equipment. The representations made in the sales brochure were held to be collateral warranties.

Even if the courts were willing to apply the doctrine to consumer transactions on a large scale, the consumer still faces major difficulties. First, the doctrine

16 Discussed below when we consider tort law

applies only to express representations. Second, the consumer must show that the representation was intended to have contractual force; and third, that he saw or knew of the representation before making his purchase and relied on it.

Through legislation some Canadian provinces have attacked the privity problem. In the early part of the century the prairie provinces effected legislation on defective farming machinery and the prevalence of the use of disclaimer clauses.[17] Prince Edward Island adopted similar legislation at a later date. Today, all these acts imply various warranties in favour of the retail buyer of such equipment and all provide that the manufacturer or provincial distributor, as well as the dealer, are liable to the purchaser to observe, keep, and perform the warranties.

In 1976 the Ontario legislature considered a bill which would have extended horizontal and vertical privity. This bill, the Consumer Products Warranties Act, Bill 110 (3rd session, 30th leg.) received first reading on 15 June 1976 but was never passed into law. Section 1(1)(a) extended the definition of consumer to any 'Natural person who is the owner or has the right to possess and use a consumer product, but does not include a natural person, partnership or association of individuals acting in the course of company or a business'; that is, it extended horizontal privity. The warranties provided for in the statute (that the consumer product would perform for a reasonable length of time and that the consumer product was free of hidden defects), could therefore be enforced by a subsequent purchaser or by anyone having the right to use the goods. Vertical privity was to be extended by the provision that both the retailer and the manufacturer were liable for breaches of these two statutory warranties. Finally, section 5 of the bill provided for a warranty, given jointly by the manufacturer and retailer, that there would be spare parts available for the repair of the goods.

There were many objections to the bill. Retail lobbies objected to the spare parts warranty on the grounds that if the manufacturer went out of business, the retailer would be helpless to live up to the warranty. Another major source of concern was that the duration of the warranties, that is, 'reasonable' length of time, was not specified in the Act. At the time of this writing, the fate of this bill has not been resolved. We argued in Chapter 3 that a policy which mandated warranties was not generally desirable (efficient). On this basis we would not favour the provision of Bill 110 which would, in essence, mandate warranties. In particular, an efficient definition of 'reasonable' length of time is an extremely knotty problem which should not be left for the courts to resolve, given the uncertainty that such an action imposes on producers. We would prefer that the legislation stay away from this problem by not getting into the business of

17 See, for example, The Farm Implements Act (SA 1913, c.15).

mandating warranties at all. The economics of the problem of privity, including a discussion of provisions in Bill 110 which would extend vertical and horizontal privity, will be taken up below.

(b) Tortious
When no contractual relationship exists between the injured party and the supplier or manufacturer of the defective goods, the injured party will have to frame his course of action in tort based on negligence. Under an action for negligence a manufacturer can be held liable for injuries sustained from a defective product if the person injured can prove that the defect resulted from some negligent act or omission on the part of the manufacturer. In other words, the manufacturer must be proved to have failed to use reasonable care in the circumstances. This failure must be proved to be the proximate cause of the injury.

Two cases illustrate both the usefulness and the limits of a tort action in relation to defective goods. In *Phillips v. Ford Motor Company of Canada and Elgin Motors Ltd.* ((1970), 2 OR 714 (SC)), an automobile manufacturer was held liable for the faulty design of power brakes containing a malfunctioning fail-safe system. On the other hand, in *Phillips v. Chrysler Corporation of Canada Ltd.* ((1962), 32 DLR (2d) 347 (Ont. HC)) an action against a manufacturer was dismissed on the grounds that an accident which was caused by a brake defect could not be traced back to the manufacturing process.

As in the last case, it will frequently be difficult to prove that negligent design etc. resulted in the particular injury to the plaintiff. In such situations the plaintiff will sometimes be able to rely on the doctrine of *res ipsa loquitur*. This is a latin phrase meaning 'the thing speaks for itself.' Under this doctrine the fact of the happening of an accident provides reasonable evidence that the accident resulted from lack of care on the part of the defendant. The facts and circumstances of each case will determine if the doctrine is applicable, but generally the accident must be one which in the ordinary course of events does not happen if those who have management and control of the product use proper care. Two cases again illustrate the uncertainty with which one can predict whether the doctrine will be held applicable. In *Wylie v. R.C.A. Limited et al.* ((1974), 5 Nfld. PEIR 147 (Nfld. SC)) the court applied the doctrine in a case where a colour television set burst into flame for no apparent reason and caused damage. In *Stewart and Stewart v. Chrysler Canada Ltd. et al.* ((1975), 13 NBR (2d), 53 (NBCC)) the doctrine was held inapplicable in a case where the plaintiff was injured when the rear window of the car she was driving shattered.

While there is some doubt whether the parliament of Canada could provide for a civil remedy for breach of a statutory duty contained in legislation based on the criminal law power, failure to comply with federally established standards could be a factor in determining whether the defendant had been negligent.

Compensation for personal injuries and property damage are clearly recoverable in tort. It is still uncertain whether pure 'economic loss' (c.g., loss of time) is recoverable when there is no damage to the plaintiff's person or property. The issue is a complicated one, but it is thought that the Supreme Court of Canada in *Rivtow Marine Ltd. v. Washington Iron Works et al.* ((1974) SCR 1189) gave judicial recognition to recovery for pure economic loss.

We argued in Chapter 3 that it may be desirable to impose producer liability for cases of product failure involving health and safety hazards. Recourse to an action in tort is not generally a satisfactory remedy, since such an action must be based on the proof or inference of negligence on the part of the producer, and the legal concept of negligence is too narrow to allow blanket imposition of producer liability. This issue will be further discussed below.

Federal-provincial co-operation
Federal-provincial co-operation is generally critical to the effective setting of product standards and to the imposition of producer liability for the wide variety of consumer goods and services markets which are national in scope. Several federal statutes, such as the Hazardous Products Act, the Motor Vehicle Safety Act, and the Food and Drug Act set product standards of various types and provide penalties to be applied to violators. If a product does not comply with these standards and it causes physical damage, personal injury, or economic loss, the consumer would presumably be more interested in compensation than prosecution of the manufacturer. The federal health and safety statutes mentioned above are silent on this point.

As we have already mentioned, there is some doubt whether parliament has the jurisdiction to create a civil course of action for breach of the standards because the legislation mentioned is based on the criminal law power. Presumably a consumer can succeed only by showing negligence on the part of the manufacturer. Although, as mentioned above, failure to comply with federally established standards (such as a national trade mark) could be a factor in the determination of whether the defendant had been negligent, it might be desirable to provide for direct civil redress.

Class actions[18]
One possible remedy for product failures affecting a number of purchasers is the class action. A class action brings together for a single determination against the

18 For a more comprehensive discussion see William (1974), and Dewees et al. (1979).

same defendant the claims of a number of individuals which arise from a common nucleus of fact. The essential characteristic of a class action is that judgment in the action will bind not only the representative party but also the persons whom he represents as fully and effectively as if they had been made parties themselves.

The appointment of the class representative is a significant factor in success of any class action. In practice the individual who sues for the rest of the class will sometimes be chosen after consultation among the members, but this procedure is not essential, and a class member can appoint himself as representative and take proceedings without prior notice to the class. Since the other class members are not parties, they have no standing in the action, which entitles them to appear at the trial and be separately represented by counsel. The importance of the appointment of a class plaintiff lies in the binding effect of the decision on all members of the class.

A peculiar characteristic of the class action procedure lies in the absence of any requirement that the class members be notified that an action has been brought on their behalf.[19] In many cases it will only be by accident – for instance, by newspaper publicity – that a class member other than the named plaintiffs will hear of the proceedings. Yet judgment in the action binds the class whatever the result, and each and every member of the class is bound, whether he had notice or not.

Until recently consumer class actions in Ontario (and Canada generally) were very unlikely to succeed. Rule 75 of the Supreme Court Rules provides: 'Where there are numerous persons having the same interest, one or more may sue or be sued or may be authorized by the court to defend on behalf of, or for the benefit of, all.' The words 'the same interest' have been very narrowly construed by the courts. For a long time it was held that an action for damages could not be brought as a class action in Ontario. This is no longer an accurate statement of the law. Instead, the position now appears to be that a class action will be allowed if the statement of claim is framed in such a way that all members of the class share the same cause of action and that the amount to which each member is entitled is readily ascertainable. In other words, the claim of the representative must typify the claim of each member in the sense that the same question is raised in all the claims and there is no need to assess facts peculiar to each claimant in order to determine if that claimant could succeed or in order to determine the amount of damages. In many situations the damages suffered by

19 However, in February 1980 an Ontario court dismissed a class action against *Time Magazine* on the grounds, among other things, that the class representative was required to notify all class members. This decision is under appeal.

purchasers of defective goods will vary considerably, so that individual assessment is required. This situation was avoided in *Naken et al. v. General Motors of Canada* ((1979), 21 OR (2nd) 780 (CA)), by a claim for only the loss in resale value of all Firenzas (regardless of their individual state) due to defective manufacturing.

SUMMARY OF ECONOMIC ISSUES

This section will review the important economic issues raised in the preceding summary of Canadian law. The specifics of social regulation in Ontario are addressed in the following chapter.

Our discussion of the division of powers between the two levels of government under the BNA Act indicated that there were significant impediments to the federal government's acting alone to legislate comprehensively in the area of social regulation. Because Canada is clearly a *national* market with respect to most consumer goods, effective social regulation of consumer goods markets will usually require that such regulation be implemented on a national basis. As we have seen, the federal and provincial levels often have recognized this fact and have found creative methods of co-operation in order to effect regulations which are, in fact, national in coverage.

Since we generally take a dim view of the utility of setting standards for consumer goods, except in some cases where health and safety hazards are important, the impediments to setting such standards on a national basis do not trouble us in most instances. Under the criminal law power the federal government has extensive scope for setting standards for products based on health and safety grounds. Since we argued in Chapter 3 that such grounds were probably the only efficiency-based justification for standard-setting, the other limitations on the ability to regulate on other grounds by national standards in our view are likely to be desirable.

On the other hand, apparently there are limits to the federal power to set informational standards, and such limits may not be desirable. As one illustration, unlike the United States, Canada has no comprehensive labelling regulations which would require, for example, that ingredients, weight, volume, etc., be listed on a label on the product. Such a regulation may very well be desirable on efficiency grounds because of its presumed enhancement of consumer information and apparent low costs.[20]

---

20 Naturally, a thorough analysis of the costs and benefits of such a regulation should be conducted in order to establish its desirability. An analysis based on an examination of the effects of such regulation in the United States would be very informative.

Although the federal level can and in some instances has enacted regulations of this type on health and safety grounds (stretched to include regulation of the use of the term 'light' in the description of beer), provision of information can be àn effective efficiency-augmenting remedy, even if health and safety are not sources of concern. It seems unlikely that the federal level could, independently, enact a general labelling regulation such as that found in the United States.[21] Furthermore, given the national nature of most markets, regulation of this kind is difficult to implement in an efficient and effective manner on an independent provincial basis. Presumably, the federal and provincial levels could find a mode of co-operation which would effect a national labelling regulation, but in the current climate of federal-provincial antagonism, such co-operation may be increasingly difficult.[22] If this is the case, there may be serious limits to the feasibility of enacting certain forms of beneficial national social regulation.

We argued in Chapter 3 that the imposition of producer liability (based on a standard of strict product liability rather than negligence) might be justified on efficiency grounds for products whose failure could entail health and safety hazards. The federal level can set standards for such products, but since such regulations derive from the criminal law power, the federal level may not be able to prescribe suitable civil remedies (i.e., civil liability) for violation of the standards.[23] Therefore, direct imposition of producer liability based on a standard of strict product liability by the federal level may not be possible. Although violation of a federal standard may bear on the finding of negligence in a case brought in tort, it seems inefficient to require redress to pursue this circuitous route, especially since negligence, in a strict sense, may not be the issue.

The issue involved here can be illustrated by the model presented in Chapter 3. In that model $(1 - s)$ per cent (<100 per cent) of the units can be expected to fail (and perhaps cause personal injury), but this result would certainly not be due to negligence, even in the instance that s was set by a government standard. The efficient policy in a particular case may require imposition of producer liability in all instances of product failure resulting in personal injury.[24] However, it is difficult to envision how such a policy could be implemented by a scheme which would specify a safety standard with some associated mechanism for civil redress in the event of non-compliance with the standard. First of all, for the reasons described in Chapter 3, imposition of standards, itself, is not generally a desirable (efficient) policy. Secondly, even if the standard achieves the desired

21 In the recent *Labbatt's* case for example, the Supreme Court ruled that the criminal power could not be stretched to include regulation of the term 'light' for malt beverages.
22 Of course this is only conjecture on our part.
23 However, see fn. 14, above.
24 Such a policy would have to be tempered by moral hazard concerns.

level of safety, the problem remains that efficiency requires that consumers receive compensation in the event of product failure, *even if a product that satisfies the safety standard fails* (for reasons other than violation of the standard). Thus, the limitations on the federal powers in this area may be a serious impediment to the attainment of efficiency.

Another problem which is difficult to remedy, given the division of powers between the federal and provincial levels, is privity of contract, discussed above. In modern consumer goods markets placing the liability for breach of contract (implicit or explicit) exclusively on the retailer seems clearly inefficient in terms of its effects on transactions, negotiations, and enforcement costs. Although we do not favour many aspects of the Ontario legislature's Bill 110 (Consumer Product Warranties Act), particularly those which, in effect, mandate warranties, its proposal to extend privity to the manufacturer would appear to have a good economic basis. We would favour such an extension of privity for breaches of warranties or conditions specified in the Sale of Goods Act. The problems of moral hazard and adverse selection (discussed in Chapter 2) make the desirability of the extension of horizontal privity more ambiguous.

Unfortunately, the provinces have exclusive jurisdiction in the area of legislation with respect to privity. Since most consumer goods markets in Canada are truly national markets, the extension of vertical privity would be most efficiently and effectively implemented by a national action. Such an action, given the division of powers between the federal and provincial levels, would have to be effected by provincial co-operation.

Thus the weighting of the division of powers between the two levels in favour of the provinces has beneficial and adverse implications. We have thus far argued that this division is beneficial in that it limits the ability of the federal level to legislate effectively in some areas where we find such limits desirable, but in other areas these limits may restrict the ability to enact beneficial policies. Our final source of concern with the division of powers is the latitude it allows for the provincial authorities to engage in actions having important national effects. The powers given under the BNA Act allow the provinces, especially the larger ones, to enact social regulation which has national repercussions. As we have seen, such action can be beneficial, but the history of regional competition in Canada indicates that such rivalries can result in provincial legislation which is undesirable from a national point of view. In particular, social regulation can be used to facilitate regional protectionism.

APPENDIX: EXCERPT FROM COMBINES INVESTIGATION ACT

36. (1) No person shall, for the purpose of promoting, directly or indirectly the supply or use of a product or for the purpose of promoting, directly or indirectly, any business interest, by any means whatever,

(a) make a representation to the public that is false or misleading in a material respect;

(b) make a representation to the public in the form of a statement, warranty or guarantee of the performance, efficacy or length of life of a product that is not based on an adequate and proper test thereof, the proof of which lies upon the person making the representation;

(c) make a representation to the public in a form that purports to be
(i) a warranty or guarantee of a product, or
(ii) a promise to replace, maintain or repair an article or any part thereof or to repeat or continue a service until it has achieved a specified result if such form of purported warranty or guarantee or promise is materially misleading or if there is no reasonable prospect that it will be carried out; or

(d) make a materially misleading representation to the public concerning the price at which a product or like products have been, are or will be ordinarily sold; and for the purposes of this paragraph a representation as to price is deemed to refer to the price at which the product has been sold by sellers generally in the relevant market unless it is clearly specified to be the price at which the product has been sold by the person by whom or on whose behalf the representation is made.

(2) For the purposes of this section and section 36.1, a representation that is

(a) expressed on an article offered or displayed for sale, its wrapper or container,

(b) expressed on anything attached to, inserted in or accompanying an article offered or displayed for sale, its wrapper or container, or anything on which the article is mounted for display or sale,

(c) expressed on an in-store or other point-of-purchase display,

(d) made in the course of in-store, door-to-door or telephone selling to a person as ultimate user, or

(e) contained in or on anything that is sold, sent, delivered, transmitted or in any other manner whatever made available to a member of the public,

shall be deemed to be made to the public by and only by the person who caused the representation to be so expressed, made or contained and, where that person is outside Canada, by

(f) the person who imported the article into Canada, in a case described in paragraph (a), (b) or (c), and

(g) the person who imported the display into Canada, in a case described in paragraph (c).

(3) Subject to subsection (2), every one who, for the purpose of promoting, directly or indirectly, the supply or use of a product or any business interest, supplies to a wholesaler, retailer or other distributor of a product, any material or thing that

contains a representation of a nature referred to in subsection (1) shall be deemed to have made that representation to the public.

(i) in any prosecution for a violation of this section, the general impression conveyed by a representation as well as the literal meaning thereof shall be taken into account in determining whether or not the representation is false or misleading in a material respect.

(4) Any person who violates subsection (1) is guilty of an offence and is liable

    (a) on conviction on indictment, to a fine in the discretion of the court or to imprisonment for five years or to both; or

    (b) on summary conviction, to a fine of twenty-five thousand dollars or to imprisonment for one year or to both.

36.1 (1) No person shall, for the purpose of promoting, directly, the supply or use of any product, or for the purpose of promoting, directly or indirectly, any business interest

    (a) make a representation to the public that a test as to the performance, efficacy or length of life of the product has been made by any person, or,

    (b) publish a testimonial with respect to the product,

except where he can establish that

    (c) the representation or testimonial was previously made or published by the person by whom the test was made or the testimonial was given, as the case may be, or

    (d) the representation or testimonial was, before being made or published, approved and permission to make or publish it was given in writing by the person by whom the test was made or the testimonial was given, as the case may be,

and the representation or testimonial accords with the representation or testimonial previously made, published or approved.

(2) Any person who violates subsection (1) is guilty of an offence and is liable

    (a) on conviction on indictment, to a fine in the discretion of the court or to imprisonment for five years, or to both; or

    (b) on summary conviction, to a fine of twenty-five thousand dollars or to imprisonment for one year or to both.

6

A summary of social regulation in Ontario

INTRODUCTION

This chapter will summarize the social regulatory activities of the Ontario provincial government. We are interested here in revealing the basic types and areas of regulation, rather than providing detailed descriptions of each piece of legislation or regulatory action. Our attention will be focused on the areas described in the terms of reference of this study, which were elaborated in Chapter 1. For this reason some of the description of ministerial responsibilities in the area of social regulation, particularly environmental protection regulation, will be brief.

Unlike Ontario Hydro, the Liquor Control Board of Ontario, the income and sales taxes, etc., which are highly visible examples of provincial government intervention, much of the social regulatory activity of the provincial government is only dimly perceived by the general populace. Therefore, one of the purposes of this chapter is to reveal the very considerable but largely unappreciated extent of provincial government activity in this area. Our second purpose is to evaluate critically a few specific social regulatory activities of the provincial government. Our choice of these activities was governed by the issues raised in the analysis developed in the preceding chapters. Naturally, we are particularly interested in provincial activities in the areas of product standards, product liability, advertising and information remedies, and occupational licensing.

The economic analysis of specific regulations which we develop in this chapter can be considered to be only suggestive. We have not done the cost-benefit calculations which would be necessary for definitive conclusions. However, the analysis developed in this study suggests that the desirability of some types of existing provincial regulation in their present form (e.g., occupational licensing) is questionable. In this chapter we shall elaborate on these arguments in the context of the specific regulations. Our conclusion will then be that these regulations deserve closer scrutiny. Finally, we shall suggest that certain new regulatory actions may be desirable, and so deserve further study.

It should be noted that our summary of provincial activity represents a 'snapshot' of provincial regulation taken at the time this was written. At least since 1977 the government has been apparently actively reviewing its regulatory activities with an eye towards possible areas of simplification and deregulation. In 1978 the provincial government took two initiatives in the area of deregulation. An agency review committee was created under the chairmanship of the Honourable D. Wiseman, minister without portfolio. This agency was charged with the task of reviewing the regulatory activities of provincial agencies and to make recommendations. A 'Customer Service and Deregulation Program' was also created, co-ordinated under a newly created associate secretary of cabinet post. At the time this was written each of the ministries had identified possible areas of deregulation or simplification of current regulation, and some policy changes were in progress. However, it appeared that most of the proposed actions were aimed at simplifying the regulatory process and making it easier for the public and business community to deal with the government rather than at actual deregulation.[1] This somewhat modest goal is perhaps to be expected, given the short period that the program has been in existence, but whether or not the provincial government has a long-run commitment to a comprehensive investigation and possible overhaul of its regulatory activities is as yet unclear. For example, the Customer Service and Deregulation Program has not produced a comprehensive survey of regulatory activity, which presumably would be a prerequisite to a major program of deregulation. Furthermore it appears that there will be no major attempt to force systematic regulatory review, such as by the use of 'sunset' provisions. The current government seems to us to have firm commitment to only a limited program of cutting provincial government red tape – a laudable, albeit restrained goal. The course of future actions will no doubt be governed by the extent of the strength and endurance of deregulation as a political issue.

In what follows we shall summarize the provincial government's regulatory activity on a ministry basis. Areas of provincial social regulation with which,

---

1 This is our conclusion derived from interviews and background documents from the Customer Service and Deregulation Program. However, the ministries were instructed to ensure that all future cabinet submissions include, as a mandatory requirement, an economic impact statement (Ontario Ministry of Consumer and Commercial Relations, 1978). However, it appears thus far that this mandatory requirement has been met in only a rudimentary manner.

based on the analysis of the preceding chapters, we are especially concerned, will be given more extensive attention and critical evaluation.

The background data on which our summary of provincial regulatory activity is based include provincial government publications, ministry annual reports, interviews, and the responses to a questionnaire which we sent to each ministry with the help of Mr Alan Gordon, associate secretary of cabinet (in charge of the Customer Service and Deregulation Program). In addition, Mr Gordon provided us with some unpublished material from the Customer Service and Deregulation Program. In our summary we shall not provide much specific discussion of most of Ontario's agencies, boards, commissions, etc., since these bodies have been catalogued and described in Bresner, Leigh-Bell, et al. (1978). Finally, the Appendix lists provincial statutes organized by ministerial responsibility.

SUMMARY OF MINISTRIES' REGULATORY ACTIVITY

Agriculture and food
The goal of the ministry of agriculture and food (OMAF) is 'to encourage the responsible development and utilization of Ontario's agriculture and food resources for the economic and social well-being of all people in Ontario' (OMAF memorandum). The main divisions of this ministry are finance and administration, production and rural development, marketing, and educational research and special services.

OMAF's regulatory powers in the areas of agriculture and food include:

Regulation of marketing of designated farm products under the Farm Products Marketing Act and the Milk Act. This regulatory activity includes the power to set quotas.

Setting and regulation of grades under the provisions of the Livestock and Livestock Products Act and the Farm Products Grades and Sales Act. Under the acts provision is made for provincial inspection.

Minimum standards are prescribed under a variety of acts. Areas subject to standards include drainage machine operators (The Agricultural Tile Drainage Installation Act), care of animals (the Riding Horse Establishment Act and the Animals for Research Act), cleanliness and construction of premises (the Milk Act and Livestock Community Sales Act), and the oil content in margarine.

Liability is imposed on owners for damages caused by animals (Dog Licencing Act, Livestock and Poultry Protection Act, and the Protection of Cattle Act), and on owners of diseased orchards, plots of noxious weeds, etc.

Various agents are licenced, such as tile drainage installation operators. In addition, OMAF has major responsibilities in the area of agricultural education and research.

(OMAF memorandum)

Of course the major social regulatory function of OMAF is the setting of standards for agricultural products and their production. On the basis of the arguments developed in Chapter 3 such regulation may be efficiency augmenting. Any individual producer has the capacity to cause harm to food consumers far in excess of his effective financial liability, and it would often be difficult to trace a problem to a particular producer. Without government standards food processors and retailers would have to attempt to set standards on primary producers in a piecemeal fashion, which in many cases would probably be more costly to implement than uniform standards. None the less, such private setting of standards is often used by name brand food manufacturers. For example, the H.J. Heinz Co. contracts for tomatoes with producers in southern Ontario, and the contractual arrangements usually require certain standards in cultivation, in use of fertilizer and pesticides, and for output. However, it is difficult to imagine such a system working for less specialized crops.

It is beyond the scope of this study to evaluate each individual standard, but it should be noted that the economic case for standards for agricultural products and production does not necessarily justify the extent of their use in Ontario. Such standards have often been used in the past in several North American jurisdictions to restrict competition (such as severely impairing the production and marketing of oleomargarine, presumably at the instigation of dairy lobbies) or for other sorts of 'mischief' having nothing to do with economic efficiency. Our discussion of the demand for regulation in Chapter 2 suggests that the 'capture' of portions of OMAF by agricultural interests (at the expense of consumers) is a possibility with which we should be concerned. For example, the Broadsmith, Huges, and Associates (1978) study of the Ontario Milk Marketing Board (OMMB) argues that the OMMB's control of the pricing and supply of milk has been injurious to consumers (and presumably to the benefit of milk producers).

Attorney general
The ministry of the attorney general (OMAG) directs and supervises the administration of justice in Ontario. OMAG is, of course, the main legal enforcement branch of the provincial government. The direct regulatory activities of the ministry are the regulation of the legal, accounting, architectural, and engineering professions. The avowed purpose of this type of regulation would clearly seem to be the setting of 'quality' standards. Since these standards include

'input' standards (such as educational requirements), the analysis developed in Chapter 4 is relevant. Of additional concern is the fact that the standards for these professions are largely determined by current members of the profession, which may give the current members the opportunity to advance their self-interest through the restrictiveness of the standards.[2] We shall return to this issue below, when we discuss occupational licensing and certification in the province.

The independent agencies of the ministry include the Ontario Municipal Board (OMB), which is a major regulatory body in the area of urban development and land use controls in the province. The OMB is a virtually autonomous, provincially appointed, administrative tribunal which is responsible for approving zoning by-laws and amendments, for approving official plans and plans of subdivision upon referral by the ministry of housing when they are subject to objections, and for hearing appeals on many types of municipal planning decisions. The OMB has a great deal of power over municipal planning. For example, in the case of appeals it can sustain, reverse, or modify municipal decisions. See Frankena and Scheffman (1980) for an extensive discussion of the activities of the OMB.

Community and social services
The primary responsibility of the Ontario ministry of community relations and social services (OMCRSS) is provision of services such as the administration of welfare, family aid, soldiers' aid benefits, etc., administration of mental retardation facilities and community programs, juvenile detention, probation, rehabilitation and group home programs, and subsidization of services of these kind provided by municipalities of citizens' groups. The basic regulatory activities of OMCRSS involve the licensing of mental health care centres, day care centres, and nurseries. These regulations include the setting of standards.

Consumer and commercial relations
The Ontario ministry of consumer and commercial relations (OMCCR) has major social regulatory responsibilities in the province. The ministry administers seventy pieces of legislation (see the appendix to this chapter), many of which are explicit social regulation. OMCCR has five main program areas: commercial standards, technical standards, public entertainment standards, property rights, and the Registrar General Program. The official description of each of the programs is revealing of the major activities and responsibilities of each program.

---

2 The professional organization committee of OMAG has completed extensive studies of the professions of architecture, engineering, accounting, and law.

a. *Commercial Standards Program*

This program consists of five activities that provide for the regulation of financial and commercial affairs to promote a high level of ethical business conduct responsive to the needs of the buyer in the market place. This is achieved through disclosure to the public of the essential elements of business transactions including the issuing of securities, registration and licencing of persons dealing with the public to assure a high degree of competence and honesty in their dealings, and examination and surveillance of the financial standing and practices of firms.

In addition this program provides services for incorporation of companies, administration of The Motor Vehicle Accident Claims Act in respect of the adjustment of claims and payment of damages occasioned by the operation of stolen, unidentified or uninsured motor vehicles, and provision for appeal hearings with respect to the matters of licencing under various acts administered by the Ministry.

b. *Technical Standards Program*

This program consists of six operating activities, co-ordinated by the Office of the Executive Director, which are responsible for ensuring public safety through the inspection of elevators, pressure vessels, upholstered and stuffed articles, the transmission, transportation, distribution and utilization of natural gas, propane and fuel oil, the storage, transportation, distribution of gasoline and associated products, and the issuance of licences for the operation of elevators and pressure vessels. The Uniform Building Standards activity is seeking to establish, through several advisory committees, a system of uniform building and fire safety standards for the Province.

c. *Property Rights Program*

The objectives of this program are to enable the ownership of and encumbrances affecting real property, and encumbrances affecting personal property to be readily ascertained. The division is responsible for the operation of Land Registry offices and branch offices of the Personal Property Security Registration system throughout the Province.

d. *Public Entertainment Standards Program*

This Program consists of activities representing the administration of The Racing Commission Act, Theatres Act and Lotteries as outlined in the Criminal Code.

e. *Registrar General Program*

This program provides for the administration of The Marriage Act and for the collection and custody of all records required under The Vital Statistics Act and supplies information and statistics to interested parties as provided for in the Act. The services are administration, issuance of certificates, recording of vital events and provision of statistical data.

(Ontario Ministry of Culture and Recreation, 1979)

As can be seen from these brief descriptions and our discussion of provincial responsibilities in the previous chapter, OMCCR's activities in social regulation are broad both in scope and type of regulation. As an indication of the scope of the ministry's activities, the seventy pieces of legislation for which it has responsibility include: Bills of Sales Act, Boiler and Pressure Vessels Act, Bread Sales Act, Building Code Act, Business Practices Act, Consumer Protection Act, Elevators and Public Lifts Act, Insurance Act, Liquor Control Act, Liquor Licence Act, Marriage Act, Motor Vehicle Dealers Act, Ontario New Home Warranties Plan Act, Ontario Water Resources Act, Paperback and Periodical Distributors Act, Petroleum Products Price Freeze Act, and the Wine Content Act. (For a complete list see the appendix to this chapter.)

Under these acts and the other legislation administered by OMCCR regulatory activities of the ministry include:

licencing of professional wrestlers and boxers;

registration and supervision of bailiffs, collection agencies, mortgage brokers, consumer reporting, paperback and periodicals dealers;

administration of a building code to ensure safety and minimize fire hazards;

regulation of cemeteries and burial grounds;

registration of partnerships, proprietorships and limited partnerships;

supervising the incorporation, management and dissolution of credit unions and caisses populaire;

inspection and licencing of elevating devices;

regulation and licencing of insurance companies, investment contract companies, medical insurance associations, mutual benefit and fraternal societies, loan companies and trust companies;

licencing of insurance agents, brokers, salespeople and adjusters;

certification, licencing and auditing of operations of those involved in distribution transportation and utilization of fuels;

administration of the New Home Warranty Program which requires registration of all new home builders, and mandates that all builders provide a specified limited warranty on all new homes;

Liquor Control Board of Ontario (LCBO) – regulates the sale of wine, spirits and beer for home consumption or to licenced establishments, and operates the only retail outlets for spirits in the province. Regulates advertising of wine, spirits, and beer;

Liquor Licencing Board (LLBO) – issues and monitors all holders of liquor licences, and regulates all advertisements for licenced establishments;

issue of licences and regulation of all lotteries and bingos;

administration of Motor Vehicle Accident Claims fund;

regulation and registration of dealers (and their agents) for new or used motor vehicles;

licencing of all participants in horse racing (except the horses);

registration of stockbrokers, salesmen and investment advisers, commodity futures dealers, salesmen and advisers;

registration of all private pension plans;

inspection of boilers and pressure vessels during and after installation, and registration of steam, refrigeration and compressor plants. Licencing of contractors and operators of such plants;

registration of real estate brokers and salesmen;

control of rents;

film censorship,

inspection and licensing of theatres and projection equipment, licencing or projectionists;

approval of motion picture advertising and classification;

registration of travel agents and wholesalers;

registration and inspection of renovators and manufacturers of upholstered furniture and stuffed articles. Testing of filling materials;

maintain standards for the baking of bread;

issue of marriage licences; and

enforcement of regulations limiting the foreign grape content of Ontario wines.

(OMCCR memorandum)

The ministry is engaged in much of the most visible SOCIAL regulation (i.e., regulation basically aimed at social, rather than economic objectives), such as film censorship.

The types of regulatory instruments employed by the ministry (as specified by the Acts it administers) include the setting of standards, mandating warranties, licensing, registration and certification, information provision, regulation of advertising, assignment of liability, and 'moral suasion.' Methods of enforcement include suspension or revocation of licence, registration or certification, and levying of fines.

Except for the Building Code (for an analysis of arguments that building codes tend to limit innovation see Oster and Quigley, 1977), the ministry's standard-setting activities are fairly compared, for example, to Agriculture and Food, and we find its use of licensing, certification, and registration less troublesome than in some other ministries which we shall comment on below. In addition, the ministry is apparently moving towards an increasing use of self-regulation (where industry takes over responsibility for education and qualification standards). Of course self-regulation can lead to restriction of competition;[3] thus, the legitimization of self-regulation by government action must proceed cautiously.

Since many of OMCCR's activities, such as the mandating of warranties, assignment of liability, provision of information, and regulation of advertising were discussed in detail in the previous chapter, we shall not consider them further here.

Correctional services
The Ontario ministry of correctional services administers a single act, the Ministry of Correctional Services Act, under which it administers correctional services in the province.

Culture and recreation
The primary responsibility of the Ontario ministry of culture and recreation (OMCR) is to support organizations and groups involved in the fields of citizenship, multiculturism, arts, cultural industries, heritage conservation, archaeology, and sports and fitness. Most of this activity falls under SOCIAL regulation (regulation aimed almost exclusively at social rather than economic objectives),

---

3 Recall in the model of Chapter 4 that it was shown that occupational licensing could be used to enhance the well-being of many existing members of a profession, generally at the expense of consumers. Self-regulation in the eyeglass market has often been used to restrict advertising and competition (see Benham, 1972).

but this regulation is largely regulated economically (through the use of subsidies). Some of the ministry's activities might be justified on economic grounds based on a public goods (art) or externalities (fitness) arguments. The minister has responsibility for licensing all archaelogical explorations, surveys, and field work in Ontario. Finally, the citizens inquiry branch of OMCR operates the provincial government's general information service (e.g., it prepared and published the *KWIK Index* (Ontario Ministry of Culture and Recreation, 1979)).

Education: colleges and universities
The Ontario ministry of education has authority in the areas of elementary and secondary education, including correspondence courses and schools for deaf and blind. Such activity may be primarily SOCIAL regulation, but public education may have important public good or externalities components which justify some sort of regulation on economic efficiency grounds.

In the context of this study we are much more interested in the activities of the Ontario ministry of colleges and universities (OMCU). This ministry has three main divisions: university affairs, college affairs and manpower training, and common services. The university affairs division is concerned with development, planning, and co-ordination of policies regarding the operation of fifteen provincially assisted universities, Ryerson Polytechnical Institute, and the Ontario College of Art. The common services division provides support services, including student assistance, information, personnel, administration, accounting, etc. The activities of these two divisions are similar to those of the Ministry of education in the areas of primary and secondary education.

The college affairs and manpower training division provides support to twenty-two community colleges, and operates industrial training and apprenticeship programs and occupational certification programs through the industrial training branch (ITB). The industrial training branch 'is responsible for the delivery of the ministry's industrial training (*manpower* training) programs. The branch is involved in training and retraining men and women for employment in industry through several programs: apprenticeship including on-the-job-training, full and part-time training of adults already in the labour force, short-term training-in-industry programs, and trade certification. The Branch administers the Ontario Career Action Program (OCAP), designed to assist unemployed youth (between 16 and 24 years) in finding gainful employment' (Ontario Ministry of Culture and Recreation, 1979, 298).

Industrial training is under the authority of OMCU because of the province's concern with secondary and post-secondary education. (The BNA gives the provinces 'exclusive' authority in the area of education.) Since the province operates the community colleges which provide the formal industrial training in the province, it is reasonable that OMCU should have jurisdiction over formal training programs. However, appended to this formal education program is an extensive apprenticeship and occupational certification system.

The main enabling legislation for this activity is the Apprenticeship and Tradesmen's Qualification Act (RSO 1970, c.24, as amended 1971–72). Under section 18 of the act the Lieutenant-Governor-in-Council (in effect, the cabinet) may make regulations:

(a) defining any trade;
(b) establishing an apprentice training program for any trade or group of trades;
(c) exempting any trade or class of persons in a trade from this Act and the regulations or from any provision of either of them;
(d) providing a system of proficiency certificates for any trade not designated as a certified trade under section 10;
(e) providing for approval by the Director of apprentice training programs established by employers;
(f) providing licences for trade schools teaching any trade to which this Act applies and respecting their issue and prescribing courses of study and methods of training in such trade schools and respecting their operation;
(g) respecting the periods of apprenticeship, qualifications and training of apprentices in any trade;
(h) approving or prescribing courses of training or study for apprentices, and fixing the credits to be allowed for such courses;
(i) prescribing, in respect of any trade, rates of wages for applicants for apprenticeship or apprentices or any class of applicants or apprentices;
(j) prescribing the maximum number of persons who may be apprenticed to an employer in a trade;
(k) respecting the ratio of apprentices to journeymen who may be employed by an employer in a trade;
(l) providing for Interprovincial Standards Examinations and standing thereunder and for the recognition of certificates or standings granted under Interprovincial Standards Examination in other provinces and the granting of certificates of qualification pursuant thereto;
(la) providing for the granting of provisional certificates of qualification and the grounds therefore and the conditions thereof;
(lb) respecting the renewal of certificates of qualification that have expired without being renewed and the conditions of renewal;
(lc) providing for the issue of certificates of qualification or licences to persons whose certificates or licences have been cancelled and the conditions upon which they may be issued;

(m) respecting the making, registration or transfer of contracts of apprenticeship;
(n) requiring and providing for the posting up in employers' premises of extracts from this Act or the regulations;
(o) defining any expression used in this Act for the purposes of this Act;
(p) providing for and prescribing fees;
(q) prescribing forms and providing for their use.

(RSO 1970, c.24, s.18; 1971, c.50, s.7 (5-7))

An extensive discussion of industrial training in Ontario can be found in the Report of the Task Force on Industrial Training (Ontario Ministry of Colleges and Universities, 1972). As explained in this report:

On March 31, 1972, there were 18,561 active apprentices registered with the ITB and these trainees were distributed among 156 different trades. These trades can be differentiated according to whether they are 'regulated' or 'non-regulated' under the Apprenticeship and Tradesmen's Qualification Act. A regulated trade is one that has been specifically identified under the Act by an Order-in-Council as an apprenticeable trade, and for which specific trade regulations are set down.

For regulated trades, there are standard training schedules and examinations. Minimum wage rates for apprentices and the maximum number of apprentices an employer may hire are stipulated. This maximum number is regulated by setting a ratio of apprentices to journeymen which an employer may not exceed.

There are also training curricula and examinations for each of the non-regulated trades, but no standards are specified. These trades are administered under the general regulations of the Act. There are neither standard trade definitions nor interim examinations; and no fixed requirements for final examinations. For most there is no provision for in-school instruction. Non-regulated trades are concentrated in the manufacturing sector, where it is difficult to specify common training requirements within a trade because of variation between industries, and even between plants within an industry, in their construction, maintenance and repair requirements.

The nature of the certification of accreditation process is different in regulated and non-regulated trades. The successful candidate in a non-regulated trade apprenticeship program receives a Certificate of Apprenticeship, but the certification is voluntary because it is not legally required before beginning work as a journeyman in the trade. In contrast, for many of the regulated trades the successful candidate receives both a Certificate of Apprenticeship and a Certificate of Qualification, and for several the latter is mandatory.

When apprentices were distributed by type of trade, it becomes evident that the regulated trades, especially those with compulsory certification, are most important. There are 16 such trades and they accounted for 13,985 of the 18,561 active apprentices on March 31, 1972. The 15 regulated trades that have voluntary certification and the two that have a Certificate of Apprenticeship accounted respectively for only 1,900 and 202 active apprentices. In the non-regulated trades there was a total of 2,474 active apprentices distributed among 123 different trades. (130)

The major trades by category (according to a number of apprentices) are given in Table 14 of the report, reproduced below as Table 17.

Since the discussion of the industrial training program in Ontario found in the Task Force Report is extensive, it is not necessary to consider the program in detail here. It should be noted that the Task Force Report made forty-eight recommendations designed to streamline and nationalize industrial training in Ontario, but most of its recommendations have not been implemented. An issue of concern to us which was not addressed by the Task Force Report is that the apprenticeship and occupational certification programs arising from the industrial training branch are generally a response to an expressed industry interest with little, if any concern given to the effect of such programs on non-industry groups. When the ITB wishes to determine the need for an apprenticeship program, it sets up a steering committee composed of interested parties *from the industry*. If the steering committee's report is favourable (which generally hinges on whether there is sufficient expected demand for formal training), a provincial advisory committee is established to develop a program.

Typically, an apprenticeship and certification program has arisen from two sources: the desire of the persons engaged in an occupation to have a certification program, or from the trained manpower requirements of employers. For example, the barbers were among the first certified occupations in the province, and in this case certification and the associated apprenticeship and formal training programs occurred because the barbers approached the province and requested such a program. Typically, if the members of an occupation or other industry interests approach the province in sufficient numbers, the province will form a steering committee to consider setting up a program.

The province's main concern in this area is whether there is sufficient demand for the relevant courses which would be offered in the community colleges. Although the province has a rightful interest in the demand for education in the province, this is a curious motivation for a system of occupational licensing. In its present form occupational licensing can and has been used by occupational groups to limit entry into their occupation. Entry generally requires both formal education *and* apprenticeship to a qualified tradesman, which naturally limits the number of entrants. Generally, when a training program is brought in, the existing members of the occupation are certified under a 'grandfather clause.'

Thus, occupational licensing in the province is even more problematic than the case where occupational licensing is explicitly motivated by an interest in

TABLE 17

Active apprentices in regulated trades by type of certification and trade, 31 March 1972

Type of certification and trade	Active apprentices	
	Number	Percentage
Compulsory certification		
Air-conditioning and refrigeration	298	1.85
Alignment and brakes	34	0.21
Auto body repairer	704	4.38
Barber	118	0.73
Electrician – construction and maintenance	3 149	19.57
Electrician – domestic and rural	46	0.29
Fuel and electrical systems	29	0.18
Hairdresser	1 034	6.43
Motorcycle mechanic	79	0.49
Motor vehicle mechanic	4 900	30.46
Plumber	1 653	10.28
Sheet metal worker	1 227	7.63
Steam-fitter	655	4.07
Transmission mechanic	23	0.14
Truck-trailer repairer	11	0.07
Watch repairer	25	0.16
Sub-total	13 985	86.93
Voluntary certification		
Automotive machinist	52	0.32
Automotive painter	42	0.26
Brick and stone mason	111	0.69
Cement mason	41	0.25
Chef	312	1.94
Dry-cleaner	10	0.06
Farm equipment mechanic	36	0.22
General carpenter	720	4.48
Glazier and metal mechanic	51	0.32
Heavy duty equipment mechanic	166	1.03
Lather	116	0.72
Painter and decorator	48	0.30
Plasterer	15	0.09
Radio and TV service technician	141	0.88
Service station attendant	39	0.24
Sub-total	1 900	11.81
Certificate of apprenticeship		
Baker	41	0.25
Ironworker	161	1.00
Sub-total	202	1.26
Total	16 087	100.00

SOURCE: (1972, 131, Table 14)

raising the quality of services provided (as discussed in Chapter 4). In Ontario there is at least some latitude for the current members of the occupation to set the standards for licensing to their benefit. There ae probably occupations for which a combination of formal training, apprenticeship, and certification is an appropriate policy, but the costs and benefits of such a policy to the public at large should be given serious weight in the decision for implementing such a policy.

Energy

The Ontario ministry of energy is involved in most areas of regulation directly affecting energy. The Ontario Energy Board, Ontario Energy Corporation and Ontario Hydro are agencies of the ministry.

The Ontario Energy Board is responsible for the regulation of gas utilities and, among other things, the establishment of environmental guidelines for pipeline projects within the province. Ontario Hydro has extensive regulatory authority over safety standards for the provision, transmission, and use of electrical power. Although electricians must be licensed, much of their work must still be inspected by Ontario Hydro inspectors, which may be excessive duplication of regulation.[4] A home-owner who does his own electrical work is required to have it inspected, and lack of inspection may invalidate fire insurance.

Environment

The ministry of the environment has four main objectives: control of contaminant emissions, establishment of environmental safeguards, management of water waste, and development and maintenance of measures intended to restore and enhance Ontario's natural environment.

The regulatory activities of the ministry of energy include:

setting of air quality (emission) standards including spot-checking of new cars for emissions;

administering the Environmental Protection Act by granting approval for waste disposal sites and issuing all permits pursuant to the EPA (which can apply to any activities affecting environmental quality);

issuing of licences to exterminators and vendors of pesticides; and

classification of pesticides;

---

4 Naturally, cost-benefit calculations would have to be done in order to be conclusive.

regulating and setting standards for pollution control for –
  septic tanks
  pleasure craft
  marinas
  ice huts
  municipal sewage treatment plants;

promotion and administration of safety certification procedures;

issuing of licences to builders of wells.

(Ministry of energy memorandum)

As we indicated in our introductory chapter, we shall not provide a detailed examination of environmental regulations in the province. The interested reader is referred to Dewees, Everson, and Sims (1975).

Government services
The Ontario ministry of government services is not a regulatory ministry. However, its activities include the purchase and leasing of property, design and construction of buildings, and integration of common government purchasing requirements. Discretionary government expenditure is, of course, a viable method of government intervention, but we have no evidence that the ministry's expenditure activities are used for such purposes.

Health
The Ontario ministry of health (OMH) is of course the main regulatory ministry in the health area. It administers OHIP, and regulates hospitals, mental hospitals, sanitaria, nursing homes, medical laboratories, summer camps, public swimming pools, etc. In addition, the ministry is responsible for the licensing and inspection of ambulances and the graduates of the ambulance and emergency care programs and the community colleges, regulations concerning medical uses of X-rays, the approval of milk containers, and the certification of pasteurization plants.

The program advisory branch of OMH has some responsibility in the area of setting standards for the safety of food (e.g., milk) in production, processing, distribution, and service. However, the ministry itself does not take a direct hand in the enforcement of the standards.

The drugs and therapeutics branch has established standards of practice for the pharmaceuticals industry, but only products used in the PARCOST (pharmaceuticals at reduced cost, which promotes generic substitution) program or in nursing homes, homes for the aged, hospitals, and government institutions are subject to inspection and quality control evaluation by this branch.

A detailed examination of public health regulation is not feasible in the present study, but we shall comment on some of the licensing and certification programs administered by OMH. Among its responsibilities the ministry regulates denturists and opthalmic dispensers. Although these two services certainly have health care components, we are persuaded that the arguments developed in Chapter 4 suggest that these two activities deserve closer scrutiny. The control of denturists in the province is clearly to the advantage of dentists and quite possibly is detrimental to the public. This issue has been given considerable attention in the media in recent years.

Regulation of opthalmic dispensers has been used in many North American jurisdictions to promote anti-competitive behaviour by opthalmic dispensers, such as restrictions on advertising (see Benham, 1972). We have not formally studied the opthalmic dispensing industry in Ontario, but our casual empirical observations suggest that average prices of glasses are higher here than in some other jurisdictions in North America where the industry is less regulated and competition is actively encouraged.

Housing
The Ontario Ministry of Housing (OMH) has major responsibilities for the regulation of development under the Planning Act. The ministry is responsible for approval of official plans and plans of subdivision, submits comments to the Ontario Municipal Board (OMB) on zoning by-laws, monitors and has the power to appeal OMB decisions of local committees of adjustment and land divisoin committees, and has the power to grant severances and impose zoning orders in areas of the province which are not organized into municipalities, principally northern Ontario.

The regulation of housing and development in the province is extensive and extremely complex. Since this regulation is fully discussed in Frankena and Scheffman (1980), we shall not develop it here. It is worth noting that Markusen and Scheffman (1977), Frankena and Scheffman (1980), Derkowski (1972, 1975), and others have argued that the current regulatory system is far more complex than is necessary for efficient regulation and, in fact, probably introduces significant inefficiencies into the system.[5]

It is interesting to note that in the past the province has attempted to use public ownership (in its 'new towns' program) as a regulatory instrument (see Frankena and Scheffman, 1980).

5 The Ontario Planning Act Review Committee Report (1977) recommended significant simplifications of provincial regulations in this area. See Frankena and Scheffman (1980).

Industry and tourism

The 'industry' part of the Ontario ministry of industry and tourism (OMIT) is involved with the promotion of domestic and foreign sales of Ontario production and in provincial government policy planning for industry and trade in the province. Industrial and commercial development policies are a major concern of the ministry, and the development corporations (Ontario Development Corporation, Eastern Ontario Development Corporation, Northern Ontario Development Corporation, Ontario Place Corporation) fall under the ministry's umbrella. An examination of regional or provincial development policies, although they are forms of social regulation, is outside the terms of reference of this study.

The tourism section of OMIT is concerned with the promotion of tourism in Ontario and licenses tourist accommodations which are not licensed by the LLBO.

Intergovernmental affairs

The Ontario ministry of intergovernmental affairs (OMIA) (formerly combined with treasury and economics) is concerned mainly with relations between foreign, federal, and municipal governments and the provincial government. As discussed in the preceding chapter, under the BNA Act municipal governments derive powers and responsibilities only through delegation by the provincial government. Co-ordination of some forms of action by different levels of government is clearly a major concern of the ministry. Most of OMIA's activities are concerned with municipal and regional governments. Some of these activities are discussed in Frankena and Scheffman (1980).

In addition, the ministry has responsibility for administering such diverse legislation as the Fire Extinguishment Act, the Public Parks Act, Public Utilities Act, the Snow Roads and Fences Act, and the Vacant Land Cultivation Act.

Labour

The regulatory activities of the Ontario ministry of labour fall into four main 'program areas': (a) labour relations, (b) employment standards, (c) occupational health and safety, and (4) human rights.

(a) Labour relations

The ministry, through the Ontario Labour Relations Board (OLRB) is responsible for the administration, and enforcement of the Ontario Labour Relations Act. The OLRB also has powers under several subsidiary industrial dispute acts. Specific regulatory actions of the OLRB include: (1) certification of trade unions as bargaining agents for employees; (2) investigation and hearing of complaints and issuing remedial orders under the Act; (3) accreditations of employers' organizations and employer bargaining agencies in the construction industry; and, (4) arbitration of disputes arising out of these or any other labour relations matters.

Under different sections of the Labour Relations Act, the ministry has wide discretion in its approaches to 'preventative' mediation. In each case at hand the ministry is empowered to choose the most effective of several options in resolving disputes. There is also discretion in the ministry's determination of appropriate bargaining units and other matters of certification.

The OCRB has extensive enforcement powers. These include the power to give orders (including cease and desist orders and orders to rectify). The board may also require compensation, assess damages, and perhaps (untested) may be able to levy fines in certain 'contempt-of-the-board' situations.

(b) Employment standards

The employment standards branch has responsibility for several acts concerning conditions of employment; the specific responsibilities are: (1) provision and enforcement of minimum wages and minimum standards for working conditions; (2) issuance of overtime permits and handicap work permits; (3) approves schedules of work jointly approved by employers and employees under the Industrial Standards Act; (4) assures that all employees working on government contracts are receiving 'fair' wages and protects contractors from 'unfair' competition via labour costs (i.e., if first part is adequately enforced, second problem is avoided); and (5) licensing and monitoring of activities of private employment agencies.

The employment standards branch has the authority to assess compensation owing and to levy fines. A referee appointed under The Employment Standards Act may issue further cease and desist orders.

(c) Occupational health and safety

The occupational health and safety division develops and enforces health and safety standards to protect employees on the job. Specific regulatory activities include: (1) inspection of workplaces; (2) issuing health certificates to workers in certain occupations; and (3) investigating accidents and refusals to work on sites alleged to be unsafe. The enforcement powers in this area are limited to issuing orders and relying upon summary convictions.

Revised occupational, industrial, and mining regulations under the Occupational Health and Safety Act, 1978 were recently filed.

(d) *Human rights*

The Ontario Human Rights Commission administers the Ontario Human Rights Code. It investigates cases of complaints. Most cases are resolved by conciliation, but when necessary, the ministry will appoint a board of inquiry to conduct quasi-judicial hearings. A board of inquiry constituted under the Ontario Human Rights Code may issue orders inclusive of requiring compensation.

Finally, the Workmen's Compensation Board is an independent organization operating an insurance plan for injured workers.

Much of OML's activities fall under a general definition of social regulation, and of particular interest, although outside the terms-of-reference of our study, is occupational health and safety regulation. Several branches of the ministry are concerned with this area:

(i) [Advisory Council on Occupational Health and Occupational Safety]: advises the Minister of Labour on matters involving *occupational health* and occupational safety. Provides liaison between the Ministry and special interest groups wishing to draw government attention to particular concerns in this field.

(ii) [Construction Health and Safety Branch]: is concerned with protecting the *occupational health* and safety of employees in the construction industry, including work on buildings, streets, sewers, water mains, underground work, and work under compressed air. The Branch periodically inspects construction sites, investigates fatalities and serious accidents and provides consultative services to all involved in the construction industry, e.g., labour, management, contractors, designers.

(iii) [Industrial Health and Safety Branch]: is concerned with protecting the *occupational health* and safety of employees in industry including the logging industry. (For the construction and mining industries, see Labour Construction Health and Safety Branch and Labour Mining Health and Safety Branch.) This branch encourages employers and employees to assume primary responsibility for *occupational health* and safety programs by establishing Internal Responsibility Systems and consulting with them so problems are recognized and ongoing safety programs are established. Periodically inspects industrial establishments and logging sites; investigates fatalities and serious accidents. Reviews plans for new buildings and alterations to existing ones to check *occupational health* and safety hazards.

(iv) [Mining Health and Safety Branch]: is responsible for the administration of the Mining Act and the succeeding legislation for mines, open pits, industrial quarries, sand, clay, shale, gravel pits and metallurgical operations. Periodically inspects these establishments; conducts air samples to ensure a safe working environment. Investigates fatalities and serious accidents. Consults with labour and management to increase their involvement in identifying and solving *occupational health* and safety hazards. Reviews and provides advice on pre-development plans of mining and metallurgical operations to check hazards before construction. Tests hoist cables and trains mine rescue personnel.

(v) [Occupational Health Branch]: operates a consulting service in *occupational health* to ministries and to industry. Occupational Health Medical Service provides consultation on medical and nursing services to those who provide in-plant health care facilities and a healthful environment for employees. Occupational Health Engineering Services provides consultation to operating branches and to industry; visits plants and sites to identify and assess health hazards from exposure to chemical, physical and biological agents and to recommend control measures. Industrial Chest Disease Services deals with identification and prevention of respiratory diseases from occupational exposure to hazardous agents. Works closely with Workmen's Compensation Board and Chest Clinic Services (Health) which conducts chest X-rays of miners. Occupational Health Laboratory Service performs chemical analyses of biological specimens, air samples, industrial materials.

(vi) [Special Studies and Services Branch]: Health Studies Services conducts *occupational health* studies and provides consultative services on the effects of occupational and environmental exposure to hazardous agents or materials on human health. Safety Studies Service conducts studies in occupational safety and maintains contact with organizations involved in accident prevention. Radiation Protection Services directs a program to protect employees and the public from harmful effects of radiation including X-Rays, radioactive materials, microwaves, lasers. Radiation Protection Laboratory analyzes radioactive materials. Develops monitoring techniques and equipment for identification of radioactive sources. The Branch also deals with contingencies related to nuclear power generating stations and heavy water plants.

(vii) [Standards and Programs Branch]: coordinates: gathering of information about and analysis of specific occupational health and safety hazards; providing detailed action plans and programs to control hazards in industry, e.g. construction industry, mining, logging industry. Assists operating branches in developing operation procedures; coordinates short and long range objectives, evaluation mechanisms; maintains occupational health statistics, e.g. injuries, illnesses. Coordinates development and distribution of standards information and guidelines. Provides information on occupational health and safety and liaises with related public and private sector advisory services. Advisory Service Section provides policy and administrative support for Provincial Lottery Fund Awards Committees on grants for occupational health research.

(Ontario Ministry of Culture and Recreation, 1979, 413–14)

As can be seen from the above descriptions, the province is not currently engaged in an extensive program of standard-setting in the area of occupational safety and health, although standards are set in some cases. Since the focus of this study is consumer goods and services, we shall not devote further effort here to analysing occupational health and safety regulation in the province. There has been a considerable volume of economics literature that evaluates the activities of the occupational safety and health administration in the United States, and this literature sheds considerable light on such standard-setting (see Owens and Schultze, 1976, Miller and Yandle, 1979, and Smith, 1976).

Natural resources
The regulatory activities of the Ontario ministry of natural resources include:

regulation and licencing of private and commercial fishing and hunting;

assessment and collection of Mining Tax;

administration of the Pits and Quarries Control Act;

issue of licences for the refining of precious metals;

issue of licences to firms extracting oil or natural gas;

arranging and licencing of timber sales; and

issue of licences to fur buyers and tanners.

(Ministry of Natural Resources memorandum)

Northern affairs
The main responsibilities of the Ontario ministry of northern affairs are the provision of services and the planning and administration of development programs in the northern part of the province. It should be noted that activities of some other ministries are handled by northern affairs in the north. It also has a role in liaison with the other ministries and putting forth the 'special needs of Northern Ontario.'

Revenue
The Ontario ministry of revenue administers the myriad of provincial taxes (income, corporations, sales, gasoline, tobacco, etc.), and its assessment division develops the assessments used for provincial and municipal property taxes. Taxation, of course, can be a form of social regulation (see Chapter 2), but the ministry of revenue is basically an administrative rather than a regulatory agency.

Solicitor general
The responsibilities of the Ontario ministry of the solicitor general include: (1) public safety: scientific investigations, co-ordination of fire safety investigations,

co-ordination of fire safety services and coroner system; (2) Ontario Police Commission; (3) Ontario Provincial Police; and (4) the Toronto Area Transit Operating Authority.

Transportation and communication
The Ontario ministry of transport and communications (OMTC) is primarily concerned with the regulation of traffic and transportation in Ontario as well as control of communications.

The specific regulatory activities of OMTC include:

regulation and investigation of radio-television services;

examination and issue of licences to drivers;

licencing and safety inspection of vehicles;

enforcing weight and safety regulation on all vehicles;

issuing permits for advertising signs along rights of way; and

regulation and issue of licences to providers of telephone services (Bell Canada comes under *federal* jurisdiction).

(OMTC memorandum)

In addition, the Ontario Highway Transport Board is an agency of OMTC.

The provincial authority to regulate radio and television and advertising on these media was discussed in the previous chapter. The regulation of communications in Canada is studied in Hartle (1978). The Ontario Highway Transport Board regulates trucking and other common carriers in the province. For a study of trucking regulation in the province see Bonsor (1978).

The required safety inspection of vehicles is an interesting example of provincial standard-setting. In this program in order to be licensed after a change of ownership a vehicle must pass a safety inspection (safety standards are specified in the Highway Traffic Act) conducted at a licensed motor vehicle inspection station. Although formally the inspection must take place only for a change of ownership, in principle all vehicles must satisfy the safety standards at all times. (This requirement is casually enforced by police through infrequent spot checks.)

The obvious benefits of such a program are the presumed reduction of unsafe vehicles on the highways. The 'amount of safety' generated by the market allocation may be inefficient owing to the externalities involved with accidents (which are partially remedied by the legal liability system) and the reduced incentives for safety which may arise from subsidized hospitalization insurance.

However, notice that the issue of interest to the province is not unsafe vehicles, per se, but instead is the reduction of the number and severity of accidents. A very safety-conscious driver may be able to drive safely in a vehicle that can't pass the safety inspection. The province is setting a design rather than a performance standard. Of course, in this instance setting an effective performance standard would be extremely difficult, if not impossible. As pointed out several times in this study (particularly in Chapter 4), design standards may have unfortunate side-effects. For example, Peltzman (1975) argues that the U.S. highway safety legislation which required safer vehicles resulted in drivers operating their vehicles less safely. We doubt that there need be a serious concern of this type for the safety inspection program in the province, but such issues should always be considered when evaluating design standards.

The direct costs of the program are the resulting higher cost of vehicles and the costs of administering the program. In addition, there may be some other side-effects, resulting from the possibility that some consumers may believe that passing the safety inspection indicates that the vehicle is mechanically sound. If this is important, it could be dealt with adequately by a suitable information provision policy.

The cost of an inspection (approximately $25) is set by the market, and in most cases will not result in a significant increment in the price of a vehicle. Furthermore, since repair work can be done by anyone, a seller or prospective purchaser can have the inspection made and conditions for passing the inspection specified, and can arrange for his own repairs. Thus, although provincial standards are set, the market is given maximum latitude in meeting the standards.

From time to time mandatory regular inspections of all vehicles is proposed as a provincial policy (such policies are already used in many North American jurisdictions). Such a policy would incur much higher costs, but it may be justified by associated higher benefits. Naturally, we would recommend that a comprehensive examination of the costs and benefits of such a policy be conducted prior to the implementation of any new program.

Treasury and economics

The Ontario ministry of treasury and economics is the treasurer of the provincial government. In addition, it has policy-planning responsibilities for fiscal, economic, and regional policies.

SUMMARY OF ECONOMIC ISSUES

Although brief, the preceding summary of the social regulatory activities of the provincial government in Ontario indicates the very extensive range of such regulation in the province. As we indicated in our introduction to this chapter, the current government has enacted a limited regulatory review process, the Customer Service and Deregulation Program, under which ministerial reviews of regulatory activity has proceeded. The main focus of this review has been on identification of opportunities to streamline current regulations by 'cutting red tape,' removing redundant regulation, and improving the co-ordination of ministerial responsibilities, particularly where there is duplication of regulation. We think that this has been a useful, albeit limited program.

The limitations of time and space in this study have precluded our developing an in-depth analysis of specific regulations in Ontario. Instead, our purpose was to develop a general conceptual framework for such an analysis. We hope that the Ontario government will initiate thorough studies of some of the basic potential problem areas which we have identified here. In addition, it would be desirable for the Ontario Economic Council to commission studies of specific regulations or the effects of regulation in particular industries. There is already a burgeoning literature on these topics in the United States, which in many cases could be replicated fairly easily for Canada.

Most of our major basic concerns with regulation in markets for consumer goods and services in the province were raised in Chapter 5 and will be summarized in Chapter 7. Of the major areas of regulation falling within the terms of reference of this study we are most concerned with the extensive occupational licensing and certification program. We argued above that in its current form this program is of dubious merit. However, there is no indication that the current deregulation program is going to take a serious look at occupational licensing and certification. We recommend that such a study be conducted.

Finally, we recommend that the requirement that ministries provide economic impact statements (i.e., calculation of costs and benefits) for new proposals be implemented in a serious manner. This might best be done by creating a provincial agency which would direct and oversee the production of such impact statements. This type of analysis is already being conducted in the federal government at the Treasury Board.[6] It would be a fairly simple matter for the provincial government to set up an agency that would conduct such analyses. However, effective operation would require that all new proposals with evident significant impact provide an economic impact statement (as has been done, to some extent, in the federal government). We shall return to this suggestion in our concluding chapter.

---

6 Under the federal government's Socio-Economic Impact Analysis Program each proposal
  for a new or amended social regulation with an estimated impact of at least $10 million must
  be subjected to a formal cost-benefit analysis.

7
Summary and policy implications

INTRODUCTION

The purpose of this chapter is to provide a brief summary of the preceding chapters, focusing on the policy implications of the study. Naturally, a comprehensive summary will not be presented. We hope that those readers who choose to begin by reading this chapter will be persuaded to delve into the preceding chapters for more complete discussions of the issues considered here.

SOCIAL REGULATION AND THE METHODOLOGY OF ECONOMICS

Social regulation has been defined for the purposes of this study as regulation concerned with the quality or safety of goods and services or their method of production. Although our study has focused on such regulation in markets for consumer goods and services, we have developed several general economic conclusions which are valid for all areas of social regulation. Although prices and quantities are the central topics of traditional micro-economic analysis, quality and safety are also basic micro-economic variables; that is, they are variables that unimpeded markets will determine by the interactions of the forces of supply and demand. The economics of quality and safety is not as well developed as the age-old study of price and quantity, but the methodology of economics is quite capable of addressing the issue of the economic efficiency and equity of the allocation of quality and safety. The efficiency of the market's allocation of resources hinges on the prevalence of potential sources of market failure and the ability of the market and non-market institutions to deal with them. As with prices and quantities, in the absence of such imperfections markets will allocate quality and safety efficiently.

Rational policy-making

Clearly, the 'real world' is littered with potential sources of market failure. Externalities and uncertainty, two particular sources, are common elements in most markets where quality or safety are important, and therefore most social regulatory activities can be casually defended by pointing a finger at a particular potential source of market failure. However, rational economic policy-making requires more than such finger-pointing. The private economy is ingenious at devising institutions which enhance efficiency in the face of potential sources of market failure. One of the most important institutions in this context is the ability of economic agents to make contracts (in a general sense) in a myriad of forms, including warranties, insurance, and financial instruments, and the implicit contracts defined by the law, such as the assignment of personal liability. Thus, the presence of a potential source of market failure is not, in itself, evidence of an actual market failure, and national economic policy-makers must recognize the role of such non-market institutions.

Rational economic policy-making must be based on an assessment of the costs and benefits of proposed policies. We realize that cost-benefit analysis is not a panacea. Performing such an analysis for the evaluation of a social regulatory action is a complicated task and the results can generally not be considered to be precise. It has been said, with some justification, that if all the economists were laid end to end, they would point in different directions. Similarly, it is possible for cost-benefit analyses of the same policy to differ. This can occur because of faulty methodology or because of different assumptions. Incorrect methodology is easy to deal with; so the major difficulty in using cost-benefit analysis lies in identifying and evaluating the assumptions used in the analysis. For a cost-benefit analysis to be useful to the policy-maker it should identify the assumptions made and the sensitivity of the results to the assumptions. The policy-maker must then make a decision about the validity of the assumptions. This task is not easy, of course, but cost-benefit analysis is not designed to make policy-making easy; rather, its purpose is to put policy-making on a rational footing. A major portion of the difficulties in applying cost-benefit analysis to social regulation is that the history of such applications is very short. As economists and policy-makers become more familiar with the general methodology, the usefulness and precision of cost-benefit analyses will improve.

We are not so naïve as to believe that economic benefits and costs are or should be the only determinant of policy decisions. However, we believe strongly that policy-makers should be forced to recognize (and publicize) the economic benefits and costs of their actions. Any policy decision involves trade-offs, and it is not sensible to ignore them. We consider the federal government's Socio-Economic Impact Analysis Program (under which each proposal for a new or amended social regulation with an estimated impact of $10 million or more must be subjected to a formal cost-benefit analysis) to be a useful beginning. However, time is of the essence in government decision-making, and under the pressure of time and politics cost-benefit analysis can be 'cooked' to justify almost any action. Therefore, for a policy such as the Socio-Economic Impact Analysis program to work effectively it is important to provide incentives for the 'proper' use of the tools of cost-benefit analysis. Opening the policy decison-making process to submissions of calculations of benefits and costs by interested parties would also be useful. This would not be a radical departure from the method by which policy-making has proceeded in the past. The new feature is to make the participants and interested parties in the policy-making process use the same logical methodology of cost-benefit analysis.

The federal and provincial governments have implemented programs requiring economic impact analyses of proposed regulatory activity,[1] and we would like to see these programs expanded to include analyses of existing regulations. This is clearly a formidable but very useful task. Of course, it could be implemented only by an ongoing, long-term program. One of the problems arising from social regulation is what James W. McKie (1970) has called the 'tar-baby' effect. This situation occurs when it is discovered that a regulatory action does not have the desired result or perhaps has an unexpected undesirable effect, and the response is to promulgate a new regulatory action in order to make the original action 'come out right.' The result can be a patchwork of regulations with large aggregate compliance and efficiency costs. The regulation of transportation and public utilities in many North American jurisdictions is the direct product of such a 'tar-baby' process. Thus, it is desirable to analyse existing social regulatory activity in that such an analysis may identify the best new policy (which may often be some type of deregulation).

DISTORTIONARY GOVERNMENT POLICIES

One of the major potential sources of market failure is that government policies, themselves, often create distortions which may lead to inefficiencies. One of the most obvious distortionary government policies is the system of subsidized hospitalization in Ontario (OHIP). In this system users of medical care do not directly bear the full marginal costs of treatment. The effects of such a system

---

1 Under the Customer Service and Deregulation Program in Ontario ministries were instructed to ensure that all future cabinet submissions include, as a mandatory requirement, an economic impact statement (Ontario Ministry of Consumer and Commercial Relations, 1978).

would be expected to include an inefficient tempering of the incentives for individuals to use preventative health maintenance and to avoid health and safety risks. We are not arguing here that on these grounds OHIP should be abolished. Rather, the effects of such government policies should be recognized, both in the design of policies such as OHIP, and in the possible need for counteractive policies (e.g., perhaps safety standards for automobiles).

REGULATORY INSTRUMENTS

There is a vast array of potential social regulatory instruments. The basic types are tax-subsidy schemes; setting standards; government owned or managed production, contract, and tort law; and information remedies. Various combinations of all of these instruments are currently used in social regulation.

The target of the regulatory instrument
In most cases social regulation arises from a concern with the *performance* of goods, services, or individuals, rather than a direct concern with product or service *design* or with the particular behaviour of individuals, except in so far as they have certain effects. For example, society's concern about children's clothing or toys is presumably a concern with the safety of these products, not with their design per se. When feasible, regulatory instruments should be directed at the perceived problem rather than attempting to reach certain goals by indirect regulation. If air pollution is the perceived problem, efficient regulation (where feasible) should regulate the amount of air pollution (properly defined and measured), not its method of production.

There are two reasons why regulation should be directed at the perceived problem, rather than at an indirect target. First, the competitive pressures of the private economy encourage the minimization of costs, so that the market will generally find the best method of achieving a particular goal. Secondly, indirect regulation often has unanticipated indirect effects. The analysis developed in Chapter 4, for example, showed that attempting to control the quality of outputs by setting standards for the quality of inputs could produce a reaction opposite from the one desired. The recent history of environmental and occupational safety regulation is replete with examples of costly, ineffective, and sometimes counter-productive indirect regulation (see Smith, 1976).

The choice of regulatory instrument
As economists we have a basic preference for regulatory instruments which allow the market maximum latitude in choosing the method by which a policy goal is achieved, because competitive pressures generally ensure that costs are

recognized when the market makes choices. Thus, when feasible, tax-subsidy schemes are preferable to other forms of direct regulation. One area in which this conclusion is becoming more widely appreciated is environmental policy, particularly control of industrial effluents and emissions, where previous attempts to regulate by setting standards have often been ineffective and costly (see Friedlander, 1978 and Kneese and Schultz, 1975).

One of the problems with other forms of direct regulation which do not make maximum use of market incentives (e.g., the setting of standards) is that the market often has strong incentives to circumvent or subvert the regulations. Obvious examples are the creation of black or grey markets when commodities are rationed, and the incentives for drivers to remove the pollution control devices on their cars. However, the methods by which regulations are circumvented or subverted are often more subtle. A class of more subtle examples was provided by the analysis developed in Chapter 3. The argument there was that competitive markets produce an allocation which purchasers would perceive as best, given their perceptions and the technological and financial constraints on suppliers. Despite purchasers' perceptions, such an allocation may not be best or most efficient from society's point of view (particularly if those perceptions are 'incorrect'). In such a situation it may be difficult to enact a policy that will lead to the best (from society's point of view) allocation, since any deviation from the present allocation will be perceived (although incorrectly) as not being as good. Thus, in the model of Chapter 3 if consumers overestimate product reliability, the market will not provide full warranty coverage, which may not be efficient. But a policy which sets standards for reliability or requires full warranty protection will result in a combination of price, reliability, and warranty coverage which is perceived by consumers to be worse than the original situation. In such a situation both consumers and producers have incentives to get around the mandated warranty. For example, one possible result of mandatory warranties is that producers offer less reliable service under the warranty.

Thus, there are strong reasons to prefer modes of regulation which make maximum usage of market incentives. For this reason tax-subsidy schemes are a preferred mode of *direct* regulation (when feasible). Information remedies (dissemination of information) are an *indirect* remedy which makes maximum use of market incentives, particularly since the source of the problem (if one exists) in markets for consumer goods and services often is that purchasers have inadequate or incorrect information. We would like to see greater use of information remedies as social regulatory instruments, at least as initial regulatory actions. For example, we believe it would have been preferable for the federal government to require warning labels on products containing saccharin and an advertising campaign on the possible dangers of the substance rather than to ban saccharin.

Although regulatory instruments that make maximum use of market incentives are preferable, such instruments are not always feasible. For example, it may not be possible to achieve the desired level of highway safety with only tax-subsidy schemes and information remedies (although both are used in this area). Other obvious examples where standard-setting may be required include regulation of the safety of drugs and the use of toxic materials. Thus, other forms of regulation, particularly the setting of standards, may sometimes be necessary. In standard-setting it is particularly important that (if feasible) the standards be set on performance rather than design for the reasons discussed above. However, performance is not always easily measured or monitored, and the performance criterion must be carefully specified. For example, it has become common in North America to set standards for the emissions of power plants, typically measured by the amount of precipitate falling in adjacent areas. One response to these regulations has been to build taller smoke stacks, which has often resulted in an undesirable spread of emissions, the recently publicized 'acid rain' phenomenon being one example.

SOCIAL REGULATION IN THE CONTEXT OF THE CANADIAN LEGAL SYSTEM

Social regulation in markets for consumer goods and services, which are often national markets in Canada, will typically require national regulation for efficiency and effectiveness.[2] As one illustration, if it is desirable to require food and some other products to have labels which list their ingredients (a policy implemented in the United States, and one which we find attractive), such a policy would generally be best implemented by a *national* labelling regulation. However, the division of powers between the federal and provincial levels provided by the BNA Act often makes social regulation on a national basis difficult, if not impossible. The federal powers, many of which are derived from the criminal law power, generally limit federal authority to issues involving health and safety. It is not clear, for example, that a comprehensive national labelling law would be upheld on these grounds. Such regulation could be implemented by provincial co-operative action, but the current climate of regional antagonisms could make this sort of action increasingly difficult.[3] Thus, the federal powers derived from the BNA Act place an effective and sometimes undesirable limit on the ability to effect national regulation.

2 Some industries, for example, construction, being basically local, may require only provincial or local regulation.
3 Naturally, this is conjecture on our part.

On the other hand, the BNA Act gives very considerable powers to the provinces in the area of social regulation. This situation is desirable in that many forms of social regulation (e.g., land use controls) are best implemented on a local or provincial level, and such powers often allow the provinces to act singly, co-operatively, or in co-operation with the federal government in order to effect useful national regulations which cannot be enacted by the federal government acting independently. However, the significant powers vested in the provinces also allow them to use social regulation for the purposes of promoting regional objectives, which can have important and undesirable effects on national markets. Any student of Canadian history is well aware of the methods by which the provincial governments have used regulation in order to promote regional objectives.

In this study we focused on two areas of social regulation in which the division of powers between the two levels of government can be a significant hindrance to effective policy. The first area is certain forms of information remedies, one example being the difficulty in enacting national labelling regulations discussed above. Other issues of concern are that it may sometimes be desirable to require manufacturers to provide information on product reliability, or to require that instances of false or misleading advertising be remedied by 'corrective' advertising (as was done in the United States in the case of Listerine and STP). Although the provinces apparently have authority to enact such regulations, the federal powers in this area are limited. Thus, effecting national regulation is difficult if not impossible.

The other area of social regulation discussed extensively in this study is the assignment of liability in cases of product failure, particularly in instances where health and safety hazards are important. Because the federal government's social regulatory activities in the area of health and safety derive from its criminal law power, its authority to specify civil remedies (e.g., producer liability) is questionable (see Chapter 5). We argued in Chapter 3 that the imposition of producer liability might be justified on efficiency grounds for products for which failure could entail health or safety hazards. The federal government can set standards for such products, and violation of the standard can be used as the basis of a civil suit; but setting standards is often not a desirable policy.

The provinces have authority (by enacting new legislation) to impose producer liability; currently, however, redress typically requires a civil action based on negligence, and negligence is difficult to prove. Furthermore, negligence may often not be the relevant issue. New legislation could also specify damages to be awarded for certain types of wrongs and can provide for multiple damages. Class action rules could be altered to encourage class action litigation in cases where the harm to individuals was so small that it was not worthwhile to sue individually. Thus, there is considerable latitude for substituting private enforcement through civil litigation for public enforcement through direct regulation.[4] The desirability of such legislation should be thoroughly studied. Finally, to be effective, in many cases such legislation would have to be enacted on a national basis, which would require extensive provincial and provincial-federal co-operation.

SOCIAL REGULATION IN ONTARIO

In Chapter 6 we summarized the social regulatory activities of the provincial government in Ontario. Some of the major areas of such regulation (environmental, health, and land use) are outside the terms of reference of this study. Of the existing policies the province's extensive program of occupational licensing and certification was the greatest source of concern to us. In Chapter 4 we developed an analysis which indicated that certification programs may be counter-productive, that is, raising the standards for entrance to an occupation may not raise the level of the quality services provided.

However, a greater source of our concern with occupational licensing and certification in Ontario is that such programs arise at the instigation of the industry or occupation concerned, with little if any regard for their effect on the well-being of other affected parties, such as the consumers of the services provided by the occupation. The only apparent issue of interest to the province in such programs is whether they generate sufficient demand for post-secondary education. The incentives for the current members of an occupation to limit entry are obvious and undesirable. We strongly recommend that the province take a broader perspective on occupational licensing and certification, considering in particular the effect of such programs on the purchasers of the services of these occupations.

We conclude this chapter with three recommendations for new policy actions for the province. First, besides our earlier comments on the desirability of rational economic policy-making, we recommend that social regulation by the province be catalogued and studied in its entirety, with an eye towards the implementation of effective new policy, including deregulation. In addition, the feasibility of the use of 'sunset' legislation should be analysed. Secondly, we advocate a closer look at the use of information remedies as a social regulatory instrument. Possible actions are labelling regulations, disclosure of product reliability, and the use of 'corrective' advertising. Finally, our analysis has suggested that the imposition of producer liability might be an efficient policy, at

4 See Dewees et al. (1979).

least for products for which failure entails health or safety hazards. Currently, civil redress for such product failures rests on an action brought in tort, based on negligence. This may be an undesirable limitation of producer liability, at least for cases in which product failure involves health or safety hazards.

APPENDIX
Ministerial responsibility for acts
December 1978*

CHAIRMAN OF THE MANAGEMENT BOARD
OF CABINET

Crown Employees Collective Bargaining
Act, 1972
Management Board of Cabinet Act,
1971
Public Service Act
Successor Rights (Crown Transfers Act),
1977
Superannuation Adjustment Benefits
Act, 1975

MINISTRY OF AGRICULTURE AND FOOD

Abandoned Orchards Act
Agricultural Associations Act
Agricultural Committees Act
Agricultural Rehabilitation and Devel-
opment Act (Ontario)
Agricultural Representatives Act
Agricultural Research Institute of Onta-
rio Act
Agricultural Societies Act

Agricultural Tile Drainage Installation
Act, 1972
Animals for Research Act
Artificial Insemination of Life Stock Act
Beef Cattle Marketing Act
Bees Act
Brucellosis Act
Commodity Board Members Act, 1976
Commodity Boards and Marketing
Agencies Act, 1978
Co-operative Loans Act
Crop Insurance Act (Ontario)
Dead Animal Disposal Act
Dog Licensing and Live Stock and Poul-
try Protection Act
Drainage Act, 1975
Edible Oil Products Act
Farm Income Stabilization Act, 1976
Farm Products Containers Act
Farm Products Grades and Sales Act
Farm Products Marketing Act
Farm Products Payments Act
Fruits and Vegetables Produce-for-Process-
ing Act, 1974 (requires proclamation)

*Ministry of Government Services ISSN 0705-4483

Fur Farms Act, 1971
Grain Elevator Storage Act
Horticultural Societies Act
Hunter Damage Compensation Act
Junior Farmer Establishment Act
Live Stock and Live Stock Products Act
Live Stock Branding Act
Live Stock Community Sales Act
Live Stock Medicines Act, 1973
Meat Inspection Act (Ontario)
Milk Act
Ministry of Agriculture and Food Act
Ministry of Agriculture and Food Statute Law Amendment and Repeal Act, 1978 (requires proclamation)
Oleomargarine Act
Ontario Agricultural Museum Act, 1975
Ontario Food Terminal Act
Ontario Producers, Processors, Distributors and Consumers Food Council Act
Plant Diseases Act
Pounds Act
Pregnant Mare Urine Farms Act
Protection of Cattle Act (RSO 1950, c. 294)
Provincial Auctioneers Act
Riding Horse Establishments Act, 1972
Seed Potatoes Act
Stock Yards Act
Tile Drainage Act, 1971
Topsoil Preservation Act, 1977
Veterinarians Act
Warble Fly Control Act
Weed Control Act
Wool Marketing Act, 1974

MINISTRY OF THE ATTORNEY GENERAL

Absconding Debtors Act
Absentees Act

Accidental Fires Act
Accumulations Act
Administration of Justice Act
Age of Majority and Acountability Act, 1971
Aliens' Real Property Act
Anti-Inflation Agreement Act, 1976
Arbitrations Act
Architects Act
Assessment Review Court Act, 1972
Bail Act
Barristers Act
Blind Persons' Rights Act, 1976
Bulk Sales Act
Business Records Protection Act
Change of Name Act
Charitable Gifts Act
Charities Accounting Act
Children's Law Reform Act, 1977
Commissioners for taking Affidavits Act
Compensation for Victims of Crime Act, 1971
Constitutional Questions Act
Conveyancing and Law of Property Act
Costs of Distress Act
County Court Judges' Criminal Courts Act
County Courts Act
County Judges Act
Creditors' Relief Act
Crown Administration of Estates Act
Crown Agency Act
Crown Attorneys Act
Crown Witnesses Act
Devolution of Estates Act
Disorderly Houses Act
Dominion Courts Act
Escheats Act
Estreats Act
Evidence Act
Execution Act

Expropriations Act
Extra Judicial Services Act
Family Law Reform Act, 1978
Fines and Forfeitures Act
Fraudulent Conveyances Act
Fraudulent Debtors Arrest Act
Frustrated Contracts Act
Gaming Act
General Sessions Act
Habeas Corpus Act
Hospitals and Charitable Institutions
    Inquiries Act
Hotel Registration of Guests Act
Infants Act
Innkeepers Act
Interpretation Act
Judges' Orders Enforcement Act
Judicature Act
Judicial Review Procedure Act, 1971
Juries Act, 1974
Justices of the Peace Act
Landlord and Tenant Act
Law Society Act
Legal Aid Act
Libel and Slander Act
Limitations Act
Lord's Day (Ontario) Act
Master and Servant Act
Matrimonial Causes Act
Mechanics' Lien Act
Mental Incompetency Act
Mercantile Law Amendment Act
Ministry of the Attorney General Act
Minors' Protection Act
Mortgages Act
Municipal Conflict of Interest Act, 1972
Negligence Act
Notaries Act
Ontario Law Reform Commission Act
Ontario Municipal Board Act
Partition Act

Partnerships Act
Pawnbrokers Act
Perpetuities Act
Petty Trespass Act
Powers of Attorney Act
Proceedings Against the Crown Act
Professional Engineers Act
Property and Civil Rights Act
Provincial Courts Act (part)
Public Accountancy Act
Public Authorities Protection Act
Public Halls Act
Public Inquiries Act, 1971
Public Institutions Inspection Act, 1974
Public Officers Act
Public Officers' Fees Act
Public Trustee Act
Quieting Titles Act
Reciprocal Enforcement of Judgments
    Act
Reciprocal Enforcement of Maintenance
    Orders Act
Regulations Act
Religious Institutions Act
Replevin Act
Sale of Goods Act
Settled Estates Act
Sheriffs Act
Short Forms of Conveyances Act
Short Forms of Leases Act
Short Forms of Mortgages Act
Small Claims Courts Act
Solicitors Act
Statute of Frauds
Statutes Act
Statutory Powers Procedure Act, 1971
Succession Law Reform Act, 1977
Summary Convictions Act
Surrogate Courts Act
Ticket Speculation Act
Time Act

Trustee Act
Unconscionable Transactions Relief Act
United Family Court Act, 1976 (part)
  (self-repealing on 1 July 1980)
University Expropriation Powers Act
Variation of Trusts Act
Vendors and Purchasers Act
Vexatious Proceedings Act
Vicious Dogs Act
Wages Act
Warehousemen's Lien Act
Warehouse Receipts Act

MINISTRY OF COLLEGES AND
UNIVERSITIES

Apprenticeship and Tradesmen's Quali-
  fication Act
Brock University Act, 1964
Carleton University Act, 1952
Colleges Collective Bargaining Act, 1975
Lakehead University Act, 1965
Laurentian University of Sudbury Act,
  1960
McMaster University Act, 1957
Ministry of Colleges and Universities
  Act, 1971
Ontario College of Art Act, 1968-69
Osgoode Hall Law School Scholarships
  Act, 1968-69
Private Vocational Schools Act, 1974
Ryerson Polytechnical Institute Act,
  1977
Sunnybrook Hospital Act, 1966
Trent University Act, 1962-63
University of Guelph Act, 1964
University of Ottawa Act, 1965
University of Toronto Act, 1971
University of Waterloo Act, 1972
University of Western Ontario Act, 1967

University of Windsor Act, 1962-63
Wilfrid Laurier University Act, 1973
York University Act, 1965

MINISTRY OF COMMUNITY AND SOCIAL
SERVICES

Charitable Institutions Act
Child Welfare Act, (RSO 1970, c. 64, as
  amended)
Child Welfare Act, 1978 (requires
  proclamation)
Child Welfare Municipal Payments Con-
  tinuance Act, 1976
Children's Boarding Homes Act
Children's Institutions Act, (RSO 1970, c.
  66, as amended)
Children's Institutions Act, 1978
  (requires proclamation)
Children's Mental Health Centres Act
Children's Mental Health Services Act,
  1978 (requires proclamation)
Children's Mental Hospitals Act
Children's Probation Act, 1978
Children's Residential Services Act, 1978
  (requires proclamation)
Children's Services Transfer Act, 1977
Day Nurseries Act, (RSO 1970, c. 104, as
  amended)
Day Nurseries Act, 1978 (requires
  proclamation)
Development Services Act, 1974
District Welfare Administration Boards
  Act
Elderly Persons Centres Act
Family Benefits Act
General Welfare Assistance Act
Homemakers and Nurses Services Act
Homes for Retarded Persons Act
Homes for the Aged and Rest Homes Act

Indian Welfare Services Act
Ministry of Community and Social Services Act
Provincial Courts Act (part)
Soldiers' Aid Commission Act (RSO 1960, c. 377)
Training Schools Act
Unified Family Court Act, 1976 (part)
Vocational Rehabilitation Services Act
Welfare Units Act

MINISTRY OF CONSUMER AND COMMERCIAL RELATIONS

Apportionment Act
Assignments and Preferences Act
Athletics Control Act
Bailiffs Act
Bills of Sale Act
Boilers and Pressure Vessels Act
Boundaries Act
Bread Sales Act
Building Code Act, 1974
Business Corporations Act
Business Practices Act, 1974
Cemeteries Act
Certification of Titles Act
Collection Agencies Act
Commodity Futures Act, 1978 (requires proclamation)
Condominium Act, (RSO 1970, c. 77, as amended)
Condominium Act, 1978 (requires proclamation)
Construction Hoists Act
Consumer Protection Act
Consumer Protection Bureau Act
Consumer Reporting Act, 1973
Co-operative Corporations Act, 1973
Corporation Securities Registration Act

Corporations Act
Corporations Information Act, 1976
Credit Unions and Caisses Populaires Act, 1976
Debt Collectors Act
Deposits Regulation Act
Discriminatory Business Practices Act, 1978
Egress from Public Buildings Act
Elevators and Lifts Act
Energy Act, 1971
Factors Act
Gasoline Handling Act
Guarantee Companies Securities Act
Income Tax Discounters Act, 1977
Insurance Act
Investment Contracts Act
Land Titles Act
Limited Partnerships Act
Liquor Control Act, 1975
Liquor Licence Act, 1975
Loan and Trust Corporations Act
Marine Insurance Act
Marriage Act, 1977
Ministry of Consumer and Commercial Relations Act
Mortgage Brokers Act
Mortmain and Charitable Uses Act
Motor Vehicle Accident Claims Act
Motor Vehicle Dealers Act
Ontario Credit Union League Limited Act, 1972
Ontario Deposit Insurance Corporation Act
Ontario New Home Warranties Plan Act, 1976
Ontario Water Resources Act (part)
Operating Engineers Act
Paperback and Periodical Distributors Act, 1971

Partnerships Registration Act
Pension Benefits Act
Personal Property Security Act
Petroleum Products Price Freeze Act,
1975
Prearranged Funeral Services Act
Prepaid Hospital and Medical Services
Act
Pyramidic Sales Repeal Act, 1978 (self-
repealing 1 January 1981)
Racing Commission Act
Real Estate and Business Brokers Act
Registry Act
Residential Premises Rent Review Act,
1975 (2nd sess.) (self-repealing, 30
June 1979)
Securities Act, (RSO, 1970 c. 426)
Securities Act, 1978 (requires
proclamation)
Theatres Act
Toronto Stock Exchange Act
Travel Industry Act, 1974
Unclaimed Articles Act
Upholstered and Stuffed Articles Act
Vital Statistics Act
Wine Content Act, 1976

MINISTRY OF CORRECTIONAL SERVICES

Ministry of Correctional Services Act,
1978

MINISTRY OF CULTURE AND RECREATION

Archives Act
Art Gallery of Ontario Act
Arts Council Act
Centennial Centre of Science and Tech-
nology Act
Community Recreation Centres Act,
1974

Foreign Cultural Objects Immunity
from Seizure Act, 1978
Historical Parks Act, 1972
McMichael Canadian Collection Act,
1972
Ministry of Culture and Recreation Act,
1974
Ontario Educational Communications
Authority Act
Ontario Heritage Act, 1974
Ontario Lottery Corporation Act, 1974
Public Libraries Act
Royal Botanical Gardens Act, 1941
Royal Ontario Museum Act
Simcoe (John Graves) Memorial Foun-
dation Act, 1965

MINISTRY OF EDUCATION

Central Algoma Board of Education and
Teachers Dispute Act, 1976
Education Act, 1974
Essex County French-language Secon-
dary School Act, 1977
Kirkland Lake Board of Education and
Teachers Dispute Act, 1976
Lake Superior Board of Education Act,
1976
Metropolitan Toronto Boards of Educa-
tion and Teachers Disputes Act, 1976
Ontario Institute for Studies in Educa-
tion Act
Ontario School Trustees Council Act,
1978
Provincial Schools Negotiations Act,
1975
Sault Ste. Marie Board of Education and
Teachers Dispute Act, 1976
School Boards and Teachers Collective
Negotiations Act, 1975
School Trust Conveyances Act

Teachers Superannuation Act
Teaching Profession Act
Windsor Board of Education and
 Teachers Dispute Act, 1976
York County Board of Education
 Teachers Dispute Act, 1974

MINISTRY OF ENERGY

Ministry of Energy Act, 1973
Ontario Energy Board Act
Ontario Energy Corporation Act, 1974
Power Corporation Act
Power Corporation Insurance Act
Rural Hydro-Electric Distribution Act
Rural Power District Loans Act

MINISTRY OF THE ENVIRONMENT

Environmental Assessment Act, 1975
Environmental Protection Act, 1971
Ministry of the Environment Act
Ontario Water Resources Act (part)
Pesticides Act, 1973
Pollution Abatement Incentive Act

MINISTRY OF GOVERNMENT SERVICES

Flag Act
Floral Emblem Act
Ministry of Government Services Act,
 1973
Official Notices Publication Act
Public Service Superannuation Act

MINISTRY OF HEALTH

Alcoholism and Drug Addiction
 Research Foundation Act
Ambulance Act
Cancer Act

Cancer Remedies Act
Chiropody Act
Community Psychiatric Hospitals Act
Dental Technicians Act
Denture Therapists Act, 1974
Drugless Practitioners Act
Fluoridation Act
Funeral Services Act, 1976
Health Disciplines Act, 1974
Health Insurance Act, 1972
Homes for the Special Care Act
Hypnosis Act
Mental Health Act
Mental Hospitals Act
Ministry of Health Act, 1972
Municipal Health Services Act
Nursing Homes Act, 1972
Ontario Mental Health Foundation Act
Opthalmic Dispensers Act
Private Hospitals Act
Private Sanitaria Act
Psychologists Registration Act
Public Health Act
Public Hospitals Act
Radiological Technicians Act
Sanatoria for Consumptives Act
Veneral Diseases Prevention Act
War Veterans Burial Act

MINISTRY OF HOUSING

Elderly Persons' Housing Aid Act
Housing Development Act
Ministry of Housing Act, 1973
North Pickering Development Corpora-
 tion Act, 1974
Ontario Housing Corporation Act
Ontario Land Corporation Act, 1974
Ontario Student Housing Corporation
 Act, 1978
Planning Act
Rural Housing Assistance Act

MINISTRY OF INDUSTRY AND TOURISM

Development Corporations Act, 1973
Ministry of Industry and Tourism Act,
1972
Ontario Place Corporation Act, 1972
Research Foundation Act, 1944
Sheridan Park Corporation Act
Tourism Act

MINISTRY OF INTERGOVERNMENTAL
AFFAIRS

City of Cornwall Annexation Act, 1974
City of Hamilton Act, 1975
City of Hazeldean March Act, 1978
City of Nepean Act, 1978
City of Port Colborne Act, 1974
City of Thorold Act, 1975
City of Thunder Bay Act, 1968-69
City of Timmins Porcupine Act, 1972
County of Oxford Act, 1974
District Municipality of Muskoka Act
Fire Guardians Act
Fires Extinguishment Act
Haliburton Act
Line Fences Act
Local Improvement Act
Ministry of Intergovernmental Affairs
Act, 1978
Moosonee Development Area Board Act
Municipal Act
Municipal Affairs Act
Municipal Arbitrations Act
Municipal Corporations Quieting
Orders Act
Municipal Elderly Residents' Assistance
Act, 1973
Municipal Elections Act, 1977
Municipal Franchises Act

Municipal and School Tax Credit Assist-
ance Act
Municipal Subsidies Adjustment Repeal
Act, 1976
Municipal Tax Assistance Act
Municipal Unemployment Relief Act,
1971
Municipal Works Assistance Act
Municipality of Metropolitan Toronto
Act
Municipality of Shuniah Act, 1936
Ontario Unconditional Grants Act, 1975
Ottawa-Carleton Amalgamations and
Elections Act, 1973
Provincial Parks Municipal Tax Assist-
ance Act, 1974
Public Parks Act
Public Utilities Act
Public Utilities Corporations Act
Regional Municipality of Durham Act,
1973
Regional Municipality of Haldimand-
Norfolk Act, 1973
Regional Municipality of Halton Act,
1973
Regional Municipality of Hamilton-
Wentworth Act, 1973
Regional Municipality of Niagara Act
Regional Municipality of Ottawa-
Carleton Act
Regional Municipality of Peel Act, 1973
Regional Municipality of Sudbury Act,
1972
Regional Municipality of Waterloo Act,
1972
Regional Municipality of York Act
Road Access Act, 1978
Shoreline Property Assistance Act, 1973
Snow Roads and Fences Act
Statute Labour Act

Tax Sales Confirmation Act, 1974
Territorial Division Act
Town of Wasaga Beach Act, 1973
Township of North Plantagenet Act, 1976
Vacant Land Cultivation Act
Village of Point Edward Act, 1972
Wharfs and Harbours Act

MINISTRY OF LABOUR

Blind Workmen's Compensation Act
Construction Safety Act, 1973
Employees' Health and Safety Act, 1976
Employment Agencies Act
Employment Standards Act, 1974
Government Contracts Hours and
  Wages Act
Hospital Labour Disputes Arbitration
  Act
Industrial Safety Act, 1971
Industrial Standards Act
Labour Relations Act
Mining Act (part IX, except s. 616)
Ministry of Labour Act
Occupational Health and Safety Act,
  1978 (requires proclamation)
One Day's Rest in Seven Act
Ontario Human Rights Code
Ontario Labour-Management Arbitra-
  tion Commission Act
Rights of Labour Act
Silicosis Act
Workmen's Compensation Act
Workmen's Compensation Insurance
  Act

MINISTRY OF NATURAL RESOURCES

Algonquin Forestry Authority Act, 1974
Algonquin Provincial Park Extension
  Act, 1960-61

Beach Protection Act
Beds of Navigable Waters Act
Conservation Authorities Act
Crown Timber Act
Endangered Species Act, 1971
Fish Inspection Act
Fisheries Loans Act
Forest Fires Prevention Act
Forest Tree Pest Control Act
Forestry Act
Freshwater Fish Marketing Act
  (Ontario)
Game and Fish Act
Gas and Oil Leases Act
Industrial and Mining Lands Compensa-
  tion Act
Lakes and Rivers Improvement Act
Mineral Emblem Act, 1975
Mining Act (part IX, except s. 616, is
  administered by ministry of labour)
Mining Tax Act, 1972
Ministry of Natural Resources Act, 1972
National Radio Observatory Act, 1962-
  63
Niagara Parks Act
North Georgian Bay Recreational
  Reserve Act, 1962-63
Ontario Geographic Names Board Act
Ontario Harbours Agreement Act, 1962-
  63
Parks Assistance Act
Petroleum Resources Act, 1971
Pits and Quarries Control Act, 1971
Provincial Parks Act
Public Lands Act
St. Clair Parkway Commission Act, 1966
St. Lawrence Parks Commission Act
Settlers' Pulpwood Protection Act
Spruce Pulpwood Exportation Act
Surveyors Act
Surveys Act

Trees Act
Wild Rice Harvesting Act
Wilderness Areas Act
Woodlands Improvement Act
Woodmen's Employment Act
Woodmen's Lien for Wages Act

MINISTRY OF NORTHERN AFFAIRS

Ministry of Northern Affairs Act, 1977
Ontario Northland Transportation
    Commission Act

MINISTRY OF REVENUE

Agricultural Development Finance Act
Assessment Act
Corporations Tax Act, 1972
Gasoline Tax Act, 1973
Gift Tax Act, 1972
Income Tax Act
Land Speculation Tax Repeal Act, 1978
Land Transfer Tax Act, 1974
Ministry of Revenue Act
Motor Vehicle Fuel Tax Act
Ontario Home Buyers Grant Act, 1975
Provincial Land Tax Act
Race Tracks Tax Act
Railway Fire Charge Act
Retail Sales Tax Act
Succession Duty Act
Tobacco Tax Act

MINISTRY OF THE SOLICITOR GENERAL

Anatomy Act
Coroners Act, 1972
Egress from Public Buildings Act
Fire Accidents Act
Fire Departments Act

Fire Fighters Exemption Act
Fire Marshals Act
Hotel Fire Safety Act, 1971
Human Tissue Gift Act, 1971
Lightning Rods Act
Ministry of the Solicitor General Act,
    1972
Ontario Society for the Prevention of
    Cruelty to Animals Act, 1955
Policy Act
Private Investigators and Security
    Guards Act
Public Works Protection Act
Retail Business Holidays Act, 1975 (2nd
    sess.)

MINISTRY OF TRANSPORTATION AND
COMMUNICATIONS

Airports Act
Bridges Act
Commuter Services Act
Ferries Act
Highway Traffic Act
Local Roads Boards Act
Ministry of Transportation and Com-
    munications Act, 1971
Ministry of Transportation and Com-
    munications Creditors Payment Act,
    1975
Motorized Snow Vehicles Act, 1974
Municipal Electric Railways Act (RSO
    1950, c. 248)
Muskoka & Parry Sound Telephone Co.,
    Limited Acquisition Act, 1978
Ontario Highway Transport Board Act
Ontario Telephone Development Corpo-
    ration Act
Ontario Transportation Development
    Corporation Act, 1973

Public Commercial Vehicles Act
Public Service Works on Highways Act
Public Transportation and Highway
  Improvement Act
Public Vehicles Act
Railways Act (RSO 1950, c. 331)
Statute Labour Act (part)
Telephone Act
Toll Bridges Act
Toronto Area Transit Operating Author-
  ity Act, 1974
Township of Pelee Act, 1978

MINISTRY OF TREASURY AND ECONOMICS

Agricultural Development Repeal Act,
  1973
Anti-Inflation Agreement Act, 1976
Audit Act, 1977
Farm Loans Act
Farm Loans Adjustment Act
Financial Administration Act
Gold Clauses Act
Ministry of Treasury and Economics
  Act, 1978
Ontario Economic Council Act
Ontario Education Capital Aid Corpo-
  ration Act
Ontario Guaranteed Annual Income
  Act, 1974
Ontario Loan Act
Ontario Municipal Employees Retire-
  ment System Act
Ontario Municipal Improvement Corpo-
  ration Act
Ontario Planning and Development Act,
  1973
Ontario Universities Capital Aid Corpo-
  ration Act

Ontario Youth Employment Act, 1977
Oxford Municipal Hydro-Electric Ser-
  vice Act, 1977
Parkway Belt Planning and Develop-
  ment Act, 1973
Peel Municipal Hydro-Electric Service
  Act, 1977
Sandwich, Windsor and Amherstburg
  Railway Act, 1977
Statistics Act
Supply Act
Venture Investment Corporations Regis-
  tration Act, 1977
Waterloo Electrical Service Areas Act,
  1977
York Municipal Hydro-Electric Service
  Act, 1978

OFFICE OF THE ASSEMBLY

Election Finances Reform Act, 1975
Legislative Assembly Act
Legislative Assembly Retirement Allow-
  ances Act, 1973
Ombudsman Act, 1975

OFFICE OF THE PREMIER

Election Act
Executive Council Act
Lieutenant Governor Act
Policy and Priorities Board of Cabinet
  Act, 1971
Representation Act
Provincial Secretary for Resources
  Development
Niagara Escarpment Planning and
  Development Act, 1973

Bibliography

Akerlof, G. (1970) 'The market for lemons.' *Quarterly Journal of Economics* 84, 488-500

Alchian, A. and R. Kessel, (1962) 'Competition, monopoly, and the pursuit of pecuniary gain.' In *Aspects of Labor Economics* (New York: NBER)

Alyluia, K. (1972) 'The regulation of commercial advertising in Canada.' *Manitoba Law Journal* 5, 97-200

Ambrose, E.R. et al. (1976) 'A quality evaluation of specific dental services provided by the Saskatchewan dental plan.' Mimeographed. Department of health, Saskatchewan

Appelbaum, E. and J. Palmer (1978), 'Too much or too little regulation? An integrated model.' Mimeographed. University of Western Ontario

Appelbaum, E. and D. Scheffman (1979), 'Occupational licencing and quality.' Mimeographed

Archibald, G. and G. Rosenbluth (1975) 'The "new" theory of consumer demand and monopolistic competition.' *Quarterly Journal of Economics* 89, 569-90

Arrow, K. (1963) 'Uncertainty and the welfare economics of medical care.' *American Economic Review* 53, 941-73

– (1964) 'The role of securities in the optimal allocation of risk bearing.' *Review of Economic Studies* 3, 91-6

Arrow, K., and R. Lind (1970) 'Uncertainty and the evaluation of public investment decisions.' *American Economic Review* 60, 364-78

Averich, H. and L. Johnson (1962) 'Behavior of the firm under regulatory constraint.' *American Economic Review* 50, 1053-69

Bailey, E. (1973) *Economic Theory of Regulatory Constraint* (Lexington, Mass.: Lexington Books)

Bailey, M.J. (1978) 'Safety decisions and insurance.' *American Economic Review* 68, 295-8

Barzel, Y. (1976) 'An alternative approach to the analysis of taxation.' *Journal of Political Economy* 84, 1177-87

Baumol, W. (1977) *Economic Theory and Operations Analysis* Fourth edition (Lexington, Mass.: Prentice-Hall)

Baumol, W. and W. Oates (1971) 'The use of standards and pricing for the protection of the environment.' *Swedish Journal of Economics*, 42-54

– (1975) *The Theory of Environment Policy* (Englewood Cliffs, NJ: Prentice-Hall)

Bell, C. (1978) 'Cost of government control reflected in rising US prices.' *London Free Press*, 4 August, 4

Belobaba, E.P. (1977) 'Unfair trade practices legislation: symbolism and substance in consumer protection.' *Osgoode Hall Law Journal* 15, 327-88

Belobaba, Edward et al. (1972) *On the Question of Consumer Advocacy: A Working Paper* (Ottawa: Canadian Consumer Council)

Benham, L. (1972) 'The effect of advertising on the price of eyeglasses.' *Journal of Law and Economics* 15, 337-52

Benham, L. and A. Benham (1975) 'Regulating through the professions: a perspective on information control.' *Journal of Law and Economics*, 427-8

Boadway, R. (1974) 'The welfare foundations of cost-benefit analysis.' *Economic Journal* 84, 926-39

Bond, D. (1974) 'Consumerism and Consumer Protection.' In Officer and Smith, eds. *Issues in Canadian Economics* (Toronto: McGraw Hill-Ryerson)

Bonsor, N. (1978) 'The development of regulation in the highway trucking industry.' In Ontario Economic Council (1978)

Boyer, M., R. Kihlstrom, and J. Laffont (1978) 'Misleading advertising.' Mimeographed

Bresner, B., T., Leigh-Bell et al. (1978) 'Ontario agencies, boards, commission, advisory bodies and other public institutions: an inventory.' In Ontario Economic Council (1978)

Broadsmith, Huges, and Associates (1978) 'The Ontario Milk Marketing Board: an economic analysis.' In Ontario Economic Council (1978)

Brown, J. (1973) 'Toward an economic theory of liability.' *Journal of Legal Studies* 2, 323-49

– (1974) 'Product liability: the case of an asset with random life.' *American Economic Review* 64, 149-61

Brozen, Y. ed. (1975) *The Competitive Economy* (Morristown, NJ: General Learning Press)

Buchanan, J. (1970) 'In defense of caveat emptor." *University of Chicago Law Review* 37, 64-73

Burness, H., W. Stuart, W. Montgomery, and J. Quirk (1977) 'The turnkey era in nuclear power: a case study in sharing arrangements involving regulated firms.' Social Science Working paper No. 175, California Institute of Technology

Calabresi, G. (1968) 'Transactions costs, resource allocation and liability rules – a comment.' *Journal of Law and Economics* 11, 67-74

- (1970) *The Costs of Accidents: A Legal and Economic Analysis* (New Haven, Conn.: Yale University Press)

Caves, R. and M. Roberts (1975) *Regulating the Product: Quality and Variety* (Cambridge, Mass.: Ballinger)

Center for Policy Process (1979a) *Proceedings – National Conference on Regulatory Reform* (Washington, DC)

Cheung, S. (1973) 'The fable of the bees: an economic investigation.' *Journal of Law and Economics* 16, 11-34

Coase, R. (1960) 'The problem of social cost.' *Journal of Law and Economics* 3, 1-44

Colantani, C., O. Davis, and M. Swaminuthan (1976) 'Imperfect consumers and welfare Comparisons of policies concerning information and regulation.' *Bell Journal* 7, 602-15

Cornell, R., R. Noll, and B. Weingaist (1976) 'Safety regulation.' In H. Owens and C. Schultze (1976)

Cox, D., ed. (1967) *Risk Taking and Information Handling in Consumer Behavior* (Cambridge, Mass.: Harvard University Press)

Dahlman, C. (1979) 'The problem of externality.' *Journal of Law and Economics* 22

Dales, J. (1968) *Pollution, Property and Prices* (Toronto: University of Toronto Press)

Demsetz, H. (1968) 'Why regulate utilities?' *Journal of Law and Economics* 11, 56-65

- (1972) 'When does the liability rule matter?' *Journal of Legal Studies* 1, 13-28

Denison, E. (1978) 'Effects of selected changes in the institutional and human environment upon output per unit of input.' *Survey of Current Business*, January

Department of Consumer and Corporate Affairs (1977) *Proposals for a New Competition Policy for Canada – Second Stage* (Ottawa: Supply and Services)

Derkowski, A. (1972) *Residential Land Development in Ontario* (Toronto: Urban Development Institute)

- (1975) *Costs in the Land Development Process* (Toronto: Housing and Urban Development Association of Canada)

Dewees, D., C. Everson, and W. Sims (1975) *Economic Analysis of Environmental Policies* Ontario Economic Council Research Study No. 1 (Toronto: University of Toronto Press for OEC)

Dewees, D., J.R. Prochard, and M. Trebilcock (1979) 'Class actions as a regulatory instrument.' Mimeo. Law and Economics Program, University of Toronto

Diamond, P. (1974a) 'Accident law and resource allocation.' *Bell Journal* 4, 366-416

– (1974b) 'Single activity accidents.' *Journal of Legal Studies* 3, 107-64

– (1978), 'Welfare analysis of imperfect information equilibria.' *Bell Journal* 9, 82-105

Diamond, P., and J. Mirrlees (1975) 'On the assignment of liability: the uniform case.' *Bell Journal* 6, 487-516

Diewert, W.E. (1974) 'Applications of duality theory.' In M. Intriligator and D. Kendrick, eds. *Frontiers of Quantitative Economics* Vol. II (Amsterdam: North-Holland)

Dixit, A. and V. Norman (1978) 'Advertising and welfare.' *Bell Journal* 9, 1-17

Dixit, A. and J. Stiglitz (1974) 'Monopolistic competition and optimum product diversity.' Technical Report No. 153. Institute for Mathematical Studies in Social Sciences, Stanford University

Doern, B. (1977) 'The regulatory process in Canada.' Paper presented at the Carleton-McGill Conference on Regulation, 3-5 March

– ed (1978) *The Regulatory Process in Canada* (Toronto: Macmillan)

Dorfman, N. (1975) 'Who will pay for pollution control?' *National Tax Journal*

Dorfman, R. and N. Dorfman, eds (1977) *Economics of the Environment* (New York: W.W. Norton)

Dorfman, R. and P. Steiner (1954) 'Optimal advertising and optimal quality.' *American Economic Review* 44, 826-36

Downs, A. (1957) *An Economic Theory of Democracy* (New York: Harper)

Economic Council of Canada (1979a) *Responsible Regulation: An Interim Report by the E.C.C.* (Ottawa: ECC)

– (1979b) 'Synopsis and recommendations from responsible regulation. An interim report by the Economic Council of Canada' (Ottawa: ECC)

Ehrlich, I. and G. Becker (1972) 'Market insurance, self insurance, and self protection.' *Journal of Political Economy* 80, 623-48

Environmental Protection Agency Economic Impact Reports (McCabe, 1978, 12)

Epple, D. and A. Raviv 'Product safety: liability rules, market structure, and imperfect information.' *American Economic Review* 68, 80-95

Evans and Williamson (1978) *Extending Canadian Health Insurance: options for pharmacare and denticare.* Ontario Economic Council Research Study No. 13 (Toronto: University of Toronto Press for OEC)

Fitzgerald, P. (1973) 'Misleading advertising: prevent or punish?' *Dalhousie Law Journal* 1, 246-64

'Ford goes to trial' (1980) *Newsweek*, 7 January, 70

Frankena, M. (1980) *Urban Transportation Financing: Theory and Policy in Ontario* (Toronto: Ontario Economic Council)

Frankena, M. and D. Scheffman (1980) *Economic Analysis of Land Use Policies in Ontario*. Ontario Economic Council Research Study No. 18 (Toronto: University of Toronto Press for OEC)

Freeman, A. and R. Haveman (1972) 'Clean rhetoric and dirty water.' *Public Interest*, 51-65

Friedlander, A., ed. (1978) *Approaches to Controlling Air Pollution* (Boston: MIT Press)

Fuchs, V. 91976) *Who Shall Live?* (New York: Basic Books)

Furubotn, E. and S. Pejovich (1972) 'Property rights and economic theory: a survey of recent literature.' *Journal of Economic Literature* 10, 1137-62

Goldberg, V. (1974) 'The economics of product safety and imperfect information.' *Bell Journal*, 683-8

Goldschmid, H. et al., eds. (1974) *Industrial Concentration: The New Learning* (Waltham, Mass.: Little, Brown and Co.)

Gorecki, P. and W. Stanbury, eds. (1979) *Perspectives on the Royal Commission on Corporate Concentration* (Toronto: Butterworth and Co.)

Grabowski, H. (1976) *Drug Regulation and Innovation* (Washington, DC: American Enterprise Institute)

Grabowski, H. and J. Vernon (1976) 'Structural effect of regulation in the drug industry.' In Masson and Qualls (1976)

– (1978) 'Consumer product safety regulation.' *American Economic Review* 68, 184-9

Grange, S. (1975) *The Constitutionality of Federal Intervention in the Marketplace – The Competition Case* (Montreal: C.D. Howe Research Institute)

Green, J. (1976) 'On the optimal structure of liability laws.' *Bell Journal* 7, 553-74

Green, M. and N. Waitzman (1979) *Business War on the Law: An Analysis of the Benefits of Federal Health / Safety Enforcement*

Greenwood, P. and C. Ingene (1978) 'Uncertain externalities, liability rules, and resource allocation.' *American Economic Review* 68, 300-10

Guzzardi, W. (1979) 'The mindless pursuit of safety.' *Fortune*, 9 April, 54-64

Halpern, P. (1972) 'Consumer politics and corporate behavior: the case of automobile safety.' Unpublished PHD thesis, Harvard University

Hamada, K. (1976) 'Liability rules and income distribution in product liability.' *American Economic Review* 66, 118-34

Hartle, D. (1978) 'The regulation of communications in Canada.' In *Government Regulation* (Toronto: Ontario Economic Council)

Hatfield, B.D. (1977) 'The constitutionality of Canada's new competition policy.' *University of New Brunswick Law Journal* 26, 3-19

Hayek, F. (1945) 'The use of knowledge in society.' *American Economic Review* 55, 300-10

Heal, G. (1977) 'Guarantees and risk-sharing.' *Review of Economic Studies* 44, 549-60

Henderson, G.F. (1974) 'Misleading advertisements.' *Canadian Policy Review* 13 (2nd), 45-51

– (1978) 'Recent developments in competition law: the limits of the federal law power.' *Special Lectures of L.S.U.C.*, 109-34

Hey, J. (1979) *Uncertainty in Microeconomics* (New York: New York University Press)

Hinich, M. (1975) 'A rationalization for consumer support for food safety regulation.' Mimeographed. Department of economics, Virginia Polytechnic Institute, Blacksburg, Va.

Hirshleifer, J. (1965) 'Investment decision under uncertainty: choice-theoretic approaches.' *Quarterly Journal of Economics* 79, 509-36

– (1966) 'Investment decisions under uncertainty: applications of the state-preference approach.' *Quarterly Journal of Economics* 80, 252-77

– (1976) *Price Theory and Applications* (New York: Prentice-Hall)

Hogg, P.W. (1977) *Constitutional Law of Canada* (Toronto: Carswell)

Hogg, P.W. and W. Grover (1976) 'The constitutionality of the competition bill.' *Canadian Business Law Journal* 1, 147-96

Hord, A.B. et al. (1978) 'The Ontario Dental Association demonstration project on dental auxiliaries with extended duties.' *Ontario Dentist* 51: 6, 14-18

Jacoby, H. and J. Steinbruner (1973) 'Salvaging the federal attempt to control auto pollution.' *Public Policy*, 1-48

James, R.W. (1978) 'Two essays on the regulation of social and economic behavior in Canada.' Economic Council of Canada Discussion Paper 113 (Ottawa: ECC)

Joskow, P. (1973) 'Cartels, competition, and regulation in the property and liability insurance industry.' *Bell Journal*, 375-427

Joskow, P. and R. Noll (1978) 'Regulation in theory and practice: an overview.' MIT Working Paper No. 218.

Kahn, A. (1970-71) *The Economics of Regulation*. Vols I and II (New York: J. Wiley)

Kaiser, G. (1976), 'The new competition law – stage 1.' *Canadian Business Law Journal* 1, 147-96

Kihlstrom, R. (1974) 'A general theory of demand for information about product quality.' *Journal of Economic Theory* 8, 413-39

Kindred, H.M. (1978) 'Consumer law developments: a note on the impact of recent federal legislation in Nova Scotia.' *Dalhousie Law Journal* 4, 383-90

Kitch, E., Mark Isaacson, and Daniel Kooper (1971) 'The regulation of taxi-cabs in Chicago.' *Journal of Law and Economics* 14, 285-350

Kleiman, E. and T. Ophir (1966) 'The durability of durable goods.' *Review of Economic Studies* 33, 165-78

Kneese, A., ed. (1980) *Research on Environment Quality* (Baltimore: Johns Hopkins)

Kneese, A. and C. Schultz (1975) *Pollution, Prices and Public Policy* (Washington DC: Brookings Institution)

Kotowicz, y. and F. Mathewson (1979) 'Informative advertising and welfare.' *American Economic Review* 69, 284-94

Kuenne, R. ed. (1967) *Monopolistic Competition Theory: Studies in Impact* (New York: John Wiley)

Lamberton, D., ed. (1971) *Economics of Information and Knowledge* (Baltimore: Penguin Books)

Lancaster, K. (1975) 'Socially optimal product differentiation.' *American Economic Review* 65, 567-85

Lave, L. and E. Seskin (1970) 'Air pollution and human health.' *Science* 723-33

Lederman, W. (1965) 'The balanced interpretation of the federal distribution of legislative powers in Canada.' In Crepeau and MacPherson eds, *The Future of Canadian Federalism* (Toronto 91-109),

– (1975) 'Unity and diversity in Canadian federalism: ideals and methods of moderation.' *Canadian Banking Review* 53

Leggett, R.F. (1971) *Standards in Canada* (Ottawa: Information Canada)

Leighton, R. (1973) 'Consumer protection agency proposals: the origin of the species.' *Administrative Law Review* 269-312

Levhari, D. and Y. Peles (1973) 'Market structure, quality, and durability.' *Bell Journal* 4, 235-48

Levhari, D. and T. Srinivasan (1969) 'Durability of consumption goods: competition vs. monopoly.' *American Economic Review* 59, 102-7

Lilley, W. and J. Miller (1977) 'The new "social" regulation.' *Public Interest*

London Free Press (1978) 'Radial 500 defended by Firestone official.' 24 May

McAvoy, P., ed (1970) *The Crisis of the Regulatory Commissions* (New York: W.W. Norton)

McCabe, L. (1978) 'Government evaluation of regulations: the United States experience.' Treasury Board, Consumer and Corporate Affairs, Ottawa

McCarthy, E., M. Finkel, and A. Kamons (1977) 'Second opinion surgical program: a vehicle for cost containment.' Paper presented at AMA Commission on Cost of Medical Care, 11 March

McConnell, W.H. (1977) *Commentary on the British North America Act* (Toronto: Macmillan)

McFadyen, G.F. (1973) 'Consumer class actions.' *Queen's Law Journal* 2, 503-8

McGuire, T., R. Nelson and T. Spairns (1975) 'An evaluation of consumer protection legislation: the 1962 drug amendments – comment.' *Journal of Political Economy* 83, 655-62

McKean, R. (1970a) 'Products liability: trends and implications.' *University of Chicago Law Review* 37, 3-63

– (1970b) 'Products liability: implications of some changing property rights.' *Quarterly Journal of Economics* 84, 611-26

McKie J.W. (1970) 'Regulation and the free market: the problem of boundaries.' *Bell Journal*, 6-26

Malinvaud, E. (1972) *Lectures on Economic Theory* (Amsterdam: North-Holland)

Manne, H. (1970) 'Edited transcript of AALS-AEA conference on products liability.' *University of Chicago Law Review* 37, 117-41

– ed. (1975) *The Economics of Legal Relationships* (Chicago: West Publishing Co.)

Manne, H. and R. Miller (1976) *Auto Safety Regulation: The Cure of the Problem?* (New York: T. Horton)

Margolis, J. (1970) *The Analysis of Public Output* (Washington DC: NBER)

Markham, J. and G. Papanek, eds (1970) *Industrial Organization and Economic Development* (New York: Houghton Mifflin)

Markusen, J. and D. Scheffman (1977) *Speculation and Monopoly in Urban Development*. Ontario Economic Council Research Study No. 10 (Toronto: University of Toronto Press for OEC)

Martin, D. (1962) 'Monopoly and the durability of durable goods.' *Southern Economic Journal* 29, 271-7

Masson, R. and D. Qualls, eds (1976) *Essays in Industrial Organization in Honor of Joe Bain* (Cambridge, Mass.: Ballinger)

Miller, J.C. and B. Yandle eds (1979) *Benefit Cost Analyses of Social Regulation* (Washington, DC: American Enterprise Institute)

Mills, E. and L. White (1978) 'Government policies towards automotive emissions control.' In *Approaches to Controlling Air Pollution* (Boston: MIT Press)

Mont, N.C. (1977) 'Comment on Ontario's Bill 110: an act to provide for warranties in the sale of consumer products.' *Dalhousie Law Journal* 4, 201

Montador, B. (1977) 'A case study: the proposed insulation requirements for ceilings and opaque walls.' Mimeographed. Treasury Board, Ottawa

Montador, B. and H. Baumann (1977) 'Government intervention in the market place and the case for social regulation.' Mimeographed. Treasury Board, Consumer and Corporate Affairs, Ottawa

Montgomery, W.D. (1977) 'A case study of regulatory programs of the federal energy administration.' Social Science Working Paper No. 147, California Institute of Technology

Morin, A. (1977) 'A case study of proposed school bus safety standards under the Canadian Motor Vehicle Safety Act.' Mimeographed. Treasury Board, Ottawa

Morphin, H.L. (1976) 'Safety standards legislation.' *Special Lectures L.S.U.C.*, 179-95

Mullan, David and Roger Beaman (1973) 'The constitutional implications of the regulation of telecommunications.' *Queen's Law Journal* 2, 67-92

Nadel, M. (1971) *The Politics of Consumer Protection* (Indianapolis: Bobbs-Merrill)

National Commission on Product Safety (1970a) *Final Report of the National Commission on Product Safety* (Washington, DC: US Government Printing Office)

– (1970b) *Industry Self-Regulation Supplemental Studies* (Washington, DC: US Government Printing Office)

– (1970c) *Product Safety, Law, and Administration* (Washington, DC: US Government Printing Office)

Needham, D. (1969) *Economic Analysis and Industrial Structure* (New York: Holt, Rinehart, and Winston)

Nelson, P. (1970) 'Information and consumer behavior.' *Journal of Political Economy* 78, 311-29

– (1974) 'Advertising as information.' *Journal of Political Economy* 82, 729-54

New York Times (1978) 'Youth awarded $127 million.' 8 February

Nicosia, F. (1976) 'Perceived risk, information processing, and consumer behavior: a review article.' *Journal of Business* 49, 162-6

Noll, R. (1971) *Reforming Regulation: An Evaluation of the Ash Council Proposals* (Washington, DC: Brookings Institution)

Oi, W. (1973) 'The economics of product safety.' *Bell Journal* 4, 3-28

Ontario Economic Council (1978) *Issues and Alternatives, 1978; Government Regulation* (Toronto OEC)

Ontario, Government of (1979) *Telephone Directory, March 1979* (Toronto)

Ontario Ministry of Colleges and Universities (1972) *Training for Ontario's Future.* Report of the Task Force on Industrial Training

Ontario Ministry of Consumer and Commercial Relations (1978) 'Identifying opportunities for deregulation and cutting red tape.' Deregulation Committee Report No. 2

Ontario Ministry of Culture and Recreation (1979) *KWIK Index to the Government of Ontario 1978/79.* Queen's Park

Ontario Planning Act Review Committee, Report (1977) Queen's Park

Orr, D. (1976) *Property, Markets, and Government Intervention* (Santa Monica, Calif.: Goodyear)

Oster, S. and J. Quigley (1977) 'Regulatory barriers to the diffusion of innovation: some evidence from building codes.' *Bell Journal* 8, 361-77

Owens, H. and C. Schultze, eds (1976) *Setting National Priorities: The Next Ten Years* (Washington, DC: Brookings Institution)

Pattison, J. (1978) 'The regulation of social and economic activity in Confederation.' Mimeographed. University of Western Ontario School of Business Administration

Peltzman, S. (1973) 'An evaluation of consumer protection legislation: the 1962 drug amendments.' *Journal of Political Economy* 81, 1049-91

– (1975) 'The effects of automobile safety regulation.' *Journal of Political Economy* 83, 677-725

– (1976a) 'Toward a more general theory of regulation.' *Journal of Law and Economics* 19, 211-40

– (1976b) 'The regulation of automobile safety.' In Manne and Miller (1976)

Phillips, A. (1975) *Promoting Competition in Regulated Markets* (Washington, DC: Brookings Institution)

Plott, C. (1965) 'Occupational study of self regulation: a case study of the Oklahoma dry cleaners.' *Journal of Law and Economics* 8, 195-222

Posner, R. (1971) 'Taxation by regulation.' *Bell Journal* 2, 22-50

– (1974) 'Theories of economic regulation.' *Bell Journal* 5, 335-58

– (1975) 'The social costs of monopoly and regulation.' *Journal of Political Economy*

– (1977) *Economic Analysis of Law.* Second ed. (Waltham, Mass.: Little Brown)

The President's Advisory Council on Executive Reorganization (the Ash Council) (1971) *A New Regulatory Framework* (Washington, DC: US Government Printing Office)

Proceedings of the N.B.E.R. Conference on Public Regulation (forthcoming)

Progress Report to Federal/Provincial Task Group on the Regulatory Process (1979) Memorandum, Alan Gordon, associate secretary of cabinet (Ontario)

Proulx, M. (1977) 'A case study of the petroleum refinery effluent regulations and guidelines under the Fisheries Act.' Mimeographed. Treasury Board, Ottawa

Romero, Louis J. (1975) *Federal-Provincial Relations in the Field of Consumer Protection* (Ottawa: Consumer Research Council)

Rosse, J. (1972) 'Product quality and regulatory constraints.' Memorandum No. 137. Center for Research in Economic Growth, Stanford University

Rothschild, M. (1973) 'Models of market organization with imperfect information: a survey.' *Journal of Political Economy* 81, 1283-308

Rothschild, M. and J. Stiglitz (1976) 'Equilibrium in competitive insurance markets: an essay on the economics of imperfect information.' *Quarterly Journal of Economics* 90, 629-49

Safarian, A.E. (1974) *Canadian Federalism and Economic Integration* (Ottawa: Queen's Printer)

Salop, S. (1977) 'Bargains and ripoffs: a model of monopolistically competitive price dispersion.' *Review of Economic Studies* 44, 493-510

Scheffman, D. (1975) 'The aggregate excess demand correspondence and the structure of economies with externalities.' *Review of Economic Studies* 42, 597-604

Scheffman, D. and E. Appelbaum (1979) 'Product reliability, warranties and producer liability and advertising.' Mimeographed

Schelling, T. (1978) 'Economics, or the art of self management.' *American Economic Review* 68, 290-4

Scherer, F. (1970) *Industrial Market Structure and Economic Performance* (Skokie, Ill.: Rand McNally)
(1980) *Industrial Market Structure and Economic Performance*. Second ed. (Skokie, Ill.: Rand McNally)

Schmalensee, R. (1970) 'Regulation and the durability of goods.' *Bell Journal* 1, 54-64
– (1978) 'A model of advertising and product quality.' *Journal of Political Economy* 86, 485-503
– (1979) 'Market structure, durability and quality: a selective survey.' *Economic Inquiry* 9, 177-96

Schultze, C. (1977) 'The public use of the private interest.' *Harpers Magazine*, 43-62

Seidman, D. (1977) 'The politics of policy analysis.' *Regulation*, 22-37

Shepherd, W. and T. Gies, eds (1966) *Utility Regulation: New Directions in Theory and Policy* (New York: Random House)
– eds (1974) *Regulation in Further Perspective* (Cambridge, Mass.: Ballinger Publishing House)

Sheshinski, E. (1970) 'Price, quantity, and quality under regulation.' *Economica* 37

Sieper, E. and P. Swan (1973) 'Monopoly and competition in the market for durable goods.' *Review of Economic Studies* 40, 333-51

Slayton, P. and M.J. Trebilcock, eds *The Professions and Public Policy*

Smallwood, D. and J. Conlisk (1979) 'Product quality in markets where consumers are imperfectly informed.' Quarterly Journal of Economics 93, 1-23

Smith, H. (1927) 'Interpretation in English and continental law.' *Journal of Comparative Legislation & International Law* 9

Smith, R. (1974), 'The feasibility of an 'inquiry tax' approach to occupational safety.' *Journal of Law and Contemporary Problems*, 730-44

– (1976) *The Occupational Health and Safety Act* (Washington, DC: American Enterprise Institute)

Spence, A.M. (1975) 'Monopoly, quality, and regulation' *Bell Journal* 6, 417-29

– (1976) 'Informational aspects of market structure: an introduction.' *Quarterly Journal of Economics*, 591-7

– (1977) 'Consumer misconceptions, product failure and product liability.' *Review of Economic Studies* 44, 561-72

Spence, A.M. and M. Weitzman (19   ) 'Regulatory strategies for pollution control' (Boston: MIT Press)

Spence, A.M. and R. Zeckhauser (1971) 'Insurance, information, and individual action.' *American Economic Review* 61, 380-87

Spengler, J. (1968) 'The economics of safety.' *Law and Contemporary Problems*, 619-38

Stanbury, W.T. (1976) 'Penalties and remedies under the Combines Investigation Act, 1889–1976.' *Osgoode Hall Law Journal* 14, 571-631

Stanbury, W. ed. (1978) *Studies on Regulation in Canada* (Toronto: Butterworths)

– (1978) 'Economic Council of Canada reference on regulation: toward a research agenda.' Economic Council of Canada, 1 September

Star, Spencer (1978) 'An economic analysis of warranties and product liability' Consumer Research and Evaluation Branch, Consumer and Corporate Affairs

Starrett, D. (1972) 'Fundamental nonconvexities in the theory of externalities.' *Journal of Economic Theory* 5, 180-99

Stigler, G. (1971) 'The theory of economic regulation.' *Bell Journal* 2, 3-21

– (1975) *The Citizen and the State: Essays on Regulation* (Chicago: University of Chicago Press)

Stigler, G. and M. Cohen (1971) *Can Regulatory Agencies Protect Consumers?* (Washington, DC: American Enterprise Institute)

Stiglitz, J. (1977) 'The theory of local public goods.' In M. Feldstein and R. Inman, eds, *Economics of Public Services* (New York: Macmillan)

Stuart, C. (1978) 'Consumer protection in markets with informationally weak buyers.' Mimeo. University of Western Ontario

Su, T. (1975) 'Durability of consumption goods reconsidered.' *American Economic Review* 65, 148-57

Sugden, R. and A. Williams (1978) *The Principles of Practical Cost-Benefit Analysis* (Oxford: Oxford University Press)

Swaigen, J. (1978) 'Polluter-pays policy called mere puffery.' *Globe and Mail*, 7 August, 7

Swan, P. (1970a) 'Market structure and technological progress: the influence of monopoly on product innovation.' *Quarterly Journal of Economics* 84, 627-38

– (1970b) 'Durability of consumer goods.' *American Economic Review* 60, 884-7

– (1971) 'The durability of goods and regulation of monopoly' *Bell Journal* 2, 347-57

Sweeney, T. (1977) 'Advertising in the context of the Combines Investigation Act.' *Business Law Quarterly* 43, 495

Takayama, A. (1976) *Mathematical Economics* (Hillsdale, Ill.: The Dryden Press)

Tamarkin, B. (1978) 'Recalls – the costs soar.' *Forbes*, 10 July, 79-80

Time (1978) 'Ford's $128.5 million headache.' 25 February

Trebilcock, M.J. (1972) 'Private law remedies for misleading advertising.' *University of Toronto Law Journal* 22, 1-32

– (1975) 'Winners and losers in the modern regulatory system – must consumers always lose?' *Osgoode Hall Law Journal* 13, 619-47

Trebilcock, M. (forthcoming) 'The consumer interest and regulatory reform.' In B. Doern, ed. *The Regulatory Process in Canada* (Toronto: Macmillan)

Trebilcock, M.J. et al. (1976) *Second Stage Revision, Combines Investigation Act, 1976: A Study on Consumer Misleading and Unfair Trade Practices* (Ottawa: Department of Consumer and Corporate Affairs)

Trebilcock, M., L. Waverman, and J. Pritchard (1978) 'Markets for regulation: implications for performance standards and institutional design.' In Ontario Economic Council (1978)

Trebilcock, M.J. et al. (1979) *Professional Regulation: A Staff Study of Accountancy, Architecture, Engineering and Law in Ontario* (Toronto: The Professional Organizations Committee)

Urban, R. and R. Mancke (1972) 'Federal regulation of whiskey labelling: from the repeal of prohibition to the present.' *Journal of Law and Economics* 15, 411-26

Walker, M., ed (1978) *Canadian Confederation at the Crossroads* (Vancouver: Fraser Institute)

Walters, A. (1975) *Noise and Prices* (Oxford: Oxford University Press)

Wardell, W. (1980) *Controlling the Use of Therapeutic Drugs, an International Comparison* (Washington, DC: American Enterprise Institute)

Weidenbaum, M. (1979) *The Future of Business Regulation* (Washington, DC: American Enterprise Institute)

Weidenbaum, M. and R. Defina (1978) 'The cost of federal regulation of economic activity.' Reprint No. 88 (Washington, DC: American Enterprise Institute)

Whincup, M. (1973) *Consumer Protection Law in America, Canada and Europe* (Dublin: National Prices Commission)

Wicksell, K. (1934) 'Real capital and interest.' Appendix 2 in *Lectures on Political Economy*. Vol I. (London: Routledge and Kegan Paul)

Williams, N.J. (1974) *Consumer Class Actions* (Ottawa: Consumer's Association of Canada)

Williams, N.J. et al. (1976) *Second Stage Revision, Combines Investigation Act, 1976: A Proposal for Class Actions under Competition Policy Legislation* (Ottawa: Department of Consumer and Corporate Affairs)

Williamson, O. (1970) 'Administration decision making and pricing: externality and compensation analysis applied.' In J. Margolis (1970)

Willig, R. (1973) 'Welfare analysis of policies affecting prices and products.' Memorandum No. 153. Center for Research in Economic Growth, Stanford University

Willig, R. and E. Bailey (forthcoming) 'Income Distributional Concerns in Regulatory Policy-making.' In *Proceedings of the NBER Conference on Public Regulation*

Wilson, J. (1974) 'The politics of regulation.' In J. McKie ed, *Social Responsibility and the Business Predicament* (Washington DC: Brookings Institution)

Wolf, C. (1979) 'A theory of nonmarket failure.' *Journal of Law and Economics* 22

Wolfe, J. (1972) *Cost Benefit and Cost Effectiveness* (New York: George Allen and Unwin)

Zinn, J. (1977) 'Let the buyer still beware.' *Business Law Quarterly* 42, 54-8